CW00346822

CHARTS OF WAR

A PROSPECTIUE VIEW
Of his Mal. Naual Yard at Mahon.

Tropicus Cancri

TERRA NOVA,
ac Maris Tractus circa
NOVAM FRANCIAM, ANGLIAM,
BELGIUM, VENEZUELAM NOVAM,
ANDALUSIAM, GUIANAM,
et BRASILIAM.

F. de Wit.

NOVA ANGLIA

NIEU NEDER-LAND.

S. SEPTENTRIONALIS.

CHARTS OF WAR

The Maps and Charts That Have Informed and Illustrated
War at Sea

JOHN BLAKE

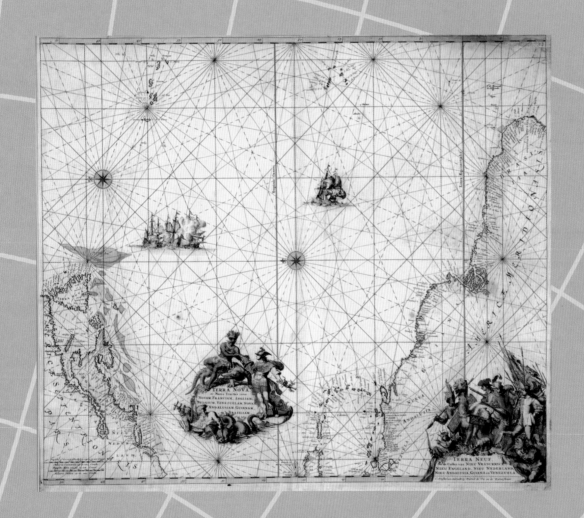

CONWAY

ACKNOWLEDGEMENTS

Charts of War is my third book and I am grateful to have had the help and guidance again of my editor, Alison Moss, for this book. Similarly, my thanks to my Publisher, John Lee, for his vision and support, and to Martin Robson in supplying his historical experience with suggestions and balance.

I am also grateful for the help from the various maritime archives who supplied the chart images: Matthew Sheldon, Head of Research Collections, and Allison Wareham, Librarian and Head of Information Services, at the Admiralty Library, Royal Naval Museum, Portsmouth (www. royalnavalmuseum.org), Geoff Armitage and many of the staff at the Map Room, Sandra Powlette, Permissions Department, Chris Rawlings, Image Library, Michael St John-McAlister, Curator, Department of Manuscripts, at The British Library, London (www.bl.uk); Dr John O'Neill, Curator, at the Hispanic Society of America, New York (www.hispanicsociety.org); Rosie Slater, Manager, at Imago Mundi Antique Maps Ltd, Museum Street, London (www.imagomundi.co.uk); Ed Redmond, Curator of the Geography and Map Division, at the Library of Congress, Washington DC, USA (www.loc.gov); Philip Curtis and Peter Stuchlik, Director, at The Map House, Beauchamp Street, London (www.themaphouse.com); Silvia Dahl, Archivo Imágenes CDM and Inma González Sánchez, Centro de Documentación Marítima, at the Museo Marítimo de Barcelona (www.museumaritimbarcelona.com); Paul Johnson, Image Library Manager, at The National Archives, Kew, London (www.nationalarchives.gov.uk); Diana Webster, Map Collections Manager, at the National Library of Scotland (www.nls.uk); Brian Thynne, Curator of Hydrography, and Sara Grove, Picture Library Manager, at the National Maritime Museum, London (www.nmm.ac.uk); Diederick Wildeman, Curator Navigation & Library Collections, Remmelt Daalder, Conservator Picturalia, Cees van Romburgh and Bart Lahr, at the Nederlands Scheepvaartmuseum, Amsterdam (www.scheepvaartmuseum.nl); Francis Herbert, Curator of Maps, the staff at the Map Room and Justin Hobson, Image Library, at the Royal Geographical Society (with The Institute of British Geographers) (www.rgs.org); Guy Hannaford, Archive Research Manager, Ann Browne, Archive Research Officer, and Helen Breeze, Archive Marketing Manager for Commercial Development, at the United Kingdom Hydrographic Office (www.ukho.gov.uk) (All UKHO images are reproduced by permission of the Controller of Her Majesty's Stationery Office and the United Kingdom Hydrographic Office).

My thanks to many who have helped me on various aspects of this wide-ranging subject, including Sir Robin Knox-Johnston CBE, Rear-Admiral Terence Loughran CB, Captain Rodney Browne CBE RN (former Captain of the RN Hydrographic Survey Squadron), Captain C J S Craig CB DSC RN, Captain N J Tobin DSC RN, Commander Ian Richards RN, Commander David Bernard RN, Commander Doug MacDonald RN (Fleet Air Arm) Andrew Brown, MA (Cantab.), Amanda Blake, BA (Hons), Dr Andrew Cook, Map Archivist, India Office Records, and to Stephen Swann, Editor of *Traditional Boats and Tall Ships* magazine.

I must, of course, include all those authors whose books I have consulted, listed in the Bibliography. I have not included specific references, as the book is aimed to interest not so much the specialist as the general public, but references can be provided by me through the Publisher.

Lastly, my thanks to my wife, Francine, who patiently read the manuscript and gave me many suggestions. I would like to dedicate this book to all my children and step-children, and their growing off-spring.

John Blake

A Conway Maritime Book

© John Blake 2006
© Volume, Conway 2006

First published in Great Britain in 2006 by Conway
An imprint of Anova Books Ltd, 151 Freston Road, London W10 6TH
www.anovabooks.com

British Library Cataloguing in Publication Data:
A catalogue record for this book is available from the British Library

ISBN 10: 1 84486 031 0
ISBN 13: 9 781844 860319

Edited by Alison Moss and Martin Robson
Design by Champion Design
Printed in SNP Leefung Ltd, China

Contents

| HALF TITLE PAGE | **VIEW OF THE NAVAL YARD AT MAHON, MINORCA, 1765**| (The National Archives {PRO} ADM 140/1318)

| FRONTISPIECE & TITLE PAGE | **CHART OF THE ATLANTIC OCEAN WITH THE EAST COAST OF NORTH AND SOUTH AMERICA AND SEA-FIGHT BY FREDERICK DE WIT, *C.* 1650** | (Courtesy of Imago Mundi, Museum Street, London)

| THESE PAGES | **NAVIGATIONAL VIEW DURING THE BLOCKADE OF BREST BY J T SERRES, 1800** | This long navigational view (in three parts from top left to bottom left and below) shows the British squadron at anchor in an unusually calm Passage l'Iroise off Isle d'Ouessant. (UKHO © British Crown Copyright)

Introduction

WE WILL never know who first grasped the essential idea of transferring a spatial mental concept of position into a two-dimensional, scaled-down representation of land and sea that could be used for both planning a voyage and recording its progress. This book looks, within the context of war, at how, from simple beginnings, the design and content of the chart grew in sophistication (and in its variety of application) through the ages. While it does not set out to be a history of naval warfare, or of sea battles and the causes thereof, it shows how the chart can illustrate, inform and comment on maritime history. I have selected 150 charts from 15 archives in the UK, Europe and the USA that present a unique opportunity for a visual understanding and appreciation of many of the wars, campaigns and actions that occurred at sea.

From the exploratory thrusts of emergent European states to war on a global scale, the selection of illustrations looks at the many purposes of the chart of war: its use for attack and defence in amphibious operations and tactics at sea; in search and rescue of survivors from ships sunk in battle; as the tool of propaganda and planning; of report, justification and excuse; of pilotage; to demonstrate prowess, nationalism, ownership and pride; and of intelligence (even the siting of harbour forts), and the means to learn from experience.

Charts trumpeted the achievements of the time, proclaiming patriotically the splendid victories achieved by their sovereign. Pages 37–38 show the triumphant record of John Pine's copy of two of the hanging tapestries depicting the defeat of the Spanish Armada that graced the House of Lords until it burned down in 1834; they had been taken from the original Robert Adams drawings made in 1588.

The captured chart is invaluable, and those of William Hack of Juan Fernandez Island and Panama that date 1682 and 1685 respectively were redrawn from the originals captured from the Spanish by buccaneers (pages 50 and 51).

Most charts have become an enduring historical record, but some started out as such, and the attractive chart by Gerard Van Keulen of the combined Dutch and British attack on Barcelona in 1705 (page 65) and the chart published by William Faden showing the prelude to the Battle of Trafalgar (pages 118–119) strongly make the point.

Forewarned is of course forearmed, and charts that provide intelligence of harbours or beachheads for attacks or as a contingency are of great value. The chart by Captain Foley (page 70), who brazenly spent the day purportedly 'fishing' in Ferrol harbour with his sailing master in 1751, during the lull between the end of the War of the Austrian Succession and the start of the Seven Years War, encapsulates the situation.

Charts that showed the sea route were naturally kept secret to maintain the commercial and territorial advantage, and part of the way the Dutch maintained their eastern possessions in the seventeenth century was to do just that, as the Portuguese and Spanish had done before them. Willem Blaeu's beautiful chart of 1674 showing the north Atlantic (pages 40–41) was not seen by anyone other than a few directors of the Dutch East India Company for a hundred years.

Other charts formed part of the official report of proceedings for a board of inquiry or court martial and one such example was produced at the court martial of Admiral John Byng following the loss of Minorca in 1756 and is featured on page 71.

The chart has been used to assess and plan the protection of the entrance to naval bases and dockyards and the charts of Chatham Dockyard of 1698 and the forts along the River Medway of 1700 (page 53) and St John's Harbour Newfoundland of 1772 (page 78) are attractive examples of this purpose.

Few charts survive that were actually used during a sea battle, although the briefing chart drawn by Lord Thomas Cochrane before his attack on Aix and Basque Roads in 1809 during the Napoleonic War (page 121) is close. But I have found many that supplement a report to the Sovereign or State on a battle or amphibious operation. Examples include the report on the bombardment of Algiers in 1816 (page 123) to the Admiralty in the UK and the naval reports to US Congress in the American Civil War (page 137).

The navigator's perspective of the chart is greatly enhanced by the elevated view and drawings of the approach to land, as advised in the Admiralty Manual of Surveying, were to be made about 4 to 5 miles offshore. They would help the navigator to recognize different parts of the coast, and identify landmarks from which he could take bearings and fix his position. The views painted by J T Serres in 1800 during the French Revolutionary War of the coast around the blockaded harbours of Ferrol (pages 106–107) and Brest (page 112), commissioned by the Admiralty, are examples of his outstanding work. They are beautifully painted, but were nonetheless used to abstract elevations of the French coast.

Charts have been used in newspapers to satisfy the public interest in wars and conflict, in particular the war map that was used as part of the report printed by the New York Herald during the American Civil War in 1861 (page 132).

Historically important charts have come to light through the journals and logbooks of naval officers, and that depicting the Battle of Navarino of 1827 (page 125) is an example held in the Admiralty Library at the Royal Naval Museum in Portsmouth. Others have survived as part of an intelligence report from an eyewitness account, and the British Naval Attaché to the Japanese drew his chart on the spot at the action against the Russians at Port Arthur in 1904 (page 144).

Amphibious operations need accurate and up-to-date charts, and those prepared for D-Day in 1944 featured in Chapter 8 include one of the coura-

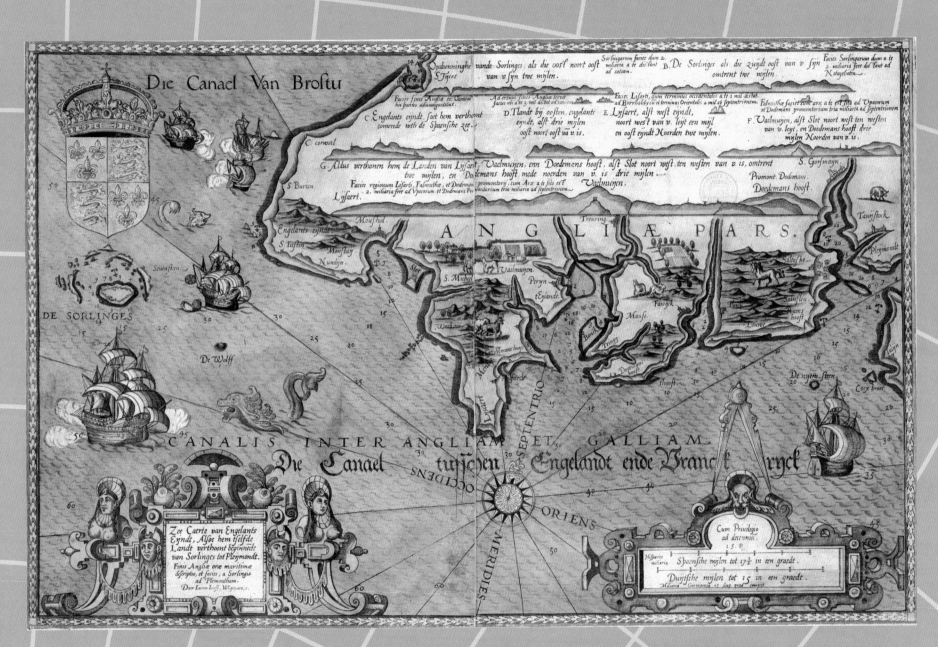

geous surveys of Lieutenant Commander Berncastle (page 153), prepared under cover of night under the German guns off the Normandy coast to provide information on the beach gradient for safe landing of troops and tanks.

By their very nature, charts were of use for the moment, so relatively few survive from before a system of collating and producing them was set up by the maritime nations. Today we value and reflect on them, celebrate their artistry and collect them, but in their time, they were merely a tool, one of many, that a navigator had to hand, to be discarded when its use had passed, or it had worn out, or been damaged by sea water, conflict or neglect.

| ABOVE | **CHART OF CORNWALL AND THE SCILLY ISLES BY LUCAS JANSZOON WAGENAER, 1584**| This chart is taken from *Spiegel der Zeevaerdt (Mirror of the Sea)* compiled by Lucas Janszoon Wagenaer, a Dutch sea pilot, and comprises a manual of navigation, pilot book and 45 charts covering from Cadiz to the Baltic and was published in Leiden in 1584. Waghenaer's book of sea charts was part of the navigational portfolio carried by the Spanish Armada and this chart taken from it shows the west of England, including the Scilly Isles and the first landfall of the Spanish Armada at the Lizard in 1588. (© National Maritime Museum, London, FO351)

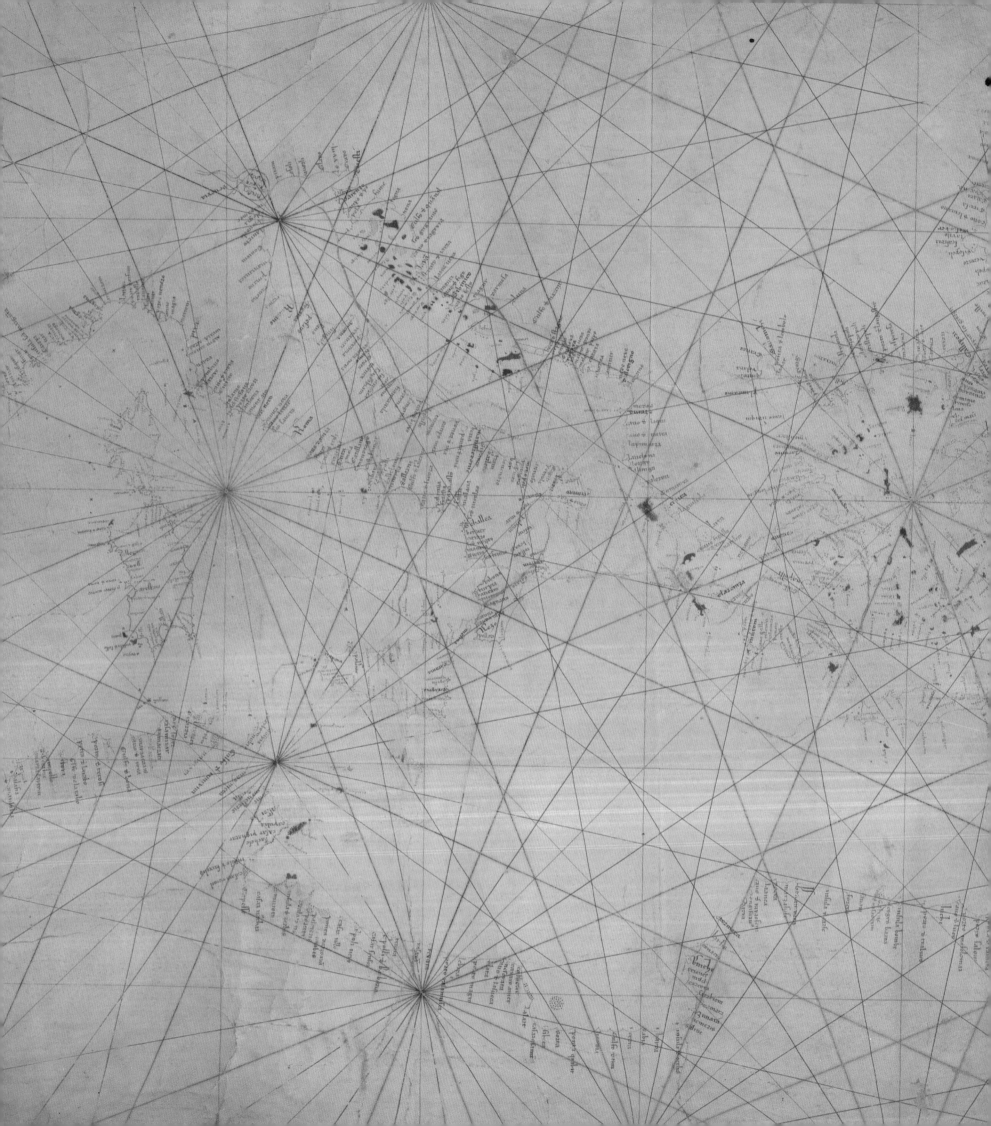

The Ancient Chart

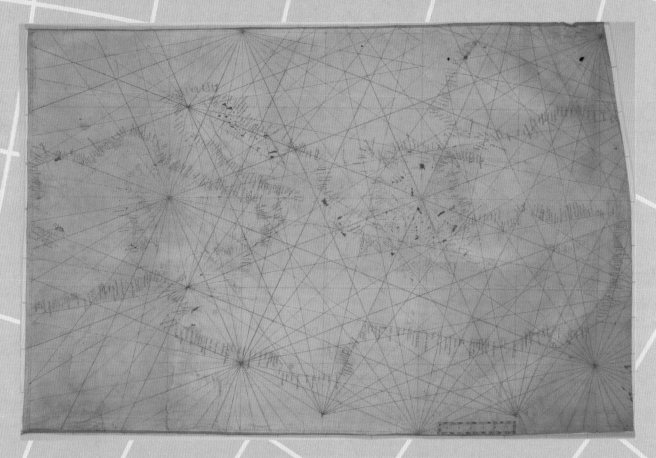

| **PORTOLAN CHART OF THE MEDITERRANEAN, *C.* 1320–50** | This manuscript chart of the Mediterranean and Black Seas on vellum is the oldest chart in the collection of the Library of Congress, Washington DC. The author is unknown, but from the portolan style it was probably drawn on vellum with green, red and brown ink in Genoa. It covers the Mediterranean from the Balearic Islands to the Levantine coast and the western part of the Black Sea and includes a bar scale with unidentified divisions. The first known mention of a shipboard chart is in 1270 when the French King St Louis sailed from Aigues Mortes to Tunis, which he intended to use as a base for his crusade. This was also the time of struggle between the two strongest maritime Italian states of Genoa and Venice, which had started in 1253 and culminated with the Peace of Turin in 1381 after four maritime wars, which strengthened Venice and ruined Genoa. The characteristic outline of Italy can clearly be seen, which is represented surprisingly accurately for this period.(Library of Congress)

EARLY navigation was a hit and miss affair. There were none of the aids to navigation we take for granted today: no compass, no means of measuring distance, and no chart. If the fog closed in sailors were lost. Harsh experience, memory and personal anecdote were passed down the generations. Chaucer summed up the oral tradition when his shipman knew from memory, 'all the havens as they were from Gotland to Cape of Finisterre, and every creek in Brittany and Spain'.

The earliest European navigational chart that has survived is the Carte Pisane, dating from the end of the thirteenth century, so called because it was acquired from a Pisan family by the Bibliothèque Nationale in Paris. It typifies a style of chart developed for a type of seamanship that was applicable in the Mediterranean, probably from the twelfth century, known as the portolan.

With the Mediterranean virtually a tideless sea and winds on average steady and reliable, a particular form of navigation and sea fighting developed there. The peculiarly predictable winds gave rise first to the wind rose, and then the compass rose. The Phoenicians are recognized as forming the wind rose with four main directions: *Boreas*, from the north; *Euros*, from the east; *Notos*, from the south; and *Zephuros*, from the west, which, depicted in simple sailing notes, formed a straightforward cross. With longer voyages, four more directions were added between the existing ones: *Kaikias*, north-east; *Apeliotes*, east, while *Euros* slipped round to the south-east; *Libs*, south-west; and *Skiros*, north-west. By ascertaining the wind direction and relating this to his understanding of the sun's movement during the day, a mariner could gain a good sense of direction. By night, the Pole Star kept a sufficiently consistent northerly bearing to set a course by. By the time of the climactic meeting of the Greek and Persian fleets at the Battle of Salamis in 480 BC, Greek mariners were steering by relating to these winds.

In turn, the Italian city states, in accord with their maritime pre-eminence, adopted the Greek system, with the northerly wind known as *Tramontana*; *Greco*, north-east; *Levante*, east; *Sirocco*, south-east; *Mezzodi*, south; *Garbino*, changing to *Africus* or *Affricone*, south-west; *Ponente*, west; *Maestro*, north-west. Each wind had its characteristics: hot, dry, cold, wet, humid, Saharan, and often a smell, which were all familiar to the experienced mariner.

Although portolan charts were initially made on a projection that utilized the wind rose, most examples that survive use the compass rose from which 16 rhumb lines (from the Spanish *rumbos*, meaning a line of constant bearing) radiated to connect to 16 more roses on a circle at maximum radius to fit on the vellum or parchment. As their construction was not to any grid, their use was spatial in that a course to steer from one point to another could be laid off on the chart by 'pricking off' with a pair of dividers, but no assessment of position along that course through dead (deduced) reckoning could be made. This is the estimate of speed and direction so as to plot progress through the water over a period of time by marking course and position, depending on the proximity of the coast and the complexity of the waters. The portolan also helped the pilot to know place name sequences, an essential feature of navigation, supported by his portolano or written sailing directions, which were used in tandem and gave details of the distance and course needed to sail from one part of the Mediterranean to another, and other information such as anchorages and depth of water.

With winds often light, the warship that developed was the manoeuvrable oar-driven galley with up to three horizontal banks of oarsmen, relying on the

| **INVASION OF ENGLAND BY THE SCOTS AND THE DANES, C. 1350** | Very few written navigational aids have survived from before the sixteenth century and what we know of navigational techniques, either in war or trade, comes from old texts and illuminated manuscripts. This image of the invasion of England by Scotland and her Danish ally comes from a verse history of England, 'Roman de Brut', by the Anglo-Norman poet known as Maistre Wace, born in Jersey and who became Canon of Bayeux. The method of sailing from Denmark to Scotland relied on knowledge gained from personal experience and handed down verbally, using the sun for direction, appreciating how long it would take to sail across the North Sea and recognizing significant headlands. Wace's descriptions of military strategic points along the coast of Normandy, for example, were used in the early stages of the Battle of Normandy in the early eleventh century. (By permission of the British Library: Egerton 3028)

ram to sink an opponent or splinter their oars by glancing down the side. On the approach, men armed with bow and arrow and sling-shot would loose off an uncomfortable volley of stones and arrows, then board with soldiers fighting hand to hand. The sailing ship started to overtake the oar as the primary means of propulsion in about 1000, although the rowed war galley continued in the Mediterranean until much later. The last significant naval action between galleys manned by oarsmen was the Battle of Lepanto in 1571 between a combined fleet of the Christian nations bordering the Mediterranean and a Turkish fleet.

The Alexandria-based mathematician and astonomer, Claudius Ptolemy, who lived from about AD 90 to 168, created the first map of the Mediterranean, or the known world, which included a latitude and longitude grid, with a prime meridian running through the Canary Islands. With the fall of the Roman Empire his major work, *Geographia*, was 'lost'. After the fall of Constantinople in 1453 it was rediscovered and had a profound influence on European cartographers in the Italian states and Majorca, the early makers of the portolan chart. In the Italian states it was translated into Latin, the *lingua franca* of the Renaissance, and his ideas of scale and projection were introduced into the portolans, forming the basis for the charting of all new discoveries in the fifteenth and sixteenth centuries. Strong influences came, too, through the Arabs, with their knowledge of astronomy and mathematics.

Some magnificent examples of portolan charts are shown in this chapter and the next. In measuring up visually to the standards of attractive classical art and sculpture of the time, they became resplendent with gold leaf and gloriously coloured flags, and the compass roses and cartouches make miniature works of art in themselves, although the cynic might argue that the less that was known the more was embellished. As well as being a working document, they were also made for a person of power or influence from kings to wealthy merchantmen, making a visual statement of authority and possession. A visiting diplomat or potentate would have the owner's territories proudly and perhaps pointedly demonstrated; a visual reminder of who he was and what he could command, and a subtle impression could be conveyed to persuade, cajole or threaten.

The portolan chart endured for five centuries and the format of its construction was to spread slowly to northern maritime countries such as England and Holland. However, the navigational tradition that developed in the northern European and Scandinavian waters had to take account of winds, tides and tidal streams that are strong, sometimes dangerous, and affect a ship's progress far more. The Vikings used no charts (although there are one or two forgeries in existence) but relied on word of mouth experience passed on. The summer was their voyaging season, with a long-lasting sun to steer by and clement weather. It was comparatively easy to leave the coast of Norway and head west, keeping the sun on a relative southerly bearing (although changing), knowing that crossing the North Sea you would hit Britain in a couple of days making landfall at obvious and conspicuous headlands, cliffs or rivers. From the eight century, regular Viking raids were made along the east coast of England, and to Ireland, the Isle of Man and Wales, where the cathedral of St David's in north Pembrokeshire, after repeated sacking, was built to a squat design nestled between hills making it invisible from the sea. From Viking poems and sagas we can strongly surmise that they would sail further to Greenland, Iceland or Newfoundland by siting high

peaks: for example the Shetlands can be seen from a low boat from 40 miles, and the Faroes from 50 miles. There is reasonable conjecture that the Vikings used the sun compass, which works by marking a horizontal wooden disc with the progressive shape of the sun's shadow cast by a gnomon during the day in your latitude. Where the gnomon curve is shortest it indicates due geographical north. They also knew of calcerite, which they used in fog or bad visibility. It bends the sun's light through 90 degrees so that, knowing the sun's azimuth, a course could be held relative to it. Their oared longships, adapted to carry a sail, were strong enough to make the journeys across the North Sea and into the Atlantic.

In the Middle Ages pilots sailed by hugging the coast and developed their own written sailing directions, known by the Dutch as *leeskaertan* (literally 'reading chart'), the Spanish as *derroterro*, by the Bretons as *routiers* and by the English, who so often anglicized the French word, as rutters. These sailing directions advised the compass course to steer from headland to headland, known as caping, with advice as to which side of a channel to keep to avoid the strongest contrary tide and to steer clear of rocks and shoals. As an aid to establishing position and navigating close to shore, knowledge of the depth of water and the nature of the sea bed was important and this could be sampled from the tallow applied to the bottom of the lead and line heaved over the side. Battles were rarely fought at sea – the ships of William the Conqueror's extensive invasion fleet were cavalry and troop transports – until Tudor times, when the concept of a national standing navy or royal fleet in being, began.

Across the other side of the world, the Chinese had developed sophisticated navigational systems well in advance of Europe. The magnetic compass is recorded as in use by ships in 1090, at least one hundred years before Europe. Chinese charts, similar in nature to the portolans but more schematic, for this period survive, and some are printed in the final chapter of the famous treatise on Chinese military and naval technology, the *Wu Pei Chih*. They have lines of travel with legends showing details of compass bearings to steer and distances divided by the number of watches, usually of four hours' duration. The notes have details of half-tide rocks and shoals with ports and havens, and advisory routes for outward- and inward-bound passage past islands. They were of sufficient accuracy to lay a course through the Singapore Strait. For timing a ship's speed, it has been surmised that the Chinese used joss sticks that burn at an even rate, or a version of the sand glass. The zenith of Chinese maritime ability was a series of remarkable voyages by Admiral Zheng He between 1400 and 1430, but after this Chinese naval power waned as the emperor concentrated on domestic matters.

The various crusades of the twelfth to fifteenth centuries kick-started and benefited the trading ports around the Mediterranean, such as Venice and Genoa. Wealthy merchant families influenced the State in sponsoring wars against other competing Italian mercantile states and neighbouring countries. The closing of the overland Silk Route that had hitherto brought desirable Eastern merchandise spurred the hunt for a sea-route. First, the Portuguese rounded the southern tip of Africa and then the Spanish expedition under Christopher Columbus, that sought a direct route west, reached America. With the opening up of the African route to the East and across the Atlantic to the New World, ships, and navigation, had to adapt to oceanic sailing, which resulted in the complex multi-masted ship designs of the caravel and carrack.

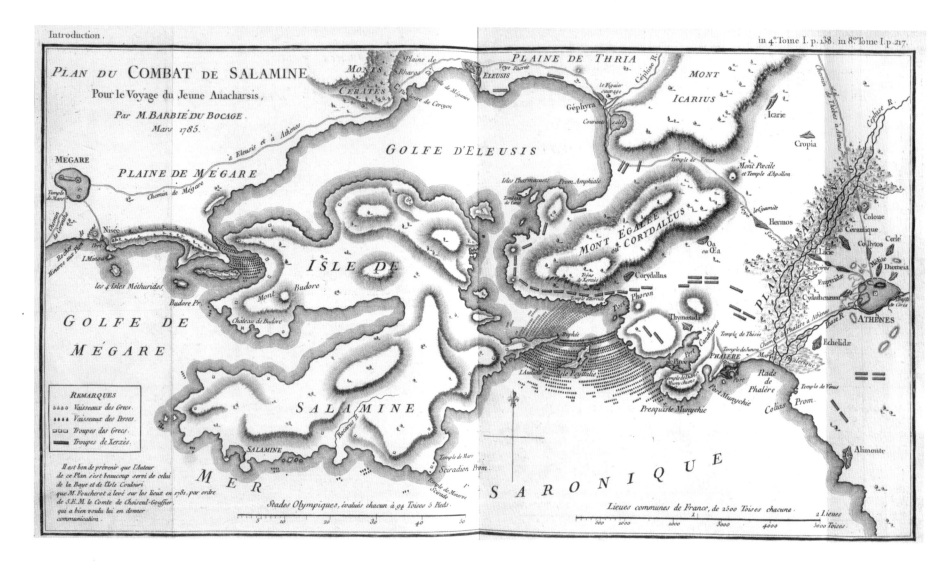

| ABOVE | **PLAN OF THE BATTLE OF SALAMIS, 480 BC, ENGRAVED BY GUILLAUME DE LA HAYE FROM AN ACCOUNT PUBLISHED IN 1785 BY J D BARBIE DU BOCAGE** | The Battle of Salamis in 480 BC was what the military historian John Keegan has described as one of the 15 most decisive sea battles in history, on a par for the Greeks with the defeat of the Spanish Armada for the English. It gave maritime supremacy in the Aegean to the Greeks and ended Persian westward expansion.

The Persians, who wanted to crush Athenian support for a revolt against their leader Darius, had already been defeated twice, the second time at the Battle of Marathon. Xerxes, the new ruler, realized the need for naval power to support his army and resolved to defeat the Greeks through the use of massive sea power: 750 galleys and 180,000 men. The Greeks had a smaller navy, deployed from Athens to the island of Salamis, about 5 miles to the west, to block the Persian fleet's entrance into the bay of Eleusis. Xerxes blocked the western channel between Salamis and the mainland with his Egyptian galleys, and sent his Phoenician and Ionian fleets into the bay. The Greek leader, Themistocles, cleverly used his Corinthian fleet to lure the Persians into the narrow strait to the north, past the island of Psytallia at the entrance, which forced them to reform from a three-line formation to a column. In a rising gale the Persian fleet, disorganized and losing the initiative, faced a devastating series of line abreast ramming attacks from the Greeks, whose marines overwhelmed the Persian archers and whose strongly built galleys sheered the oars of the Persians. By sunset 200 Persian ships had been sunk, as compared to 40 Greek.

This chart, engraved by Guillaume de la Haye, is taken from the account published in 1785 (by J D Barbie du Bocage) of the re-enactment of the travels of the Sythian philosopher Anarchasis, inspired by his teacher, the French geographer and cartographer Jean Baptiste Bourguignon D'Anville, and gives the positions of the Greek and Persian ships and troops, based on contemporary writings. (Reproduced by courtesy of the Royal Geographical Society with IBG: 3.E.13 plate III)

| RIGHT | **THE BATTLE OF ACTIUM, 31 BC, BY JEAN BAPTISTE BOURGUIGNON D'ANVILLE, C. 1775** | This was the key battle to decide who would rule the Roman Empire after the assassination of Julius Caesar in 44 BC. The power struggle was between Octavian, with Agrippa his commander, and Mark Anthony, allied with Cleopatra of Egypt. Agrippa had sailed from the Roman port of Tarentum, by the heel of Italy to take Methone in the Peloponnese, and then north to the Gulf of Arta where Anthony had established a camp on the promontory with the old name of Actium. The Egyptian fleet had 230 bigger and more solidly built galleys to the Romans 400. But their lightness gave the Roman galleys manoeuvrability and instead of relying on ramming they ran alongside, smashing the slave's oars. As the Romans took the advantage, Cleopatra, followed by Mark Anthony, slipped away and the remainder of the fleet surrendered. Octavian took the title Augustus as the first Roman Emperor, a legacy that has lasted with the month of August.

There are no known charts of this time and navigation relied on local knowledge, the lead and line, and Stella Maris, the Pole Star which, in describing a circle each day of only 2°25′, remains a reasonably constant pointer to true north.

The map is from *A Complete Body of Ancient Geography* by M. D'Anville, Member of the Royal Academy of Belles-Lettres, at the Academy of Sciences, Petersburg, and Secretary to the Duke of Orleans. (This version was published in London by Robert Sayer in about 1775.) This was the period of the Enlightenment and as part of the 'Grand Tour', it was *de rigeur* to explore ancient civilizations. Both D'Anville and his pupil, Bocage, mapped afresh most of the countries of the pre-Christian world. (Reproduced by courtesy of the Royal Geographical Society with IBG: 1.C.7 Map 6)

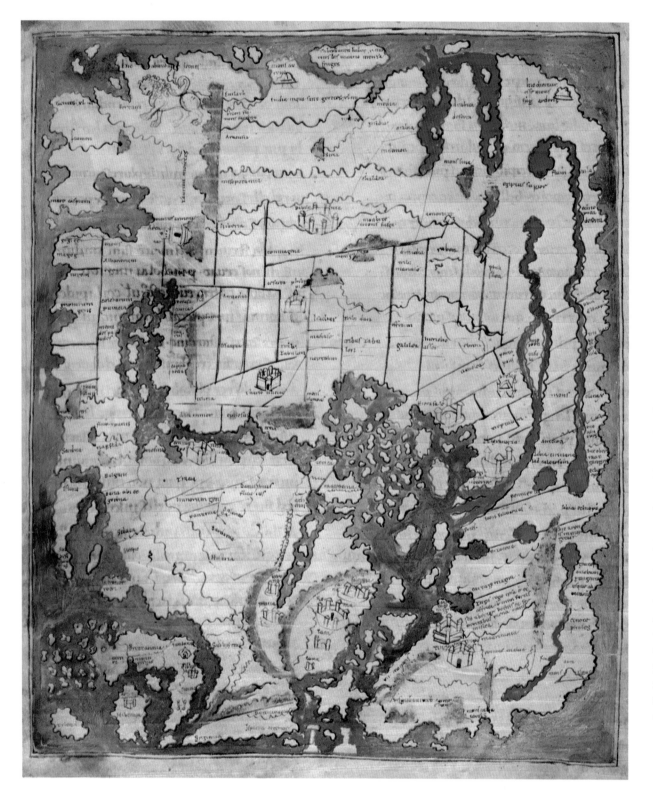

| SEA BATTLE BETWEEN CRETE AND ATHENS, C. 1285 | The Fourth Crusade led in 1204 to the temporary disintegration of the Byzantine Empire and the creation of a feudal state under the rule of French, Flemish, Italian nobles and Venice. The restored Byzantine Empire of 1261–1453 recovered only parts of Greece, most of which continued under the rule of French and Italian princes until conquered by the Ottoman Turks (completed in 1456). Genoa held Khíos until 1566; Venice retained Crete, sold to them in 1204, until 1669 and the Ionian Islands until 1797. In its numerous wars with the Ottomans, Venice also held Athens, Évvoia, and several other ports and islands for brief intermittent periods prior to 1718. This sea battle depicted between the fleets of Crete and Athens in about 1285, from a contemporary French history, represents the independence attempts by the islanders.

Typically, war galleys would be sent in divisions against the enemy, selecting their target on an opportunity basis, firing arrows and sling-shot to immobilize the slaves or kill the captain and officers, aiming to either ram and sink an opposing galley or to steer hard at the last moment to parallel the other's course, break the oars in succession, and probably killing the rowers, then boarding and taking the galley with soldiers. (By permission of the British Library: Add. 15268)

| THE TIBERIUS MAP, 11TH CENTURY | This map, unusually drawn in rectilinear form rather than the medieval circular norm, is the only world map to survive from Anglo-Saxon England. It is thus representative of the European understanding of the world at that time, with the British Isles emerging from the Dark Ages, subject to the raids and settlement of the Vikings. Believed to have been drawn by monks around the time of the First Crusade of 1095, maps at that time placed the Holy Land in the middle, because Jerusalem was considered to be the centre of the world and was the prime destination for pilgrims, as well as the military expeditions of the eleventh, twelfth and thirteen centuries by the Christian powers to recapture the area from the Muslims. The map is divided into the three continents of Europe, Asia and Africa, showing the Mediterranean with the Nile delta clearly marked. The British Isles and Ireland (Armagh) are passably accurate with the River Thames identifiable, while the Faroe Islands, Orkneys, Shetlands and the Isle of Man are indicated. (By permission of the British Library: Cotton Tiberius B. V., Part 1)

| ZHENG HE, CHINESE ADMIRAL (1371–1433) | Zheng He (also translated as Cheng Ho) was the highly successful Chinese admiral who, under the Ming dynasty, oversaw an extraordinary period of Chinese expansion and trade between 1405 and 1433. He built huge Chinese junks with which he made seven voyages into the Indian Ocean, probably south to the East Indies and Australia, and he may even have sailed to America. He put China into a trading position strong enough to have pre-empted the Portuguese trading empire. With Zheng He's death and the 1449 capture of the Emperor by the Mongols, China's expansionist inclination faltered and she turned inwards. Japanese coastal raiding increased but China ignored it failing to build a navy and banning all coastal shipping, while vital grain and other commodities were sent inland along the new Grand Canal. As coastal shipping declined, so did overseas trade and any idea of protective shipping. The last of the Ming emperors committed suicide in 1644 and China became quiescent until the late nineteenth century. This was unexpected behaviour from a country that had introduced the mariner's compass to the world, made careful study of the tides and understood latitude and longitude and the use of the sun and stars to assess position. The illustration comes from a Chinese account of Zheng He's voyages, dating from the 1600s. (By permission of the British Library: 15331.f.2)

| SPANISH CONQUEST OF THE CANARY ISLANDS, 1402 | The Canary Islands, originally discovered by the Romans, who were so impressed by the indigenous wild dogs that they called the islands Canarii, were largely forgotten until, with Portuguese exploration south along the coast of Africa, and then Spanish voyages to the New World, their strategic position attracted interest. The Norman nobleman Sieur Jehan de Béthencourt learned of an earlier Spanish plundering expedition to the islands and sailed from Cadiz in 1402 to conquer them. His shipmaster would probably have been Spanish – both Spanish and Portuguese pilots were highly respected by English, Dutch and Italian mariners for their pilotage skills. He would have had access to the Spanish King Henry's portolan to plan the voyage, but would otherwise have relied on his portolano or rutter of sailing directions in coastal waters and, once out of sight of land, the compass and dead reckoning to steer to the islands and check position and progress. Béthencourt took two Franciscan monks, Pedro Bontier and Juan le Verrier, who chronicled the conquest. King Henry encouraged and rewarded Béthencourt with a lordship of the islands, starting a 100-year process of the islanders' annihilation, subjugation and assimilation to the Catholic faith, a precursor of what was to happen in the New World. The illustration is taken from the account and depicts the invasion. (By permission of the British Library: Egerton 2709)

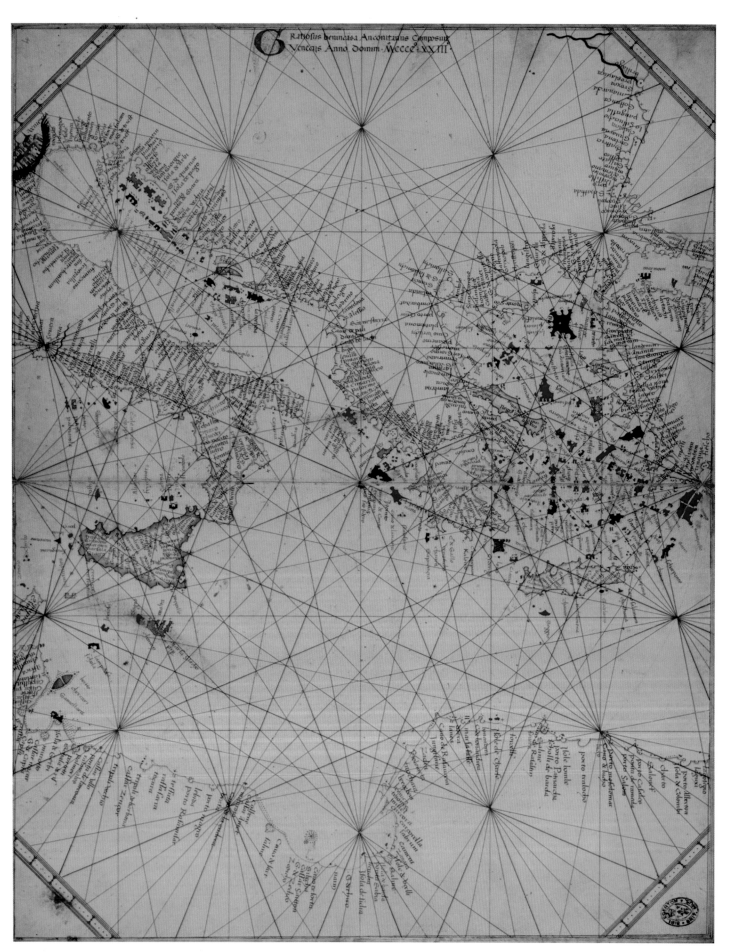

**| CHART OF THE
MEDITERRANEAN AND
ADRIATIC SEAS, FROM
SICILY TO THE BLACK SEA,
BY GRAZIOSO BENINCASA,
1473 |** Improvements in navigational
techniques slowly appeared due to
advances in mathematics brought to
Europe by the Arabs and enhanced
by the Jews in, for example, the
previous Arab territory of the
Balearic Islands, who stayed on after
the Arabs were vanquished. This,
along with the introduction of the
Hindu numeral system by the Arabs
(including the numeral concept 0),
bought about the possibility of
creating the geometry needed to
draw a chart with bearings that could
be used to assess a course to steer. By
1109 seamen in the Italian port of
Amalfi had adapted the magnet as a
compass and sailing directions were
already well in use by 1250.

Claudius Ptolemy, gave the
Europeans their first map of the
Mediterranean, which included a
latitude and longitude grid system.
Although no actual map of his has
survived, medieval copies based on
his co-ordinates have.

This portolan chart by Grazioso
Benincasa, a Venetian cartographer,
uses Ptolemy's square grid. North is
orientated two 'points' of the
compass or 22½° to the right, and
there is the characteristic circle of
16 compass roses. The chart dates
from 1473, twenty years after the fall
of Constantinople, which resulted
in the expansion of so much
mathematical and astronomical
talent that fuelled the upsurge in
navigational methods. The chart
shows the battleground of much of
the eastern Mediterranean, where
constant rivalry between Greece and
Turkey spilled over into
neighbouring islands, such as Crete
and Rhodes (shown with a red
Christian cross or sword hilt). (By
permission of the British Library:
Egerton 2855)

| LEFT | **RHODES BY BARTOLOMMEO DALLI SONETTI, 1485** | This illustration is from the *Isolario* or Island-Book, drawn by the Venetian shipmaster Bartolommeo dalli Sonetti in about 1485. It depicts the island of Rhodes and was, according to Sonetti, constructed with his compass. Each of the 49 charts in the *Isolario* has the eight-pointed Mediterranean compass rose with the symbols for each direction from the older wind rose – in use before the magnetic compass arrived. Coastal rocks are shown by dotted lines, the symbol still used today. Sonetti's real name was Zamberti, but his pseudonym 'dalli Sonetti' came about because he wrote his sailing instructions in verse, for example:

> In summer the island is full of fine roses
> That comfort the senses with their sweetness
> From these the island takes its name
> For from 'Roses' in Greek derives.

Each page of the *Isolario* is left relatively plain, it is thought so that the owner could write in his own navigational notes, and a number that survived are annotated in this way. What this shows is that, although navigation was a very personal business and information was not much shared, there were those prepared to do so and this sort of information was very useful for ships both trading and conquering. (© National Maritime Museum, London, F1607)

| BELOW | **VIEW OF VENICE, 1488** | The influence of the Renaissance ideas of perspective and spatial design on painting, sculpture and architecture also affected cartographers, and ways of representing coasts and continents in two dimensions took shape accordingly. This view of Venice symbolizes artistic advances and the power of the merchant. The crusades brought trade and prosperity to Venice, as it did to Genoa, its main Mediterranean rival, which brought war, too. Pisa had been a rival as well, but was eliminated in 1284 by Genoa at the Battle of Meloria. The markets of the Levant and Byzantium ensured continuing conflict, which was not settled until the fourth and decisive war of 1378–81. Although Venice was silting up as a harbour, the war established her as the pre-eminent Mediterranean power for the next century, until the expanding Ottoman Empire eclipsed her.

This 1488 view of Venice shows the wealth and prosperity of the port which had developed its maritime and trading skills because the hinterland and the lagoon on which the city was built would not support much agriculture, and the early inhabitants had to look to the sea for survival. Many of the early portolans were drawn at the cartographic schools that developed, rather as Fra Mauro, the monk who created the first map of the world through the reports of visiting and returning sea captains, describes. Knowledge was built up from hard won sea-going experience.

This view of Venice, by featuring an array of beautiful and opulent buildings, such as the Doge's Palace, the dome of St Mark's cathedral and the famous Campanile or bell tower, shows off her mercantile prosperity. (By permission of the British Library: G. 7203)

s Countrie

Mc Guyes Country

Mc Guyes.

Enis Killin

Logh Earne

Mc Glonnoghes
Countrie

Logh
wittaghe

Logh Care

Lough Derg or
St Patrickes
purgatorie.

Balle M^c
Glanny.

A^o. 98, 0^e
campsed by
Logh ro^per
men did se
Horses of a
huge bignes

ew Benbo

Drum
Bradnelen.

Court.

Grange.

Belleck

Nether

Dunawna. Lisha
Hill.

Ballech
H. auen.

Dun
carbury.

Bondows.

Artar
men.

Ascaro

Barnesmore.

The Fryers bed wher the
Fryers doe rest, themselues
goinge vp the Mountaines
from Dongall.

3. Spanyshe Shippes
cast awaye in
a^o 88.

In this Ilande there dwe
man named Oscanlon of
contrie people holde
opinion, that if he be
one c^o doe turne 5. sp^e
vppon them, wch he ke
they shall dye w^ith in

Logh
Laskel

Donagall.

Inismurray.

The
B. OBoile.

In this Begg a
is scene in euery
somtime wth foote
on a sodaine, som
dryuinge and f
scene by Sr Geo
dyuers others

The Age of Discoveries

The Renaissance Chart, 1493-1599

| THE NORTH-WEST COAST OF IRELAND WITH WRECKS OF SPANISH ARMADA GALLEONS BY BAPTISTA BOAZIO, *C.* 1600 | This chart of part of the north-west Ireland was drawn on linen by Baptista Boazio in the early 1600s. Orientated with North at 270° and a scale in Irish miles, from observations by Captain John Baxter, it became part of the collection of maps and plans put together for George Legge, 1st Baron Dartmouth, Master General of the Ordnance in 1682, responsible, amongst other jobs, for all fortifications in England. It gave an insight into the topographical situation and opportunities to land troops or build defensive structures. The chart aims to explain the approaches to the territories belonging to the local Irish clans of the O'Donnells and McGuyres (Maguires) in Tyrone and the McWilliams in Sligo. The defeat of the Irish at the end of the nine years' war resulted directly in the later policy of placing Protestants from England and Scotland into Ulster known as the 'Plantations', not dissimilar in its political implications from the Highland Clearances after the Jacobite rebellions of the mid-eighteenth century.

In addition to the notes regarding local folklore, such as 'a holy man who can, by turning stones, cause the death of people who anger him' and 'a bog where scenes of battles, castles and cattle can appear' and others, it depicts the position of '3 Spanish shippes cast awaye in ao 88'. (© National Maritime Museum, London, F2013)

THE Renaissance, generally regarded as starting in Florence in the early fourteenth century, was much more than a re-birth in art and literature. In harking back to the classical influence of Greece and Rome, it was a fillip to the concept of visual representation by such great sculptors as Donatello, and architects such as Brunelleschi and Bramante, who worked on and developed the theory of perspective and naturalistic representation, further advanced in the innovative frescoes and paintings of Massacio and Peiro della Francesca. These artistic and stylistic influences spread themselves into the ground-breaking, two-dimensional representation required by a committed community of seafarers in the burgeoning Mediterranean ports such as Venice and Genoa – the portolan chart and the navigational elevation or coastal view.

As we have seen in Chapter 1 the tradition of navigation was to use personal notes and drawings, called portolano or sailing directions, which would include a portolan chart. In aspirational maritime states, speculators and adventurers were motivated to seek, conquer and forcefully retain lands in the New World. It was inevitable that navigational techniques would advance to meet the demands of ocean voyages and that cartographic production would grow in response. Initially it was concentrated at two main centres: in northern Italy around Ancona, Genoa and Venice, and in the western Mediterranean in Majorca and Barcelona. During the course of the fifteenth century, the Portuguese took the lead, largely due to the committment of Prince Henry, who supported Portuguese explorations of the Atlantic islands and down the west coast of Africa. The portolan became more useful and embellished. Although originally lacking scale, latitude bars were added from around 1500 and longitude measurements were being included as the impact of Ptolemy's grid spread.

The Arabs had adapted the astronomical astrolabe, essentially used for time-measurement and perfected by Persian and Indian astronomers to make charts of the coastlines they traded and attacked. Introduced into Europe the mariner could now use this in conjunction with the magnetic compass, portolano, portolan charts, and the sand glass to create a complementary supporting arrangement of navigational techniques.

The Portuguese developed the forerunner of the modern sextant, the Seamen's Quadrant for their navigators' use on voyages along the African coast. It was a simple quarter circle in brass or wood with a plumb line to measure the angle of a heavenly body, usually the Pole Star. With the introduction of *Regimento do Astrolabio a do Quadrante* in Lisbon around 1495, to be included in William Bourne's navigational vade mecum *A Regiment for the Sea* in 1574, which was in use for a century, a navigator could use these tables to work out his latitude – giving rise to a technique of sailing the latitude or 'plane sailing' until you made a landfall you recognized. This was a mixed blessing because an enemy could simply patrol at that point until you sailed into their trap. Francis Drake used this successfully at Cape Sagres, catching a number of Spanish and Portuguese ships aiming to make for Cadiz after landfall.

The discovery of America in 1492 would almost inevitably lead to a dispute between Portugal and Spain, the two leading maritime nations of the day, over territorial rights. Both being Roman Catholic countries, they appealed to the Pope to issue a ruling. An imaginary line was drawn 100 leagues west of the Azores: all new lands to the east fell to Portugal, and to the west to Spain, thereby giving the eastern sea-route to the Portuguese and the western route to the Spanish. This was known as the Treaty of Tordesillas

(1494). Unbeknownst at the time of the treaty was the trending of the Amazonian coast of South America to the south-east, and Pedro Cabral's discovery of land at 16° South of the equator in 1500 gave Portugal that territory which is Brazil. Ferdinand Magellan's voyage into the Pacific through the strait that took his name in 1520 was primarily to ensure that the Spice Islands were placed within the Spanish sphere. Portugal was able to build up an unchallengeable monopoly of trade with India and the East through a chain of fortified ports along the African coast across the Pacific and lead the design in the most powerful of ships.

With exponentially expanding empires that needed to be maintained, Spain and Portugal realized that charting and navigation needed to be given State support and in 1500 Portugal set up the *Casa da India* in Lisbon followed quickly by Spain's *Casa de Contratación* in Seville in 1504. They administered chart distribution and checked and examined ocean pilots. All charts were accounted for and to knowingly disseminate charts or their information carried the death penalty. But this deterrent was not always successful, as pilots and navigators sometimes changed their allegiance with impunity One of the best examples of 'cartographic espionage' was a copy made by an Italian agent Alberto Cantino and smuggled out of Lisbon in 1502 to his employer, the Duke of Ferrara in Italy. Known as the Cantino chart and held in the Biblioteca Estense in Modena, Italy, it shows the delineating longitudinal line that divided the world as accorded by the Treaty of Tordesillas.

England was quick to respond to the news that Columbus had reached the Indies via a route to the west. In 1497 Giovanni Caboto, a Venetian navigator known as John Cabot in England, sailed with letters patent from Henry VII and sponsored by a group of Bristol merchants in response to Columbus's discovery of America. He landed on the island of Newfoundland and took possession of it in the King's name, thus beginning Britain's interest in that part of North America. He was probably the first to introduce the portolan chart to Bristol. However, the divide between northern European and Mediterranean styles of navigation was still marked and most English ship captains and masters continued with the rutter well into the next century, scorning the Mediterranean seafarer and his 'sheepskins'.

During the reign of Philip II (1556–98) Spain reached the peak of her power, ruling over a vast Empire, which included parts of Europe, America and the Far East. Phillip instructed viceroys in all his realms to commission cartographers to draw up maps and charts. The Viceroy in Naples, for example, in 1575 was told that, 'every day there arise matters in which for greater clarity it is necessary to know distances of the places in that realm, and the rivers and frontiers it has'. The same applied to his lands across the oceans, and Philip clearly needed to know about them for defence and expansion. In a flurry of cartographic activity he ordered a survey of Spain and the coasts in 1566. Now kept in the Escorial Museum, it is the most impressive survey of its kind undertaken in any European state in the sixteenth century. In 1570 Francisco Dominguez, a Portuguese cosmographer, was commissioned to survey all of New Spain and an official 'cosmographer-historian', Juan Lopez de Velasco, was appointed for America. But a great boost to Philip's collection was the *Theatrum Orbis Terrarum* published in 1570 by Abraham Ortelius, who worked closely with Europe's most successful printer Christopher Plantin. Ortelius dedicated the *Theatrum*, with 53 maps covering the world, to Phillip, who was delighted with it.

State-sponsored expeditions aside, in northern European waters in the sixteenth century conflict was characterized by wars of religion. Henry VIII broke away from the Catholic Church and created himself head of the Church of England in 1534, thereby making enemies of Catholic France and Spain. Such antagonism fuelled the design of the warship, which became a fighting unit in its own right rather than merely a carrier of soldiers (in the forecastle and aftercastle). The introduction of gunpowder from China, and the casting of guns lead to the obvious consequence of mounting guns on a ship. To give the ship stability, the guns were placed as low as possible and so moved to the waist from the fore- and aftercastles. To diminish the disadvantage to the ship's sailing qualities of a high freeboard blowing the ship to leeward, castles were reduced in height, although this sacrificed a good field of fire for the sharp-shooters and a commanding position against boarders. The caravel, a compromise rig that utilized the Mediterranean lateen (fore-and-aft) sail set on the mizzen (after) mast with square-rigged sail on the main and forward masts, was the forerunner of the galleon.

By the time of Elizabeth I's reign in England two prominent seamen, Sir Walter Raleigh and the Earl of Cumberland, George Clifford, understood very well the need for better navigation. They respectively engaged Thomas Harriot, an Oxford scholar, and Edward Wright, a Fellow of Caius College, Cambridge, to study the problems of navigation. Both young men had experienced at first hand the difficulties of navigation with a voyage: Harriot to the colony of Virginia in 1585 and Wright to the Azores in 1589. Wright published his *Certaine Errors in Navigation Detected and Corrected* in 1599 in which he strongly urged seamen to adopt Mercator's chart projection with its greater accuracy than plane sailing. Published in 1569, Gerardus Mercator had constructed his projection of parallels and meridians at right angles, which overcame the problem of representing a three-dimensional globe on a two-dimensional surface. It allowed the mariner to plot a single straight rhumb line from one point to another as a course to steer, which would not need to be constantly corrected to make allowances for the earth's curvature. On this type of chart the coastlines in the northern and southern latitudes appear stretched and Wright's analogy of a pig's bladder blown up inside a cylinder and then opened flat slowly took root with English seamen, although taking until at least 1640 to be implemented, mainly through French support.

It is interesting also to note that along with improvements in navigational techniques, a mechanical invention would slowly kill off the portolan and manuscript chart produced by hand. While in China printing was already in use by the sixth century, and a moveable type metal printing was invented in Korea in 1234 by Chwe Yoon Eyee, it was only in 1440, probably after the technology had diffused through India and the Arabic world, that Johann Gutenberg developed a printing press in Mainz. But it was to alter, slowly, the nature of charts from the manuscript style. William Caxton had been governor of the English merchant community in Bruges, and then as secretary to Edward IV's sister, Margaret, who married the Duke of Burgundy, he learned the new art of printing at Cologne and set up his own printing press in London in 1476, printing the first book in English, a history of Troy. It took over 100 years before manuscript charts died out; indeed The Thames School of chartmakers continued making charts to order until the early eighteenth century. Many captains preferred to choose and direct their own personal chart portfolio, but these were eventually out-priced by the far cheaper and more readily available printed charts.

But the obvious practical advantage and convenience of the successor to the portolan could not be long coming, and the Dutch led the way. Cornelis Anthonisz, cartographer to Emperor Charles V, whose famous painted map of Amsterdam, combining skills of perspective, painting, cartography and topography, can be seen in the Weigh House, published in about 1550 the first *paskaertan* or passage chart which would supersede the *leeskaertan* or Flemish rutter.

In 1584 the Dutchman Lucas Janszoon Wagenaer published *Spiegel der Zeevaerdt*, which would have a huge impact on chartmaking. It comprised a collection of charts of the European Atlantic coastlines, from Cadiz northwards into the North Sea and the Baltic. Although he constructed charts without latitude or longitude indications, they had revolutionary new features, including coastal views, a decrease in distance between harbours, bays and rivers, thus enlarged to take information such as depth of water (at half tide), new symbols for navigational buoys and landmarks such as beacons, churches, windmills and rocks awash at half-tide. He incorporated symbols adopted from portolans, such as an anchor for anchorages, a cross for dangerous submerged rocks and dotted areas for sandbanks. England's Lord High Admiral Lord Howard of Effingham was shown a copy of *Spiegel der Zeevaerdt* by the Netherlands' ambassador and he saw immediately how useful it would be for the Queen's navy. He ordered a translation by Anthony Ashley to be known as *The Mariner's Mirrour*, which was finished just after the Armada in 1588. It was hugely successful in England and was in use for a century, giving rise to the English term for a chart: waggoner – a corruption of the Dutch author's name.

Luiz Teixeria, cartographer to the Spanish Crown, copied some of the charts from *Spiegel der Zeevardt* for the ships of the Spanish Armada to carry. These covered the coastline of Cornwall, where they made a landfall, sighting the Lizard, and the Dover Strait, showing Nieuport and Dunkirk on the European continent, where Parma intended to embark his troops to make the crossing to land in Kent.

In addition, the Spanish had a portolan chart of western Europe by Domenico de Vigliarolo, a Neapolitan cleric and cartographer in the Casa de Contratación in Seville, which gave a better idea of the outline of the British Isles, and some reasonable maps of western Europe and the British Isles from *Theatrum Orbis Terrarum*.

However, none of these charts showed the Gulf Stream, although it was known to the Channel Island fishermen who worked the Newfoundland cod banks, and the Spanish knew of it after Ponce de Leon's Pilot Major, Anton de Alaminos, recorded its beneficial flow in the log of their voyage from Vera Cruz to Spain in 1513. But the fleeing Armada was ignorant of the need to allow for the westerly push of the Gulf Stream as they headed south, and having rounded Scotland, they were surprised to find the Irish rocks close on the port beam, with, for many, disastrous results.

Likewise, an official set of sailing directions, *Derrotero de las costas de Bretana, Normandia, Picardia, hasta Flandes, y de la de Inglaterra, Manga de Bristol y Sant Iorge, y parte de la costa de Irlanda*, published by Antonio Álvarez in Lisbon on 30 March 1588 on the orders of the inexperienced commander of the Armada, the Duke of Medina Sidonia, had no information of the English coast north of 'Tierra bermeja' (The Naze near Harwich) along the east coast or, to the west, north of 'a Isla de Baldresay' (Bardsey Island).

The entrance from Belkerbert.

The greate bote wth 67 men for breache ar goinge.

Eneſkillin Caſtell.

Two Cotts wth 30 men for Scale.

A fence made by th curr to impeache o botes

Stakes

A fence croſſe the ryuer

Magwiersbote

A table ditche deepe water

My bettur

The ſowe wth 30 men

Captaine Dow dall gouernor

Three falcons

The gouerners battle.

A quadrent to ſeconde y^e neede

The paſſ to y Iland

An Ilande

A dyche cutt

Cotts for the vſe of the Campe

The houſe of munition

Gouernor Dowdalls Campe

A Scale for paſſes

10	20	30	40	50	60	70	80	90	100	110	120
30			60			90			120		

A hard won lesson for many navigators – always to have the next chart beyond your planned destination to hand – seems not to have been adopted by the Armada, which never expected to sail further north than Kent, but was blown to Scotland before the surviving ships could make a westerly heading and try for Spain. The chart of north-west Ireland reproduced in the opening pages to this chapter shows the position of some of the wrecked Spanish galleons.

Philip sent a second and third Armada in 1596 and 1597 sailing with a set of five sketches made by an English Catholic pilot, Nicholas Lambert, held in the Museo Naval, Madrid. They are some of the earliest surviving charts of the ports where landings were considered – Milford Haven, Falmouth, Plymouth and Dartmouth, and in the vicinity of the Isle of Wight, Southampton and Portsmouth.

The Spanish and Portuguese, with their respective Casas focussed on the New World, were better cartographically informed to voyage to America than to England. And the English were in comparison barely informed at all. This accounts for Drake's solution to the problem of navigation in strange waters; he captured a Spanish pilot. Described in Richard Hakluyt's well-known contemporary accounts of sixteenth-century English voyages, Nuno da Silva was a pilot for the Viceroy of New Spain who had stopped at St Iago in Cape Verde Islands in 1578. Towards the beginning of his circumnavigation, Drake sailed in with his six ships to restock on water and provisions and took da Silva, keeping him as pilot across the Atlantic to Brazil, then south and through the Strait of Magellan, the first European after Magellan to do so. He attacked and sacked many Spanish ports along the western seaboard of South America and released da Silva at Guatulco on the Pacific coast of New Spain (Mexico today). It is difficult to understand the shock, and so undermining confidence in the Spanish monarchy, that Drake's sudden appearance in the Pacific generated, out of all proportion to the actual damage caused. Conversely Drake's voyages of attrition gave England a huge boost and the publication of the charts in his accounts, examples of which are featured on page 34, were avidly taken in.

|LEFT | **SIEGE OF ENNISKILLEN CASTLE, 1594** | The Elizabethans regarded the conquest of the Ireland as a first step in emulating Spain's empire. Partly, too, control of Ireland was seen as a necessary step in preventing an invasion by Spain – or France. And a faction wanted to impose Protestantism on a Catholic populace, although the intertwining of religious and political motives is hard to disentangle. Elizabeth established a strong standing army and rebellions such as that of the Desmonds in the 1580s were put down with ruthless efficiency. Of the four provinces of Ireland, Ulster, Leinster, Munster and Connaught, the last two to the south were under English control, and Ulster was to follow. Rebellions by clans along the southern Ulster border were put down in 1593, but real trouble for the English followed the rebellion of the O'Neills under Hugh, made Earl of Tyrone by the English for, paradoxically, his service with the royal army. O'Neill had asked Philip of Spain to help, but it was too little, too late and too far when a Spanish expedition landed in the south west at Kinsale in 1601.

There were three sieges of Enniskillen Castle in 1593 as control was wrested by one side then the other, ending ultimately with the defeat of the Maguires (owners of the castle and lands surrounding) and their allies the O'Donnells. Looking at the map of the siege one can see the galley with two small 'cotts' (small shallow boats) with '30 men for Scale' which had been rowed in an early example of combined amphibious force operations with another 'bote ankered to breach'. The breach in the castle wall is shown after shelling from the howitzers by Captain Bingham's camp. By the sharp bend in the creek stakes have been driven into the riverbed to control the passage of boats. A warning is given against resistance by the impaled heads in Governor Dowdall's camp, while other cotts nearby are pulled onto the bank ready for any minor use, such as the cott full of firewood being rowed to the shore. (By permission of the British Library: Cotton Augustus I.ii.39)

| **PORTOLAN CHART OF THE KNOWN WORLD BY VESCONTE DE MAGGIOLO, *C.* 1508** | By the time of this Genoese portolan chart of 1508, made by Vesconte de Maggiolo (variously de Maggiola or Maiolo), the New World was already discovered and the European race to take its wealth had begun. This chart has little on it to commend it to navigation; it has a crude scale with the tropics and equator marked, but no wind rose, directional rhumb lines or navigational hazards. However, it is an indication of Europeans' evolving knowledge of the world. It shows the Fortunate Islands (Canaries), Madeira and the Cape Verde Islands, parts of Central America that bound the Caribbean, including Cuba, Africa with S. Vincentii (Madagascar), the Persian Gulf, India and Asia along with a naïve outline of Japan.

Vesconte was one of an important family of Genoese cartographers, and was probably the first Italian cartographer to draw a Madonna onto a portolan chart, so acknowledging the driving force of the Catholic Church in proselytizing the American continent with all of its unhappy consequences. Any ambitious European would have looked at this chart and sensed from it the possibilities of trade and conquest. (By permission of the British Library: Egerton 2803)

| **THE WEST INDIES AND CENTRAL AMERICA BY VESCONTE DE MAGGIOLO, *C.* 1508** | Maggiolo also drew this portolan of Central America that shows the Caribbean coastline of modern Colombia and Venezuela from the mouth of the great River Magdalena, near Carthagena at Barranquilla, including the islands of Cuba and Trinidad. Its construction, based on eight compass roses of 32 rhumb lines, only one of which can be seen, against a grid of parallel lines is typical of the portolan, and he uses the traditional Mediterranean symbols, taken from the winds, to indicate north, south, east and west.

Of course any map can be used to show actual or aspiring territorial ownership and many portolans fulfilled that role. European rulers commissioned portolans specially for this purpose, with national flags on fortresses and castles to emphasize their rule on land and flown from the masts of caravels to reflect their dominance at sea. (By permission of the British Library: Egerton 2803)

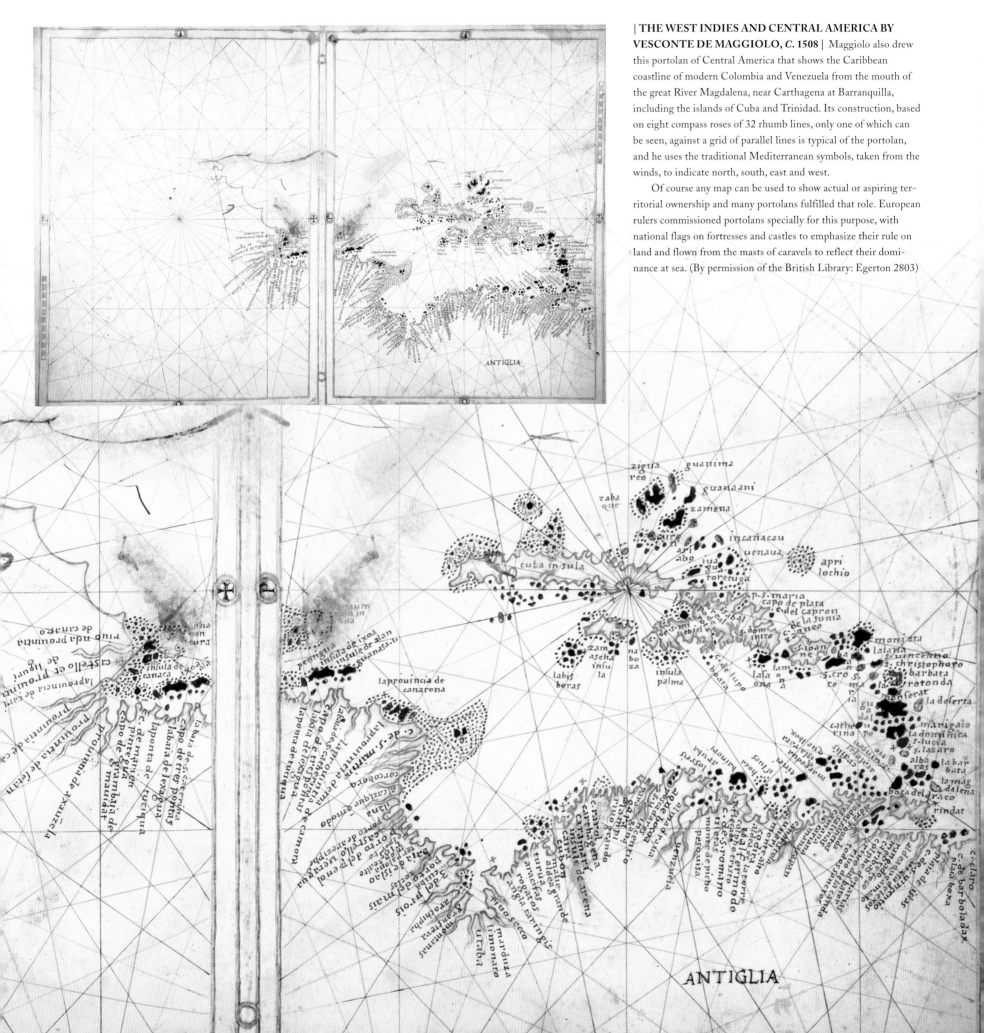

| FRENCH RAID ON BRIGHTON, 1514 |

Although this attack on an obscure fishing village called Brighthelmstone that happened to be well within range of the French coast would seem insignificant, it was the 'finale' of a greater scene. Louis XII of France was at war with the Holy Roman Empire, fighting between 1494 and 1559 to gain control of Italy. A Holy League was formed against France, which from 1512 to 1514 included England. In retaliation to the attack on Brighton, Henry VIII sent a large force but the French evaded them and the fleet had to be content with a final burning of Breton villages before both sides, mutually exhausted, sought peace, sealed by the marriage of Henry's favourite sister Mary to Louis.

This chart records the attack by the Mediterranean galleys and landing craft of Pregént de Bidoux while, with warning beacons lit and many houses burning, the local defence force attempts to repulse them – a chart drawn to both record and stimulate reaction to the event. (By permission of the British Library: Cotton Augustus I.i.18)

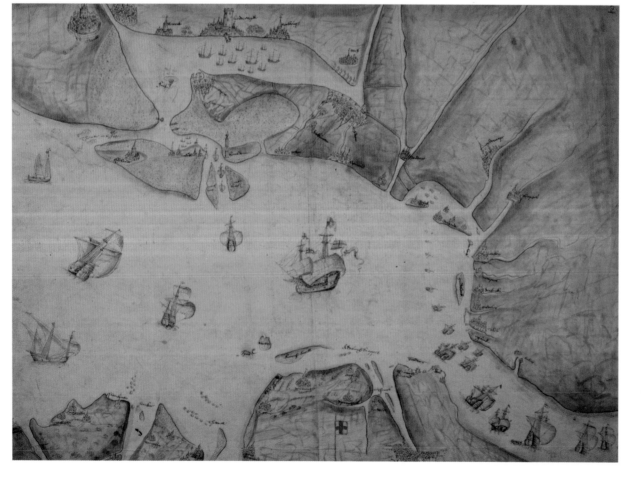

| PROPOSED ROUTE OF ANNE OF CLEVES TO HENRY VIII, 1539 |

Following the death of Henry VIII's third wife, Jane Seymour, in 1537, the King's chief minister, Thomas Cromwell, found a politically advantageous match in Anne of Cleves. An alliance though marriage into one of the myriad German and Dutch states would strengthen England's position in Europe, in danger of isolation at a time when France and Austria had declared a truce. Seeking to avoid any risks by minimizing the journey overland, it was decided to bring her by sea from Harderwijk in Guelderland, by the Zuider Zee to England. Unfortunately, and this reflects the general state of English charting at the time, there were no charts available, and the *Rutter of the Sea*, the only book of sailing directions printed in English, was essentially a guide to the English Channel.

Two sailing masters, John Aborough from Devon and Richard Couche from Dover were chosen in 1539 to discreetly survey the route. They produced this chart of the Zuyder (Zuider) Zee and Zeegat van Texel, and showing the east coast of England (marked with the cross of St George), including London and the Thames Estuary, parts of Flanders, Holland and the North Sea, with the proposed route indicated by a succession of ships of decreasing size, and the perspective adjusted to emphasize the more relevant bays and islands. In the event, Anne travelled by land to Calais and across the English Channel to marry Henry, so the chart was never used. (By permission of the British Library: Cotton Augustus I.ii.64)

| SEA MAP OF THE ENGLISH COAST BETWEEN FOWEY AND SALCOMBE, INCLUDING PLYMOUTH, 1539 | Henry VIII's territorial ambitions in France, his suspicion of the Low Countries, and his deteriorating relations with Scotland laid his country open to retaliatory attacks and even invasion, as was to happen in 1545 when France, incited by his proclamation of 1543 allowing unrestricted private warfare at sea, landed troops on the Isle of Wight and brought a combined fleet of 25 galleys and 150 ships up to Spithead, where it was repulsed by the English fleet with the loss of Henry's flagship, *Mary Rose*. A review of the south coast defences was urgently needed and a sea map of the coast and hinterland from Land's End to Exmouth was produced to help in this endeavour. One of the earliest existing charts made for navigational use, the features for which a seaman would need to keep a lookout have been exaggerated, widened and foreshortened, which lends the view much charm. This excerpt shows the Devon coast between Fowey and Salcombe and includes the important naval base of Plymouth, home to many of England's sea heroes, such as the Hawkins brothers and Drake. (By permission of the British Library: Cotton Augustus I.i.38)

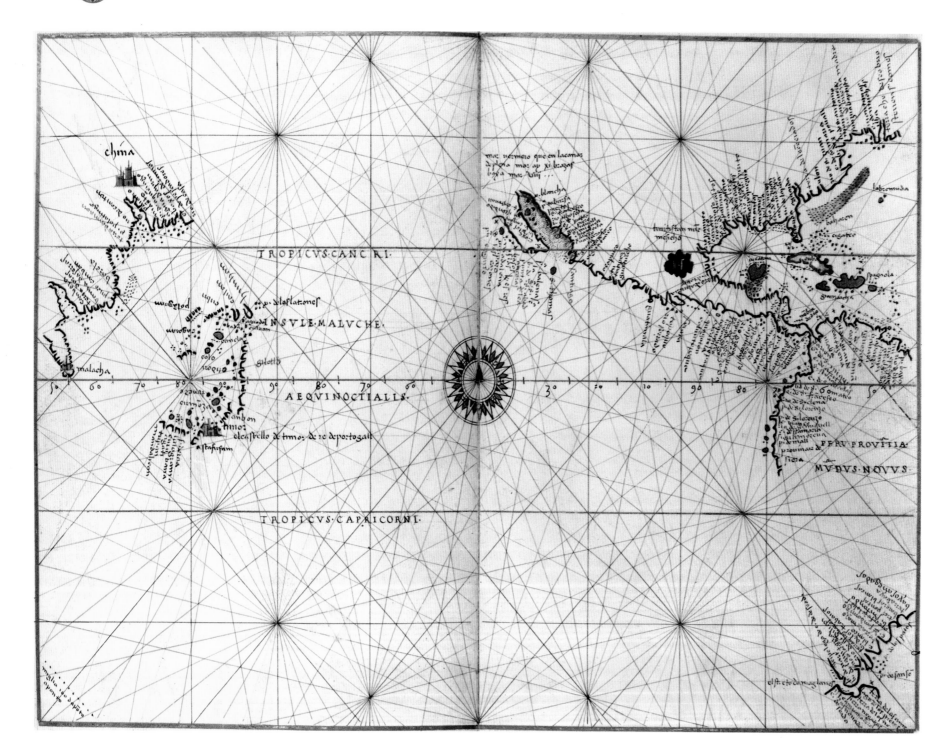

| ABOVE | **PORTOLAN OF THE AMERICAS AND THE PACIFIC OCEAN, INCLUDING HERNÁN CORTÉS' DISCOVERIES ALONG THE WEST COAST BY BATTISTA AGNESE, *C.* 1540** | While England and France were preoccupied, Spain and Portugal were exploring the New World. This portolan was one of the first to show the Magellan Strait and includes Cortes' discoveries along the Gulf of California. It is a chart used to illustrate conquest and was drawn for a wealthy merchant family of Florence, the Guadagnis. Niccolo Machiavelli mentions Bernardo Guadagni, who was the Gonfalonier or chief Italian magistrate of the Republic, in his history of Florence. It is an example of the patronage such wealthy families extended towards trade and exploratory voyages. The Magellan Strait clearly suggests the understanding of the route into the Pacific, while in the Caribbean the Gulf Stream is portrayed by a bold brushstroke. California is correctly shown as a gulf and not an island. In the Pacific a shy intimation of the Philippines (named after King Philip of Spain) and the coast of China and Cochin is included along with a longitude scale on the equatorial line. (By permission of the British Library: Egerton 2854)

| RIGHT | **SOUTH ASIA AND THE SPICE ISLANDS BY DIOGO HOMEN, 1558** | At a time of burgeoning interest in the possibility of England's own colonial empire, speculation as to sidestepping Spain and Portugal's monopoly of the East by a northern route across the top of Europe or North America stimulated exploration to find the North-East and North-West Passages. It became a peculiarly English obsession, with the formation of the Muscovy Company in 1555, the East India Company in 1601 and the Hudson's Bay Company in 1670. During her reign Queen Mary ordered an atlas of the world from one of the leading Portuguese portolan-makers, Diogo Homen, son of the famous hydrographer, Lopo Homen. Diogo had been exiled from his native country and arrived in England in 1547. He produced what is acknowledged as the first printed passage sea chart in 1569. This chart-style map of the Spice Islands and Asia comes, imbued with iconoclastic designs, from Mary's atlas. The value of spices such as nutmeg was greater than gold and the denial of this trade to England as well as the trade of gold and silver of South America and slaves from Africa, pushed England, the Netherlands and France to seek and take their own territories. (By permission of the British Library: Add.5415A)

| RIGHT | **LISBON, 1553** | Julius Caesar appreciated the strategic location of Lisbon and made the city the western capital of the Roman Empire. By the fifteenth century its position on the western seaboard of the Iberian peninsula had enabled it to become an entrepôt for the distribution of goods that came from China and the East over land along the Asian silk route. When Portugal captured Ceuta from the Moors, gold started to flow into the royal coffers and the search for the African source instigated the succession of exploratory thrusts south along the African coast that culminated in Bartholomew Diaz's rounding of Cabo d'Esperanza (Cape of Good Hope) in 1487–8, which opened up the sea-route to India and beyond.

The patronage of Prince Henry the Navigator, Prince of Portugal, who set up a navigational school at Sagres in 1438, brought and kept Portugal at the forefront of navigational and cartographic development, so that she was well placed to take advantage of the Treaty of Tordesillas in 1494 with Spain, which inadvertently gave Brazil to her. A similar treaty agreed at Saragossa in 1529 in the wake of Magellan's circumnavigation that ceded Portugal the Moluccas and Spain the Philippines underlined that advantage. As a result, Lisbon became the capital of a huge Portuguese empire, only to suffer grievously in the earthquake and tidal wave of 1755, when many charts were lost in the resulting fire.

This attractive north and south view of Lisbon from the River Tagus is taken from a 1553 translation of the work of the Latin author Polybius by L Domenichi and shows a busy commercial port with ocean-sailing carracks and smaller Mediterranean trading craft. Its style is also indicative of the development of perspective and how this could be applied to coastal views on the chart. (By permission of the British Library: C.29.c.1 Volume 1)

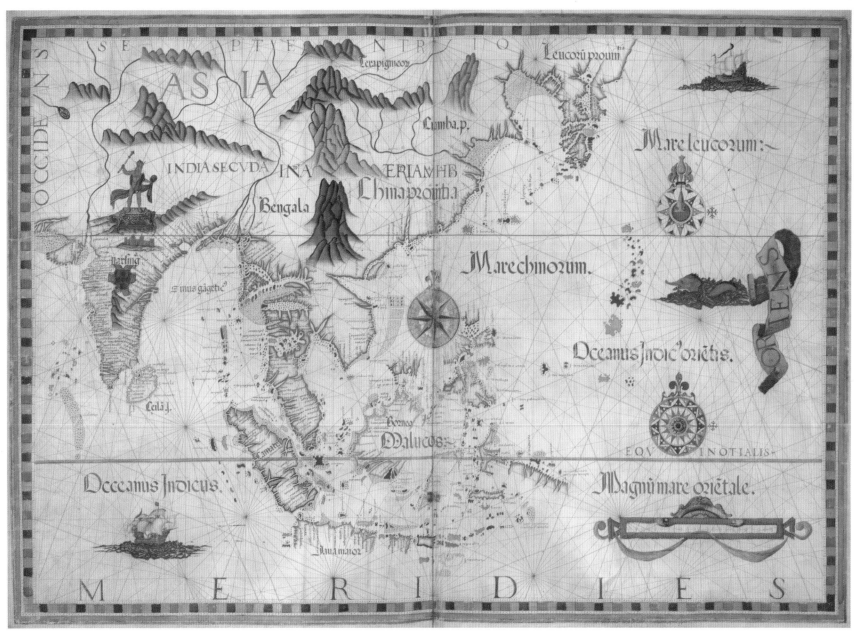

| ABOVE | **MEDITERRANEAN COAST IN THE PORTOLAN STYLE BY DIOGO HOMEN, 1558** | Also from Homen's atlas made for Queen Mary, this portolan-style chart outlines the world's most prolifically mapped coast of the Mediterranean, from the Pillars of Hercules (Strait of Gibraltar) to Morea and Greece in the east. The banners and coats of arms of the rulers of the surrounding countries lend the map a regal feel. (By permission of the British Library: Add.5415A)

| RIGHT | **VIEW OF THE BATTLE OF LEPANTO, 1571** | The momentous Battle of Lepanto of 1571 was fought between a combined fleet of Christian nations bordering the Mediterranean and the Turks with squadrons of galleys from Tunis and Algiers. It broke the Turkish command of the Mediterranean and cemented the maritime power of Venice and Spain. Allegedly each galley was captained by a nobleman from every European aristocratic family, including Don Miguel de Cervantes Saavedra, author of *Don Quixote*, and the English commander, Sir Richard Grenville.

No chart would have been used as the ship masters would have had their own sailing directions from which to navigate, but the battle was well recorded afterwards in oil paintings and etchings. This one is by the well-known Flemish engraver Adriaen Collaert and is held in the Scheepvart Museum in Amsterdam. The battle was the last sea action fought solely between rowed galleys, and could only have taken place in the relatively calm waters of the Mediterranean. The development of the carrack, the caravel and its derivative, the galleon, was a direct response to the need for a seaworthy ship that could weather the seas and storms of the Cape of Good Hope or the Cape Horn. (Scheepvart Museum, Netherlands)

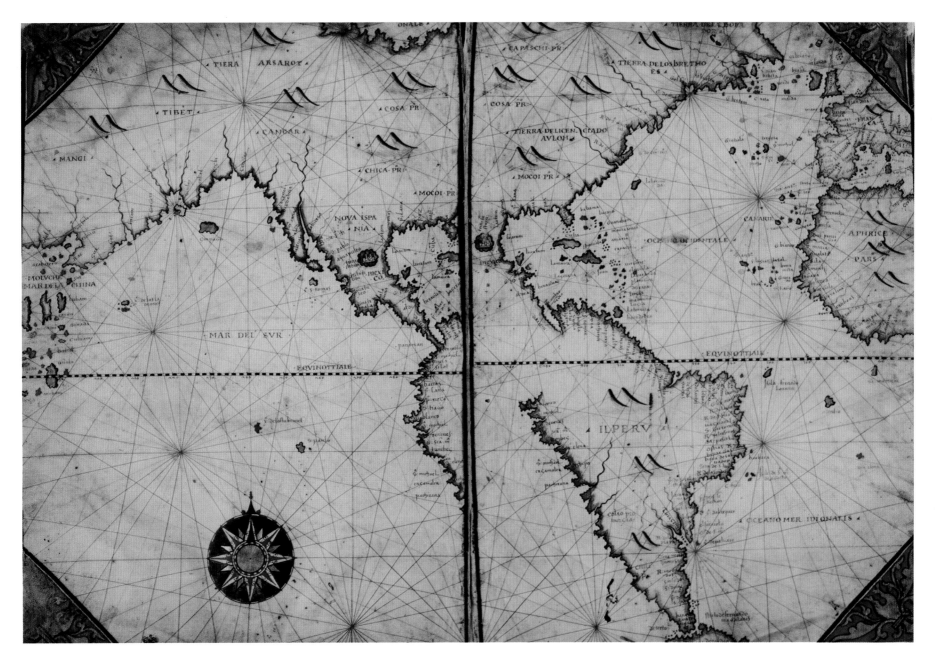

| ABOVE | **THE PACIFIC AND ATLANTIC OCEANS BY GEORGIO SIDERI, 1562** |
The Venetian nobleman and ship captain Leonardo Emo commissioned one of the principal
cartographers of the day, Georgio Sideri, to produce a personal atlas of portolans for, as it says on the
binding: 'attinente a soggeto della nobile familia Emo Veneta per il suo passagio a Coustinopoli' – for
his use on a voyage to Constantinople.

In the competitive world of the Mediterranean, war over trade between states was frequent, as
between Genoa and Venice and Turkey. In time of war merchant captains would take command of
ships and Emo needed a worthwhile portfolio of charts to discuss and plan operations.

This portolan gives a good picture of the New World, one which has an innocence as there is so
little to indicate the territorial wars that would take place there. (By permission of the British
Library: Egerton 2856)

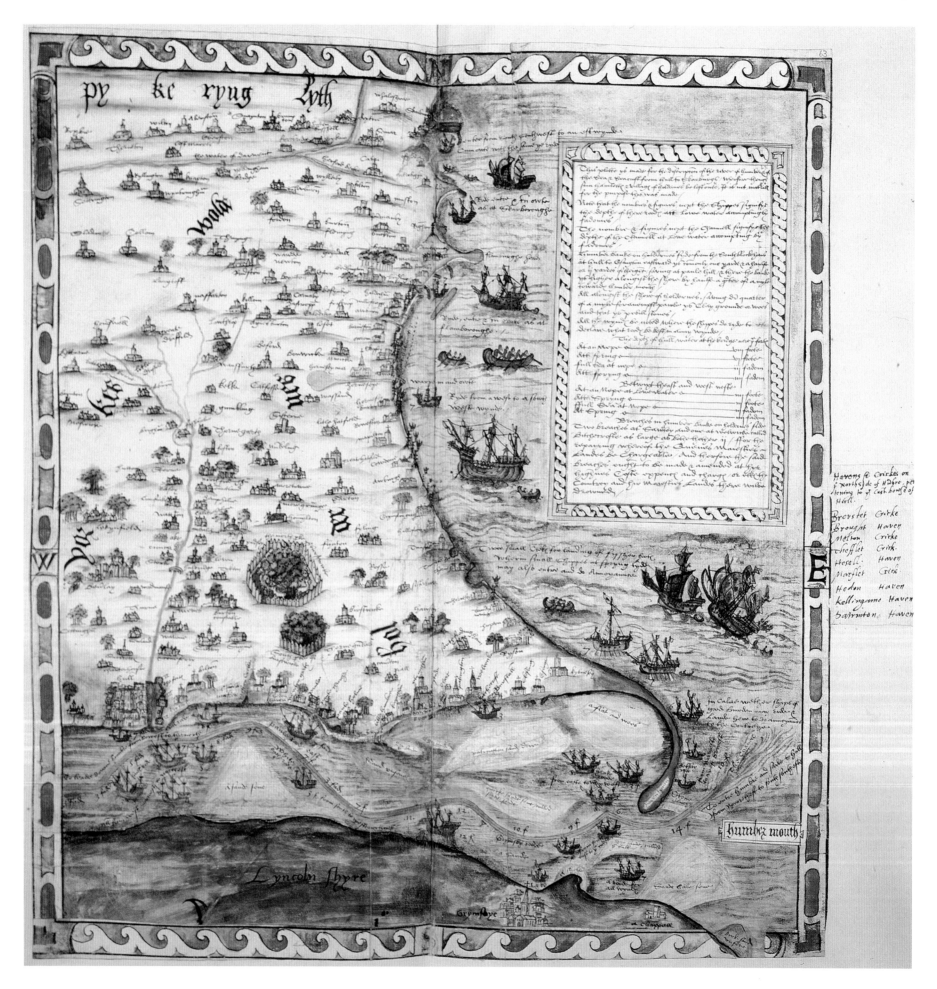

| LEFT | MANUSCRIPT PLAN OF THE RIVER HUMBER AND NORTH SEA COAST FROM HULL TO SCARBOROUGH, 1579 | Lord Cecil Burghley was Elizabeth I's chief adviser, and served her well for 40 years. Although the 1560s had been peaceful between England and Spain, various incidents aroused mutual suspicion in the 1570s. France was at war with itself and the French Huguenots, with Elizabeth's naval support, attacked not just the French Catholics but rich Spanish shipping in the Channel, too. The Hawkins family, operating out of Plymouth, had traded slaves from east Africa to the Spanish West Indies (with local Spanish approval) and had thereby broken Spain's monopoly. The Queen's ship *Jesus of Lubeck* had sailed from Plymouth in October 1567 and was part of John Hawkins' squadron, with his young cousin Francis Drake commanding a pinnace, that sheltered in the harbour of San Juan de Ulúa (the port for Vera Cruz) for repairs when the Viceroy of New Spain unexpectedly made harbour the next morning. Disregarding an agreed truce, the Spanish attacked. Although Hawkins and Drake escaped, this incident particularly marked the start of the hostilities between Spain, the superpower of the day, and England, hitherto regarded as a diminutive country off the European map which was following an unrecognized variant of the Catholic faith.

With buccaneering against Spain, which was unofficially condoned by the Queen, increasingly irritating Spain, Burghley needed to review the country's defences and he put together an atlas of coastal maps and charts of which this manuscript plan is one. This sea map of the River Humber clearly showed that its 40 miles of navigable river and estuary, whilst providing trade access into the heart of Yorkshire could also allow an opportunity for attack. With his own margin notes on the 'Havens & Crickes on y Northside of Humber pertening to y Cust. Howse of Hull', Burghley was forming a defensive picture of the geographical and administrative structure of the kingdom. (By permission of the British Library: Royal 18D.III)

| AMPHIBIOUS LANDING, ANTWERP, 1582 | Towards the end of the Dutch struggle for independence from Spain, William the Silent invited the Duc d'Anjou, youngest son of Henri II of France and Catherine de Medici, to become the hereditary sovereign of the United Provinces. In so doing he gained the support of France, and Spain was left with no access to any northern European port.

This engraving comes from a book that was produced to mark the arrival of the Duke to take up his new position. It shows how, after an unsuccessful courtship of Elizabeth I, he had sailed from Dover with a large fleet and army embarked to be given a magnificent reception in Antwerp. The Duke died aged 29 in May 1584 leaving the Huguenot Henri of Navarre the heir presumptive, re-fuelling the French Wars of Religion. Britain found herself no longer able to rely on France's role as a block to the power of Spain.

The illustrations and 21 engravings for this book were completed by Crispin van den Broeck and Adam de Bruyn and printed by Christopher Plantin, a Frenchman who fled to Antwerp in 1542 from a country where religious intolerance was so great that printing atlases was regarded as a form of heresy and printers were burnt at the stake. The text describes the journey from Dover and the Duke's ceremonial investiture as Duc de Brabant. (By permission of the British Library: C.22.c.12)

| FRENCH CHART OF THE COAST OF SCOTLAND BY NICOLAS DE NICOLAY, 1583 | Nicolas de Nicolay, a well-travelled French spy, prepared the first printed sea chart of Scotland. It was produced in France in 1583 for his translation of the Spanish navigator Pedro de Medina's *Arte de Navegar* (*Art of Navigation*). It was based on an earlier manuscript sea map drawn for a rutter in about 1546 by Alexander Lindsay, pilot to James V that Nicolay as Hydrographer to Henry VIII managed to acquire before he left England for France to work similarly as Cosmographer to Henry II (the scale in Milliaria Scotica supports this). (Reproduced by permission of the Trustees of the National Library of Scotland)

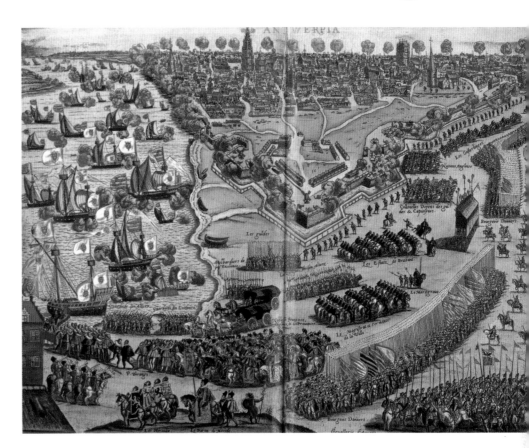

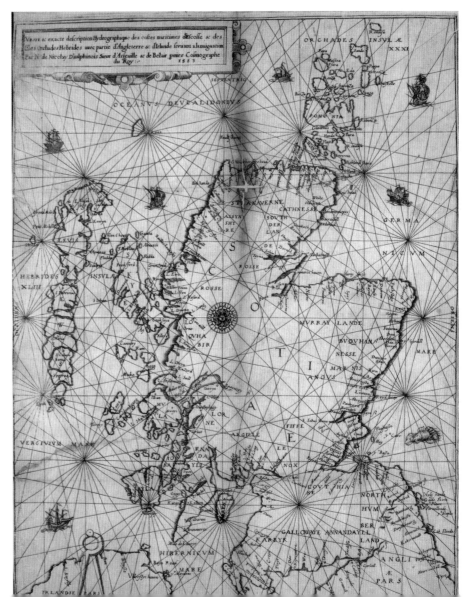

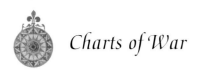

| RIGHT | **ATTACK BY FRANCIS DRAKE ON ST JAGO, CAPE VERDE ISLANDS, 1585** | As relations rapidly deteriorated between Spain and England a powerful mix of London courtiers and merchants backed a privateering voyage put together by Francis Drake. Planned in secret, with a cover story that the 29 ships were sailing to Alexandria, the fleet was to take Panama, controlling the isthmus across which bullion was brought from Peru to Nombre de Dios, then destroy Havana, Cuba and take any *flota* or bullion fleet that assembled there. The ships sailed from Plymouth on 14 September 1585 with Drake in the aptly named *Elizabeth Bonaventure*. Sailing south, taking advantage of the trade winds and the Canary current along the African coast, the fleet first anchored off the island of Santiago in the Cape Verde Islands. While a detachment of ships distracted the town batteries, 1000 men were rowed ashore out of sight and divided into three companies (to the right). In standard formation with pikemen surrounded by infantry armed with harquebus, two companies marched across the mountains to the tune of fife and drum, as appealingly drawn on the chart, and the town was quickly overwhelmed. Finally, the English can be seen on the left chasing the enemy. Drake stayed 14 days, long enough to stock up on water and provisions and to take revenge for the 1568 Spanish 'treachery' at San Juan de Ulúa, where as a young man with Hawkins they were attacked by the Viceroy of Spain.

Baptista Boazio, an Italian cartographer who worked in England, is usually credited with drawing this sea map. His work was widely copied: that of Ireland, for example, was used by Ortelius in his famous atlas *Theatrum Orbis Terrarum*. (By permission of the British Library: Egerton 2579)

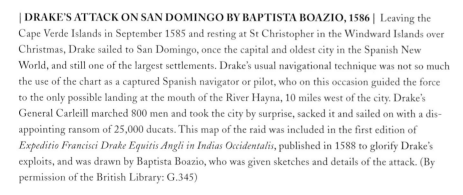

| **DRAKE'S ATTACK ON SAN DOMINGO BY BAPTISTA BOAZIO, 1586** | Leaving the Cape Verde Islands in September 1585 and resting at St Christopher in the Windward Islands over Christmas, Drake sailed to San Domingo, once the capital and oldest city in the Spanish New World, and still one of the largest settlements. Drake's usual navigational technique was not so much the use of the chart as a captured Spanish navigator or pilot, who on this occasion guided the force to the only possible landing at the mouth of the River Hayna, 10 miles west of the city. Drake's General Carleill marched 800 men and took the city by surprise, sacked it and sailed on with a disappointing ransom of 25,000 ducats. This map of the raid was included in the first edition of *Expeditio Francisci Drake Equitis Angli in Indias Occidentalis*, published in 1588 to glorify Drake's exploits, and was drawn by Baptista Boazio, who was given sketches and details of the attack. (By permission of the British Library: G.345)

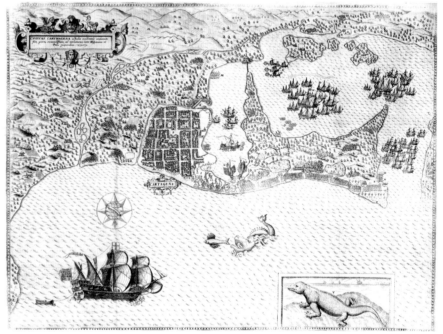

| **DRAKE'S CAPTURE OF CARTHAGENA BY BAPTISTA BOAZIO, 1586** | Drake continued his privateering expedition to Cartagena, Spain's most important city on the Spanish Main, which stored the spoils of her colonies – gold, silver, pearls, hide, cochineal and other produce bought locally. The sea map, oriented with North to the bottom of the page, shows Cartagena weakly defended and Drake's fleet sailing into the bay and thence to the inner harbour. He set fire to a number of buildings, extracted a ransom of 107,000 ducats, but stayed for two months, his crew stricken with sickness. He had to abandon his intention to attack Panama, returning to England via Virginia where he picked up the survivors of the failed settlement at Roanoke. However, the psychological effect of Drake's raids throughout Spain and her colonies was immense, far greater than the actual cost and damage he wrought, particularly with regard to Philip II's reputation. Such impudence could not go unpunished and the Spanish started to plan an invasion of England. (By permission of the British Library: G.345)

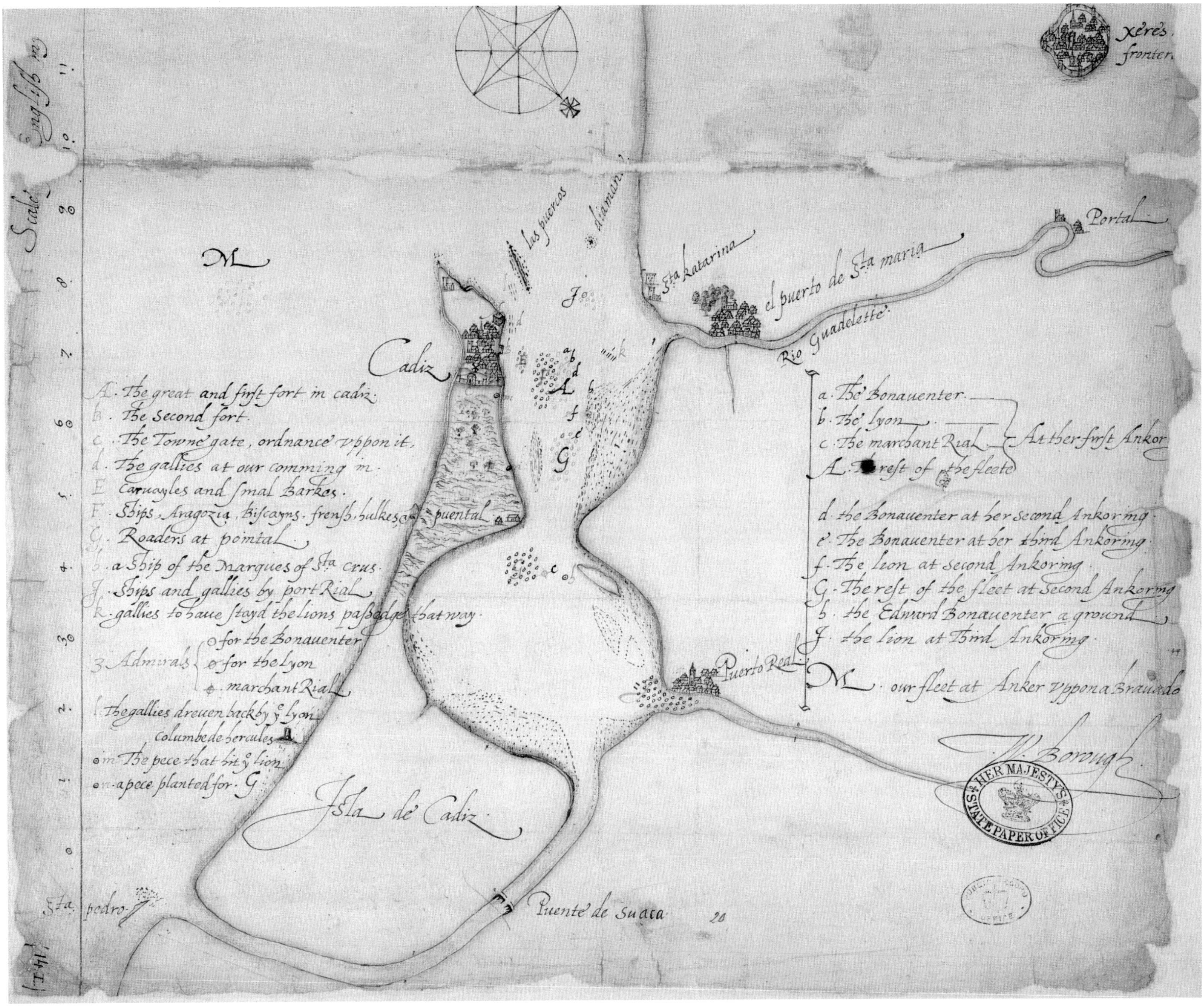
Xeres fronter
Scale English
M
las puercos
Sta katarina
el puerto de Sta maria
Portal
Rio Guadelette
Cadiz
A. The great and first fort in cadiz
b. The second fort
c. The Towne gate, ordnance vppon it
d. The gallies at our comming in
E. Caruoyles and smal Barkes
F. Ships, Aragozia, Biscayns, frensh, hulkes
puental
G. Roaders at pointal
h. a Ship of the Marques of Sta crus
J. Ships and gallies by port Rial
k. gallies to haue stayd the lions passedge that way
3 Admirals
for the Bonauenter
for the lyon
marchant Rial
l. The gallies dreuen back by ye lyon
columbe de hercules
m. The pece that hit ye lion
n. a pece planted for G
Jsla de Cadiz
Sta pedro
Puente de Suaca
a. The Bonauenter
b. The lyon
c. The marchant Rial
A. The rest of the fleete
At ther first Ankor
d. the Bonauenter at her second Ankoring
e. The Bonauenter at her third Ankoring
f. The lion at second Ankoring
G. The rest of the fleet at second Ankoring
h. the Edward Bonauenter a ground
J. the lion at third Ankoring
Puerto Real
M. our fleet at Anker vppon a Brauado
W. Borough
HER MAJESTYS STATE PAPER OFFICE

| **PLAN OF DRAKE'S ATTACK ON CADIZ BY WILLIAM BOROUGH, 1587** | William Borough, son of John Aborough, the ship master from Devon who drew the chart for Anne of Cleves' passage to England (see p. 26), first learned navigation and cartography as an ordinary seaman during Sir Richard Chancellor's voyage in 1553 to search for the North-East passage to China, on which his brother Stephen was sailing master. He trained as a navigator at the Spanish Casa de Contratación in Seville, to become Clerk of the Queen's ships.

In April 1587, as Drake's vice-admiral, Borough commanded the *Lion* in a fleet boosted by a London squadron originally aiming to intercept Portuguese carracks returning from the East Indies. Portugal had reluctantly accepted Spanish rule after Philip II marched into Lisbon in 1581, lasting 60 years until they rebelled. The London squadron met up with Drake to create a fleet of 22 ships, and sailed to Cadiz. With the discovery of America in 1492, Cadiz had developed into the wealthiest port in Europe, the destination of all the American *flota* or treasure ships. All the more testimony to Drake's attack, which achieved complete surprise as they entered the harbour in a pre-emptive strike designed to hinder Spain's Armada preparations. Drake had indeed singed the King of Spain's beard.

With the Spanish unable to dislodge them, Borough had three days to draw this accurate and pleasing chart plan. He included much useful information to scale, such as shoals, with a graphic account of Drake's attack that sank 24 ships, including the Spanish Admiral Santa Cruz's galleon (marked at 'h'). This plan was to be very useful for Lord Howard of Effingham's successful attack nine years later. (The National Archives {PRO} MPF 318)

| RIGHT | **PLAN OF THE FORTIFICATIONS AT CAPE ST VINCENT BY WILLIAM BOROUGH, 1587** | Drake sailed south from Cadiz to Cape Sagres, just past Cape St Vincent, intending to attack the port of Lagos. Borough questioned Drake's intentions as they were at variance with the Queen's instructions. Drake had had an officer executed in similar circumstances during his circumnavigation (1577–80), but Borough was saved through his well-placed friends. Drake captured the castle at Cape St Vincent and idled under the fort awaiting shipping on its return journey from the Spanish Main or East Indies which used this identifiable cape as a landfall to make for either Lisbon or Cadiz. He was rewarded. He captured his biggest prize, the Portuguese carrack *San Felipe*, valued at £114,000.

Borough was able to draw this plan of the castle and fort, which would not only give an account to the Queen's Councillors, but be used for future planning. Santa Cruz, who had been appointed commander-in-chief of the Spanish Armada by Philip II, was frantically trying to assemble the fleet in Cadiz. In retaliation, he managed to put together a fleet of 37 ships, but Drake was already back in Plymouth and Santa Cruz , joined by Juan Martinez de Recalde's squadron, finished his fruitless search in October returning to Cadiz with dejected and sickly crews. (By permission of the British Library: Cotton Augustus I.ii.113)

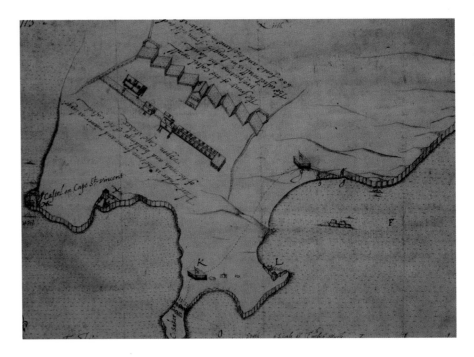

| BELOW | **ELIZABETH I'S ROUTE TO TILBURY AND DEFENCE OF THE THAMES BY ROBERT ADAMS, 1588** | Elizabeth travelled down the River Thames to Tilbury in August 1588 where Robert Dudley was commanding the troops amassed to repel any Spanish landing, and made her famous speech to rally her troops, best known for the line: 'I have the body of a weak and feeble woman; but I have the heart and stomach of a king'.

This pictorial chart of the River Thames was made by the Queen's Surveyor of Works, Robert Adams, to show the route the Queen followed from 8 to 10 August to inspect the army at Tilbury, and is based upon a similar chart made by him earlier in the year to record the military defences of the Thames, with gun emplacements and arcs of fire, in case of an attack up the river. The chart shows her progress along the Thames, including a stop at the port of Erith, a graving dock (graving or breaming was the necessary operation of burning off the weed and barnacles from a ship's bottom to maximize way when sailing), staying overnight there on the 9th. She returned from Greenwich to Lambeth overland on the 10th.

The chart has a colour wash and is made with South to the top of the page to a scale of 1 inch to 1 mile. Signed on the front 'Rober: Adamo authore 1588', Adams also wrote, 'The Pricked Line sheweth her Ma:[ties] progresse to the Campe'. (By permission of the British Library: ADD.44839)

| RIGHT | **SIEGE OF SLUYS, 1587** | Sluys (Sluis) lies near the mouth of the Scheldt, positioned then at the southern channel along the Swarte Gat, giving access for ships and trade to Antwerp in Holland, and was an important medieval port. The Dutch rebellion had denied Spain a northern European port, and it was essential to Philips's plan to invade England to have a base from which to embark his army for the Channel crossing. The Duke of Parma was sent out to suppress the rebellion and wrest back the port. Realizing it was politically expedient to assist the Dutch, Elizabeth sent out her favourite, Robert Dudley, Earl of Leicester, in command of the English army. He was enthusiastically received, but was unable to raise the siege. As Sir Roger Williams points out on this chart he sent to Dudley as part of his brief, after a siege of three months over June to August: 'the narrowest passage to the towne [was] surprised by the ennemy' and 'the sconce [small fort] taken by the ennemy'. With the fall of Sluys Philip was able to secure Ostend and the canals as an invasion base for his army. Now he needed to send a sufficiently strong Armada to embark Parma's army and hold the Channel to land it. (By permission of the British Library: Cotton Augustus I.ii.102)

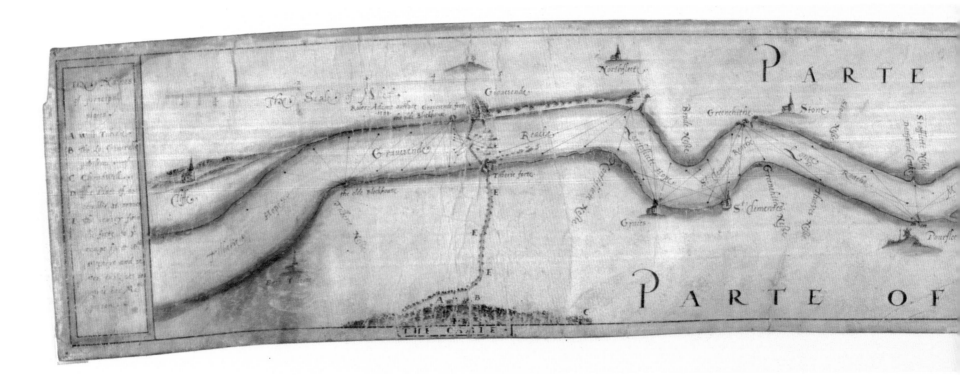

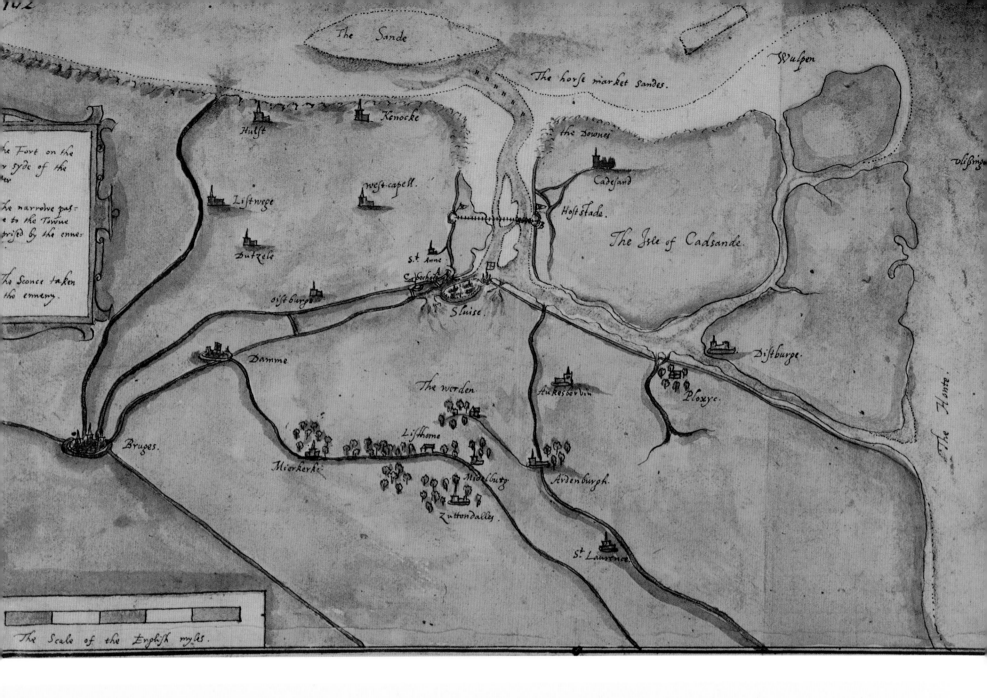

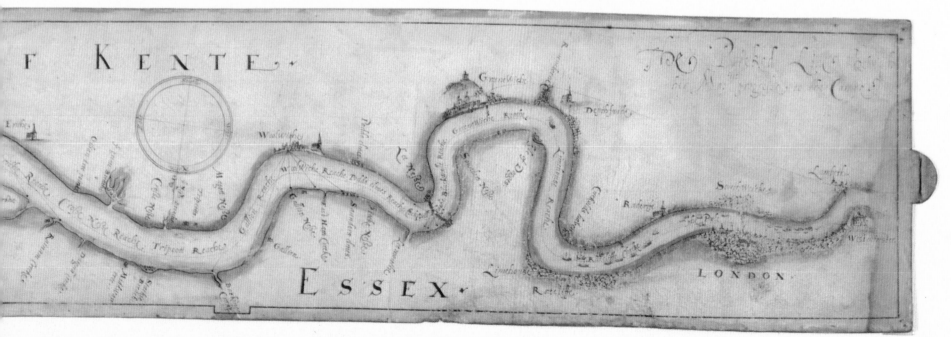

| THE SPANISH ARMADA BY JOHN PINE, 1588 |

The Spanish Armada (meaning fleet) of 130 ships set sail from Lisbon carrying 30,000 men, led by a general who was prone to sea sickness, Don Alonzo Perez de Guzman, Duke of Medina Sidonia, one of the richest noblemen in Europe. Many who sailed with the Armada thought the English would immediately rise in revolt against Queen Elizabeth and replace her with a Catholic monarch.

The hand-coloured print is part of a set illustrating the defeat of the Spanish Armada by the English fleet in 1588. Robert Adams, as well as being an architect and surveyor for Elizabeth, was also an engraver, well-known for his engravings of Anthony Ashley's translation of Wagenaer's book of sea charts. He drew the original series of charts showing the day-by-day development of the battle, completed by 1590. These in turn inspired a set of tapestries made for Lord Howard of Effingham, Lord High Admiral of England, who had led the English navy against the Armada. Howard sold the tapestries to James I in 1616 and they hung in the House of Lords until it burned down in 1834. Writing on the Library of Congress web site, scholar Hans P Kraus has noted that John Pine's 1738 engravings after the tapestries are important historical documents of the stages of the battle, 'as we may be sure that the designs had been examined and approved by Howard'.

The engraver, John Pine, was born in London and spent his life there, becoming the city's finest heraldic and decorative engraver of his generation, and producing numerous book illustrations. Of Moorish extraction, he has been described as the first black man in England to join the Masons. Among his close friends was the painter William Hogarth. (Courtesy of Imago Mundi, Museum Street, London)

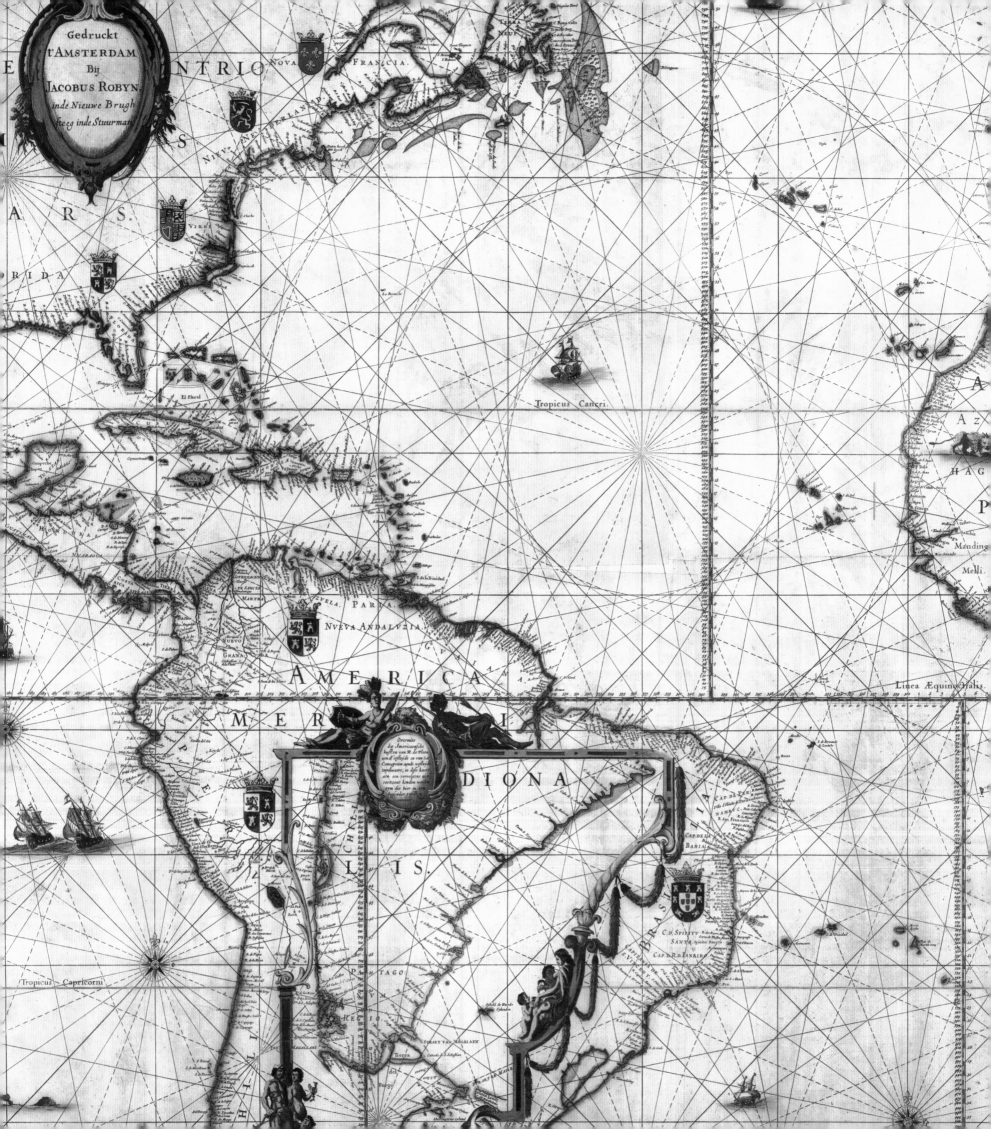

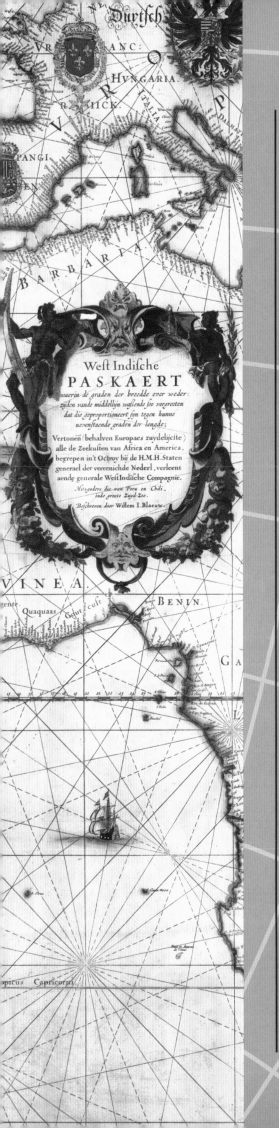

American Gold

Attrition of Spanish and Portuguese Empires, 1600-1715

| CHART OF NORTH AMERICA BY WILLEM BLAEU, *C.* 1674 | This spectacular chart is of great significance, as it is the first sea chart to portray North America using Mercator's projection. Blaeu worked in Amsterdam and was the greatest mapmaker of his time. He was commissioned by the Dutch East India Company to provide this chart for the company and court use during the period when the Dutch were at war with most of their European colonial rivals, and it was kept as a state secret for nearly a century. Its contemporary significance is underlined by the superb hand-colouring and the lavish use of gold leaf. There are only four other recorded examples, all in European institutions. (By kind permission of The Map House, London)

CAPTURING a rival's charts gave access to their territories, and perhaps knowledge of their intentions. One example when Spanish cartographic secrecy suffered a blow is illustrated in this chapter on page 50. The buccaneer Bartholomew Sharpe seized a Spanish *derroterro* in 1681. It was then copied and widely distributed in England as the *Waggoner of the South Seas*, which facilitated and encouraged privateering and piracy on the Spanish Main. These captured charts opened up the route to the Spanish Pacific South American colonies. Although the South Pacific seaboard was impractical for other Europeans to run as colonies, privateers and buccaneers, who often descended into piracy, raided Spanish ports. The period covered by this chapter could be described as the century that decided the contest between England and Holland as to which country would achieve maritime supremacy over the other. While Spain and Portugal already controlled large tracts of land across the world, England and France were making inroads into Canada, India and the West Indies. India was big enough for the two countries to avoid any serious clash until the following century, as was North America, and Spain was too powerful in South America and the Philippines. But the West Indies became a hotly contested area. Protestant Holland had managed to break away from Spain in 1581, although present-day Belgium, mainly Catholic, remained within Spain's Empire. The Dutch had traditionally taken the incoming American and Far East trade arriving at Spanish and Portuguese ports to be distributed into northern Europe, and learned much about their empires in consequence. With the setting up of the Dutch East India Company in 1602, the Netherlands now concentrated on challenging Spanish and Portuguese territory around the Spice Islands of present-day Indonesia. England's Honourable East India Company (HEIC) was set up in 1601 and when attempts to take over Dutch interest in the East were bitterly resisted, she turned her attention to India where there were fewer Dutch settlements, but fought three bloody sea wars in home waters while a bewildering succession of alliances and treaties shifted allegiances between the European powers as political advantage was sought, fought, gained and lost. Of course the contest with the Dutch was, for England, compounded by Irish rebellion and civil war, and it is surprising that the Dutch tried no more than an incursion up the River Medway on the English mainland as portrayed in the Dutch chart in this chapter.

England was realizing the strategic importance of overseas bases to sustain extended operations, and so, too, the charts necessary to get there. Gibraltar was taken from Spain in 1704 as a superbly positioned naval base affording and commanding access to the Mediterranean or the route south to India and South America. The various northern Atlantic islands such as Cape Verde, Madeira and the Azores were unreliable provision stops as they were Portuguese or Spanish possessions.

With bigger, more expensive and sophisticated ships safe pilotage assumed greater importance. The pilot, in acknowledgement of his status, had his own cabin in the forecastle where he kept his charts, under lock and key, and instruments. These would comprise a magnetic compass (although magnetic variation was not yet understood and caused problems on longer voyages), dividers and an astrolabe or backstaff for position finding out of sight of land. But he would have taken his altitude of, say, the Pole Star at twilight when he could see the horizon and star clearly, from the quarterdeck, aft. To assess speed, to give him a sense of distance covered (dead reckoning) he had a chip log. With the 'Regiment of the Sun', declination tables that showed how the sun's altitude varied with latitude, he could take a sun sight at midday to obtain a position line on the chart. He would be assisted by the master's mate or midshipmen under training. But within sight of land he would still use his rutter, with navigational notes. A practical physical environment for chart-work on board ship was also a necessity. By the mid-seventeenth century galleons were built with accommodation aft for the captain and admiral if embarked, and a cabin for the master called the coach, in the forward part of the cabin space under the poop deck.

As ships developed into mobile gun platforms increasingly able to deliver a punchy message worldwide to back up the political policy of the time, so their ability to act in concert grew and it became essential to have some guidelines as to how a multi-ship formation could be fought. While the admiral could get his sailing master to check the chart to ascertain one of the most important factors before engaging the enemy – the amount of sea-room he had available – he would also brief his team of captains as to the general conduct and fluidity of the battle scene at sea. He needed flexibility once engaged. Another form of chart was created that needed to explain the tactics, and then be used to 'wash-up' (in modern naval parlance) or de-brief afterwards, and to be incorporated into a report of proceedings; a tactical chart as opposed to a navigational one.

To impose some sort of tactical order on the fleet the first Fighting Instructions were formulated in England in 1653 by Generals-at-Sea Robert Blake, Richard Deane and George Monck, later the Duke of Albemarle. There were 21 instructions, but the main provision was to establish the line of battle whereby a rigid column was held as the fleet bore down on the enemy, and, assuming they formed a line ahead, each ship in turn would then engage the next astern. These instructions were formalized in 1672 as the Sailing and Fighting Instructions. Where admirals scored in future fleet actions was in recognizing the moment to break up the formation and allow ships discretion to attack opportunity targets, as in a mêlée or general chase, which the Fighting Instructions only allowed for much later. The French similarly came to appreciate the necessity for tactical discipline and issued *Orderes et Signaux Generaux* in 1690, although a number of theoretical treatises came out such as *pere hoste's l'art des armees navales* in 1697 and one by Morogues and Pavillon in the eighteenth century. However, the rigid adherence to these fighting instructions, which the admiral concerned felt he was forced to follow, could caused calamitous outcomes, especially regarding the particular instruction laid down that battle could not be joined with an enemy fleet until the line had been formed and was directly opposite the enemy's line. Examples include Admiral Mathew's action off Toulon in 1744, depicted as a schematic chart for tactical analysis by the Dutch Admiral van Braam and charts of Admiral Byng's action off Minorca in 1756, which lost the British the useful base at Port Mahon, both of which are were used at subsequent court martials and are illustrated in Chapter 4.

In Jean Baptiste Colbert, Louis XIV had a brilliant reforming first minister. Appointed in 1669, four years before Charles II appointed Samuel Pepys as Secretary of the Admiralty, Colbert, in his role as Minister of Marine brought the French navy to its peak of excellence so that by 1690 the French fleet, from virtually nothing 20 years before, was a formidable force. Colbert

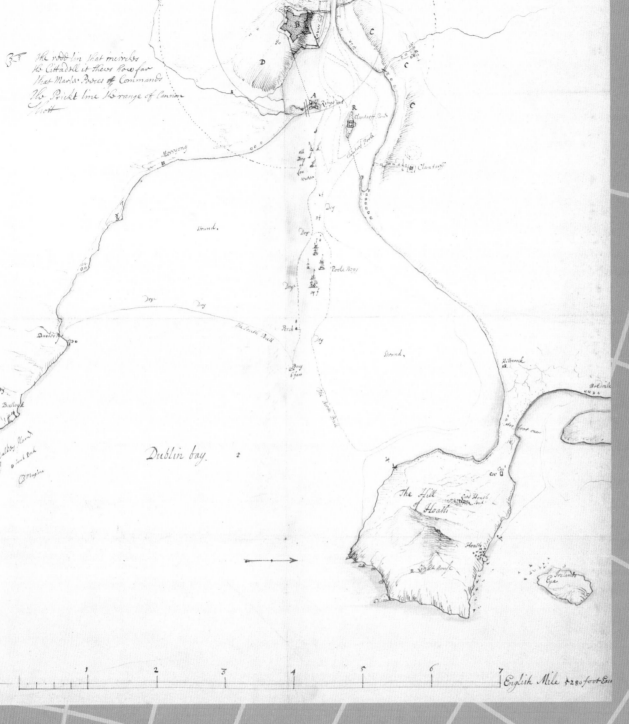
organized the rebuild of the naval port at Toulon, and built a new naval base at Rochefort, although its disadvantage was a hostile tidal system, as at Le Havre, also updated. He started naval schools at these ports and at St Malo and Dieppe where navigation and surveying were taught. He had well-designed new ships built and reformed the manning of them with a system of service whereby seamen served for six months every three, four or five years and were given pensions. Louis' ambitions also aroused French interest in the sciences and the Paris Observatory was set up in 1667, and from there the survey of the coast of France by the very accurate method of triangulation was started.

The result of the French surveys was the beautiful and much more accurate charts of *Le Neptune François*, the official French chart neptune (sea atlas) used and prized by all European navies. This was much superior to the nonetheless laudable charts of Greenvile Collins' *Great Britain's Coasting Pilot*, first published in 1693, which sold well and ran to 21 re-issues until 1792, and was taken to sea in British warships. Pepys had appointed Collins, under the title of Hydrographer to the King, to complete the first real survey of the British Isles, when he compared a chart of the south-west of England in John Seller's *The English Pilot*, hitherto the navigator's chart 'bible', with the triangulated charts of France and found the Cornish coast some 20 miles out of position. However, even *Le Neptune François*, from its publication in 1693 until finally superseded in 1822, was found to have placed Brest out by some 35 miles. But the French lead in chart production continued with the establishment of their Hydrographic Service in 1720.

| PORTOLAN CHART OF THE
ATLANTIC OCEAN BY JOAN
MARTINES, LATE 16TH CENTURY |

A maritime map rather than a navigational
chart, the portolan is by Joan Martines, a
prolific Spanish master cartographer from
Catalan (possibly Majorca) who worked in
Messina, Italy. Since most of his work (and
the Hispanic Society of America, for example,
has 23 atlases) dates around the period 1560
to 1582 we can presume this chart is from a
similar time. It is drawn with latitude but no
longitude scale in the traditional portolan
style of a central, attractive, compass rose with
the 16 main compass directions extended to
16 further compass roses drawn in a circle
from each of which 32 radiating lines form a
latticework. This grid template was then used
to fix the coastline.

Covering from Labrador to Brazil and
east Africa, it shows the important islands in
the Atlantic – the Azores, Madeira and the
Cape Verde Islands – used by ships of all the
maritime powers to water, provision or rendezvous, and which were, in consequence
much fought over. English, Dutch and French
privateers, pirates or war fleets would lie in
wait for the Spanish *flotas* bringing silver and
gold to Spain from the New World. Warships
escorting convoys of merchant ships stopped
on their way to and from the East and West
Indies. (By permission of the British Library:
Add. 9814)

| ABOVE | **DUTCH VICTORY OVER THE PORTUGUESE NEAR BANTAM (JAVA) BY HERMANUS ALARD AND JOHANNES CLOPPENBURGIUS, 1603 |** As they gained maritime strength through fighting the Spanish for independence the Dutch became the first to contest the Portuguese monopoly in the East, and as this bird's-eye view shows, they smashed the Portuguese fleet off Bantam in 1601. The Portuguese attempts to keep crucial navigational information secret, even on pain of death, could not last with such persistence to discover new lands and it leaked out to other European nations.

The view was engraved and published in Amsterdam by Hermanus Alard and Johannes Cloppenburgius in 1603 to broadcast and celebrate the victory. It shows in detail Admiral Wolffert Harmensz with five galleons attacking 30 Portuguese. Analysis of the flags hoisted in each ship is interesting, for they include not just the Dutch tricolour, but the Maltese cross and St Andrew's cross. The inset chart, originally by Visscher, shows the location of Bantam (by present day Jakarta in Java) but with North at 180°. This victory stimulated the formation of the Dutch East India Company that year, the VOC (*Vereenigde Oostindische Compagnie*). In the later years of the sixteenth century the Dutch had been involved as the trading intermediaries between the Portuguese and the northern European countries, and slowly put together the charts and sailing directions that were crucial to successful navigation to India and on to the Spice Islands. (Scheepvart Museum, Netherlands)

| RIGHT | **SPANISH BLOCKADE OF THE SCHELDE BY WILLEM BLAEU, 1603 |** By the early seventeenth century the balance of maritime power was shifting to the Dutch. The Jews had fled Spain and brought their financial expertise to Amsterdam and cartographers came, too, with their knowledge. Dutch shipbuilding and gun-casting was outstripping both Spain and Portugal's. Spain tried unsuccessfully to retain control of the Spanish Netherlands and this engraving by Willem Blaeu shows the battle with the Spanish galleys of Frederico Spinola, from the Genoese banking family who did much to finance Spain, at the Schelde near Sluis. Sea battles were conducted without charts: safety was the job of the sailing master who relied on lookout and the sounding lead to sail the ship clear of navigational hazards, which could become very difficult in the heat of battle when ships became too engrossed in fighting to notice they were being blown onto a lee shore or about to run aground. (Scheepvart Museum, Netherlands)

This crude Dutch sketch, drawn in brown ink shortly after the battle, shows the sandbanks in the vicinity of the Downs, including the 'Goodings' (Goodwin) and Queens, and the port of Margat (Margate), Santwÿck (Sandwich) and Dover with the three main fleets bunched together, and the Dutch squadron under de With watching the English in case they made a move to support the Spanish – Charles I, an ardent Catholic, might support Philip. (Scheepvart Museum, Netherlands)

| RIGHT | **MAP OF PLYMOUTH SHOWING FORTIFICATIONS, 1643** | Early in the English Civil War (1642–51) the Royalists laid siege to Plymouth, but were never likely to sustain it without control of the sea. When Charles I was forced to flee London, Parliament took control of the navy. Whichever side held the ports could starve out the other and Parliament was able to supply Plymouth by sea so that the Royalist siege collapsed in 1643. This map of that year is an unsigned copy of an original, as evidenced by prick holes round all the details. It shows the Royalist positions and Parliamentary ships bringing in supplies, and, acknowledging its importance, the route of the water supply that Sir Francis Drake had organized for the city some 60 years before. (UKHO © British Crown Copyright)

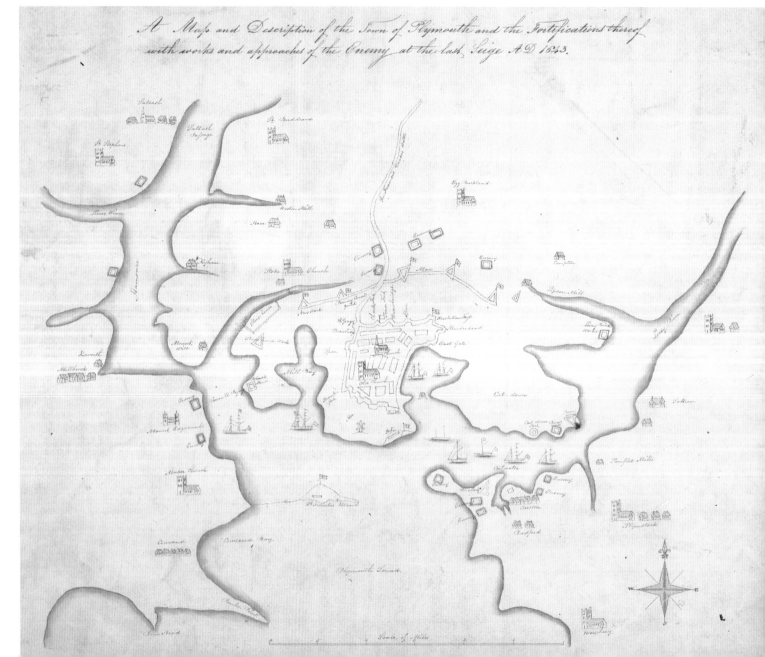

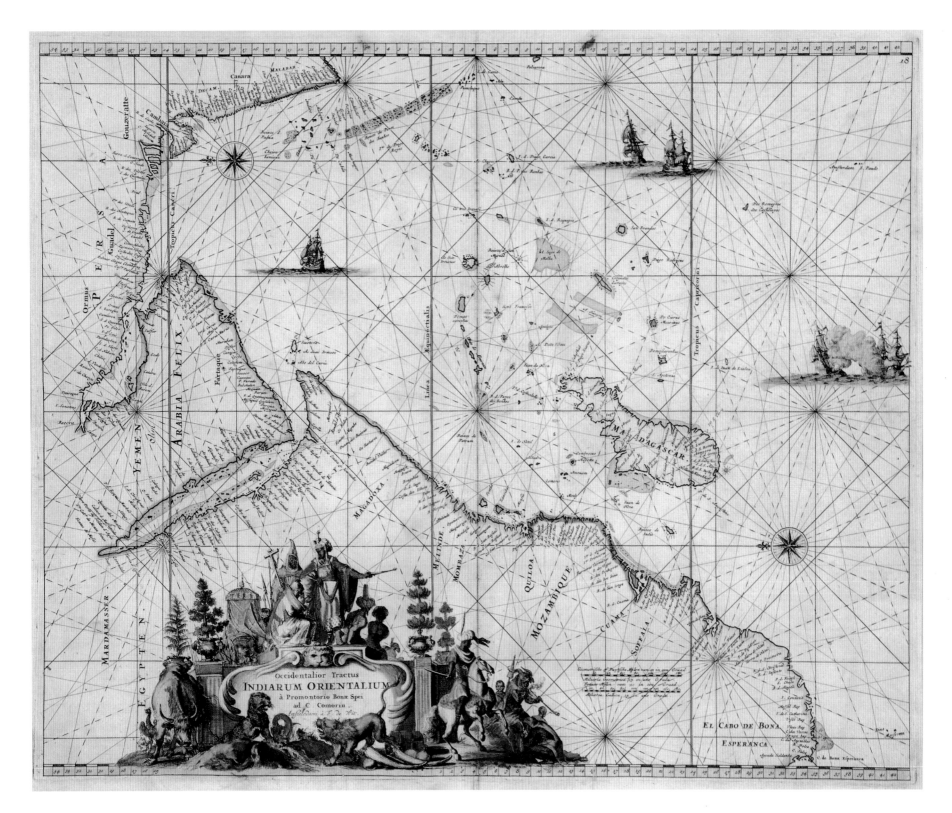

| CHART OF THE INDIAN OCEAN WITH SEA-FIGHT BY FREDERICK DE WIT,
C. 1650 | As a quintessential symbol of the inexorable rise of Dutch sea power this is a reso-
nant example. The Dutch by this time had smashed the Portuguese chain of forts along the
route from Europe around the Cape of Good Hope and across to the Indian Ocean. Ceylon
(Sri Lanka), Java and the Spice Islands were theirs, and they were making overtures to China,
through Macao, and Japan.

Frederick de Wit was one of the most successful map engravers in Amsterdam, producing
beautiful engraving and rich colouring, in a style that was still based on the portolan, with and a
magnificent cartouche – a characteristic of de Wit's work. The detail and accuracy of the coastline
reflects the quality of the surveys being brought back to Amsterdam by sea captains, which he
copied. Dutch power is symbolically represented on the chart by galleons winning a sea battle
against the Portuguese. (Courtesy of Imago Mundi, Museum Street, London)

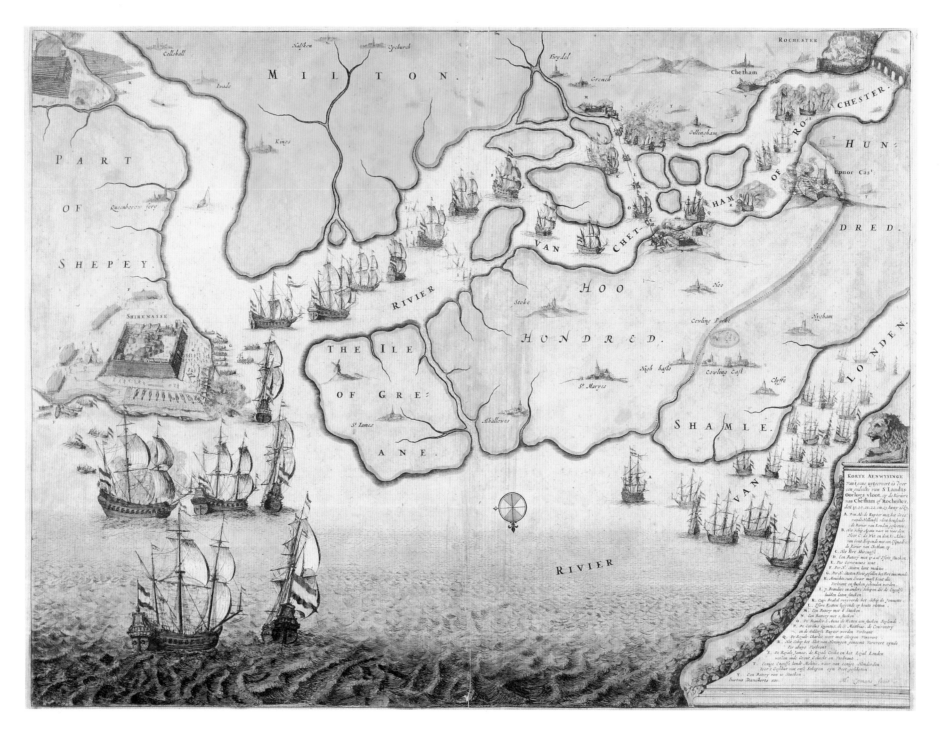

| MAP OF THE THAMES ESTUARY WITH THE ROUTE OF THE DUTCH ATTACK
ON CHATHAM, 1667 | With such enormous riches in the East, and the setting up of the
English and Dutch East India Companies at about the same time, it was inevitable that competition between the two countries would lead to war. The first of the three Anglo-Dutch wars
during the seventeenth century was fought under Oliver Crowell's Commonwealth government
from 1652 to 1654. Admiral Robert Blake, who laid the foundations of naval discipline and tactics through the Articles of War and the Fighting Instructions, met the Dutch Admirals Tromp
and de Ruyter four times, with two defeats and two victories. The final Battle of the Gabbard, a
sandbank off Orford Ness, forced the Dutch to retreat to Texel where they were blockaded. The
subsequent peace treaty was favourable to the English.

The second war was triggered by an attack by Sir Thomas Allin on a homeward bound
Smyrna Dutch convoy off Cadiz in December 1664. The navy of Charles II was well led, and
with good ships from the Commonwealth, but the government was chronically short of money,
and this stymied the opportunity to follow up advantages gained from the sea fights of Lowestoft
in 1665, off North Foreland in June 1666 and about 10 miles east of Foulness in August 1666.

With the distractions of the Fire of London in 1665 and the ravages of the plague in 1666, and in
spite of the fact that the 1667 'fighting season' during the warmer months was approaching, peace
talks had started and it was unwisely decided to keep the ships laid up 'in ordinary' over the winter, out of commission. The Dutch meanwhile prepared a fleet to attack London.

As can be seen on the Dutch chart Admiral de Ruyter sailed up the River Medway unmolested on 10 June 1667, after an aborted attempt to force the Thames, occupied the unfinished fort of
Sheerness then sailed through the boom to attack shipping up the Gillingham Reach and at
Chatham dockyard and thence to Rochester. Three ships of the line were burned and the *Royal
Charles* was towed back to Holland as a prize. The peace treaty at Breda was agreed afterwards on
much more favourable terms to the Dutch. King Charles suffered the political consequences,
with Parliamentary recriminations and suspicion of a Catholic link with France.

However, within three years the third and final war started, culminating in the Battle of
Texel in June 1673. The Medway attack hastened the reform of the Royal Navy's administration
under Samuel Pepys and the Board of Admiralty was formed that decided and executed naval
policy for the next 300 years. (Scheepvart Museum, Netherlands)

| ADMIRAL SIR ROBERT HOLME'S ATTACK ON THE SMYRNA FLEET, 1672 |

Admiral Holmes had gained much experience fighting the Dutch. He had regained English territory in West Africa and occupied the Dutch settlement of Nieuw Amsterdam, renaming it New York in honour of Charles's brother, the Duke of York. He fought in two battles during the Second Anglo-Dutch war. By torching 170 merchant ships at Vlie, on the mouth of the Zuider Zee, he inflicted the heaviest damage of any of the three wars, an event known afterwards as Holmes's Bonfire. On 12 March 1672 he chanced upon the Dutch Smyrna convoy returning from the Mediterranean and immediately attacked. This action started the Third Anglo-Dutch War.

The fighting lasted two days. The chart, topographically correct, was drawn by a Dutchman and shows the positions of the two fleets in the English Channel during the first day, with hand-written details. The Dutch always fought well and persistently and Holmes suffered much damage, although losing only one of the rich Smyrna ships. (© National Maritime Museum, London, PW5525)

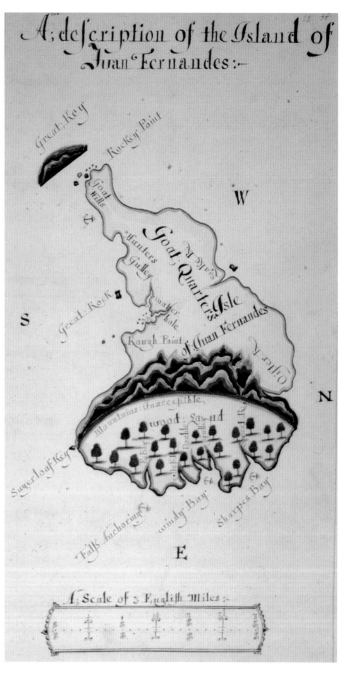

| THE CHANNEL ISLANDS BY THOMAS PHILLIPS FOR BARON DARTMOUTH, 1680 | This beautiful chart, with an attractive cartouche, which shows the main Channel Islands of Guernsey, Jersey, Sark and Herm, was prepared by Thomas Phillips in 1680 for George Legge, Baron Darmouth, as part of the report on the defence of the Channel Islands he prepared with Sir Bernard de Gomme, at the time as much for use against the Dutch as to prevent the Channel Islands' continued use as an unofficial privateering base against the French. (By permission of the British Library: Kings 48)

| JUAN FERNANDEZ ISLAND OFF THE COAST OF CHILE, *C.* 1682 | Bartholomew Sharp learned buccaneering under the famous pirate Henry Morgan and led an attack on Panama in 1679. Sharp and his band marched across the Isthmus of Panama and captured a Spanish ship, naming her *Trinity*. He cruised the Peruvian and Chilean coasts and in 1681, off the coast of Ecuador, captured the *Rosario*. On board he found 'a Spanish manuscript of prodigious value', a secret *derroterro* or atlas with charts and sailing instructions for Spain's South American ports covering from Acapulco to Cape Horn, which had been compiled in Panama in 1669. It was to open up the coast to British plunder and trade. When Sharp returned to England, he asked William Hack (one of the Thames School of manuscript cartographers, and himself a one-time buccaneer) to copy the charts and coastal views, one of which is this chart of Juan Fernandez Island, and had the sailing instructions translated by Philip Dassigny. He presented the volume as the 'Wagoner of the South Seas' to Charles II in 1682, who, in recognition of its value, acquitted Sharp on charges of piracy, saving him from the noose. (By permission of the British Library: Sloane 46A)

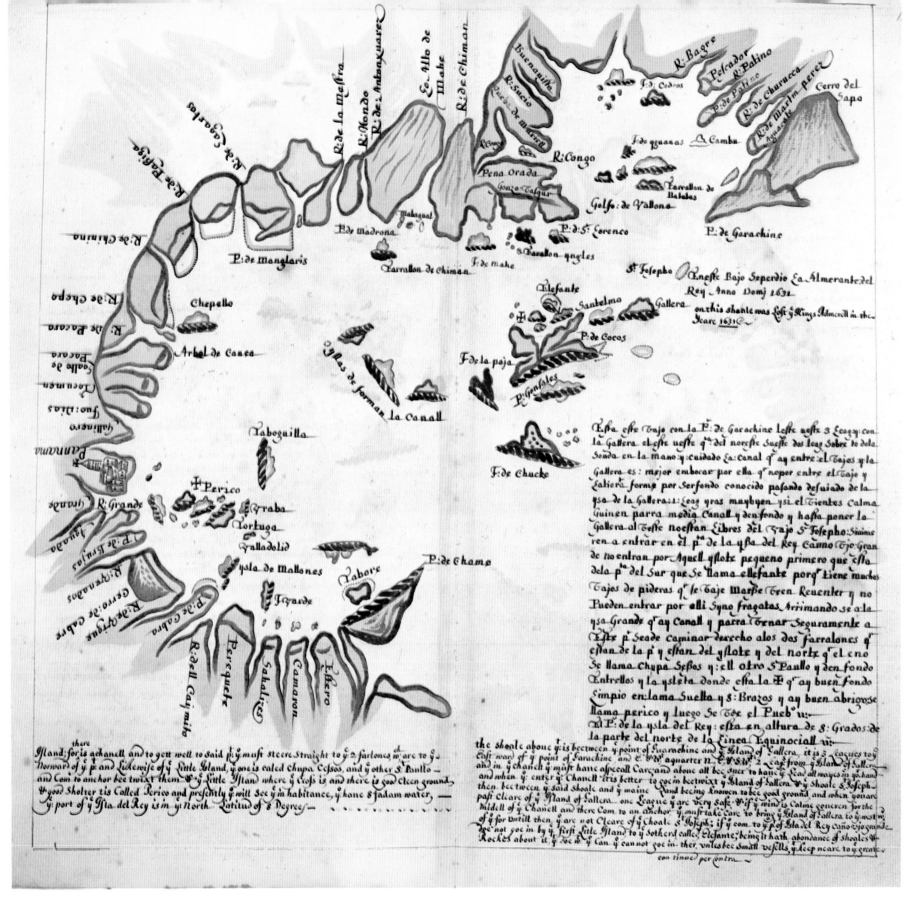

| PANAMA BAY BY WILLIAM HACK, C. 1685 | The Spanish had tried to keep the other European maritime nations ignorant of the South American west coast, withholding all charts and even spreading false rumours that there was a counter-current through the Strait of Magellan, which made it impossible to return west to east and that, as the South American continent was only separated by the narrow strait from the Great Southern Continent, no other route was possible.

The chart of the bay of Panama between Point Guarachine and the island of Gallera, including sailing directions, is copied from captured Spanish charts, permitting future attacks on the port where the Spanish treasure ships unloaded Peruvian silver to be taken across the isthmus by mule.

The capture of Jamaica in 1655 allowed a base for English buccaneers to maraud shipping in the Caribbean and later the Pacific seaboard of South America once the possibility of sailing the Strait of Magellan was known. Buccaneers, who styled themselves as privateers, but operated without commission or letters of marque, were excellent seamen, and they valued and used charts to extend and plan their freebooting activities. Many, such as William Dampier, Woodes Rogers, Basil Ringrose and William Hack, made and recorded remarkable voyages and circumnavigations and did much to disseminate information from charts seized from captured ships. Once England declared war on France in 1689, it brought buccaneering to a close because they were commissioned as legitimate privateers. (By permission of the British Library: Harley 4034)

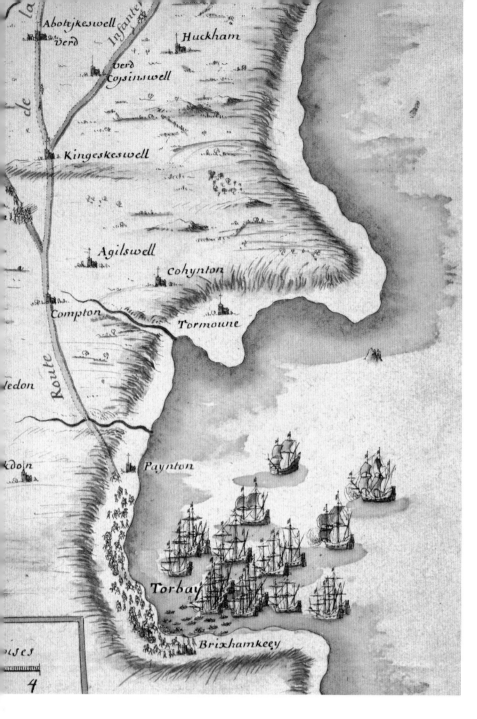

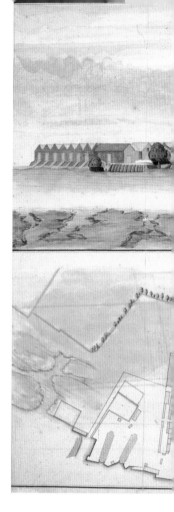

VIEW OF CHATHAM AND DOCKYARD WITH IMPROVEMENTS, 1698 |
This plan is one of a number ordered by the Surveyor of the Navy, Edmund Dummer. It shows a perspective view from the opposite bank of the Medway with two plans, one showing the dockyard as it was in 1688, and the other showing improvements. A re-assessment of naval dockyards became apparent for a number of reasons, and one became compelling after Admiral Lord Torrington prevented French troops landing to help James II recover his crown at the Battle of Bantry Bay in 1689. Afterwards Torrington had to take his ships to Portsmouth to repair and refit, leaving Irish waters wide open to James and the French for two months.

'A Survey and Description of the principal Harbours with their accomodations and conveniences for erecting, moaring, secureing and refitting the Navy Royall of England … with an account of the emprovements which have been made at each yard since the Revolution 1688', was completed in 1698. The views are neatly drawn, and many of the plans are on a large scale. The plans included a chart of the Thames and Medway, and a view of the Medway from Rochester to Sheerness, surveys of Chatham, Sheerness, Woolwich, Deptford, Portsmouth and Plymouth dockyards, and a 'Description of all the forts and castles scituate upon the river Medway'.

Britain was ahead of her competitors in the building of dockyards, enabling ships to spend longer at sea and less time having hulls cleaned and on general repairs. Whereas by 1750 the French had only four dry docks, the British had 16, increasing to 24 by the end of the century. The Spanish built the first Mediterranean dry dock at Cartagena in 1754 and had two at Ferrol (their Brest equivalent). (By permission of the British Library: Kings 43)

THE RIVER MEDWAY WITH (INSET) GILLINGHAM AND COCKHAM FORTS, C. 1700 |
This chart of the River Medway is based on Captain Greenvile Collins' 1688 survey, which was included in his important *Great Britain's Coasting Pilot*, the first complete survey of the British coastline and instigated by Samuel Pepys, Secretary of the Navy. With North orientated to the right, a scale of 1760 yards to a mile (giving a land mile), the depth of water based on low water spring tide and a relatively new convention showing the soundings in fathoms with black figures and the feet in red underlined, the survey shows the defence of the Medway from Rochester to Sheerness and dates to about 1700. Of added interest are the inset drawings of Gillingham and Cockham Wood forts.

The defence of London, her docks and associated ports, was naturally of paramount importance and the Dutch raid of 1667 had brought home the vulnerability of two of the Royal Navy's key dockyards, Chatham and Sheerness. By 1669 the two forts had been built. The chart shows a formidable river defence with Sheerness Fort at the entrance to the Medway, supported by three batteries totalling 50 guns along the shore opposite, around two bends a further 40 guns at Bishops Ness on the south easterly bank, around the next bend on the opposite shore 27 guns at How Ness. Before the final bend defending Chatham dockyard and the town of Rochester were the two newly built forts on opposite sides of the river – Cockham Wood fort with 40 guns and Gillingham fort with 24 guns. At the end of the bend by the boom across the river were two more gun batteries, the Birdsnest with 18 guns and Midletous with 10 guns. Today there is no sign of Gillingham fort, and some overgrown remains are all that are visible of Cockham (Cookham) Wood fort. (The National Archives {PRO} MPHH 1/76)

| ABOVE | **WILLIAM OF ORANGE LANDS AT TORBAY, 1688** | James II succeeded his brother, Charles II, to the British throne in 1685. However, his stubborn intention to promote the Roman Catholic faith made him an unpopular monarch. As Duke of York he had learned much about the navy and had worked with Pepys to modernize it: he had every reason to think it would remain loyal. In the Netherlands Prince William of Orange, as Stadholder, could see that his wife Mary's inheritance to the throne (she was James's daughter) could remove Britain as a threat to Holland, and that the combined strength of the two countries would counter Louis XIV's predatory intentions towards the Dutch. William planned to invade England by invitation and secretly assembled a fleet totalling 463 ships, including 49 warships and troop transports with 40,000 men. Easterly winds kept the British fleet paralysed, unable to clear the Kentish Knock and Goodwin Sands, but William managed to tack down Channel until miraculously the wind veered south westerly and, although originally intending to land along the Yorkshire coast, two days of calm allowed him to land his army at Torbay and march on London. Although James had sufficient, if grudging, support to hold the country against William, he miscalculated and fled, aiming to land later in Ireland with French support and regain the throne.

A contemporary French account, *Journal du voyage d'Angleterre commence le 28 Octobre*, has 20 coloured route maps and gives the names of the commanders of each regiment and the quarters they took each night. This one shows William's fleet at the point of landing and the start of the route he took to march to London on 16 November 1688. (By permission of the British Library: Add. 33970)

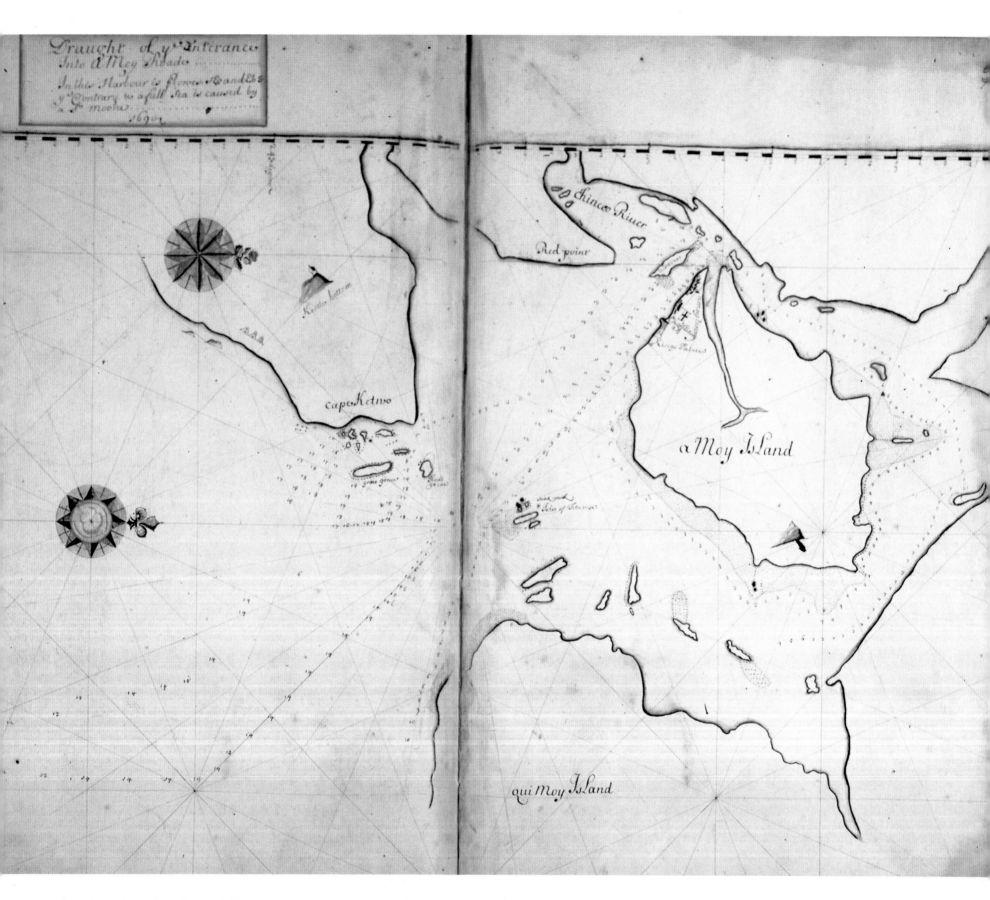

| AMOY ISLAND, CHINA, BY CAPTAIN JOHN KEMPTHORNE, 1690 | Amoy, named Xiamen today, is the port at the mouth of the Jinglong Jiang (Nine Dragon) river and has always been one of the main trading ports of Asia. The Dutch had taken control of the neighbouring island of Taiwan in 1624 and traded through Amoy, but they were driven out in 1662. In 1684 the Qing Government set up a customs house and the British and Spanish carried out much trade there. Kempthorne carried out this survey on his fourth voyage in his ship the *Kempthorne*. His charts, although still based on the portolan style of construction, have a distinctive, attractive style with beautifully rendered compass roses, and are full of navigational information with soundings, rocks and a comment on the ebb and flow of the tides. (By permission of the British Library: Sloane 3665)

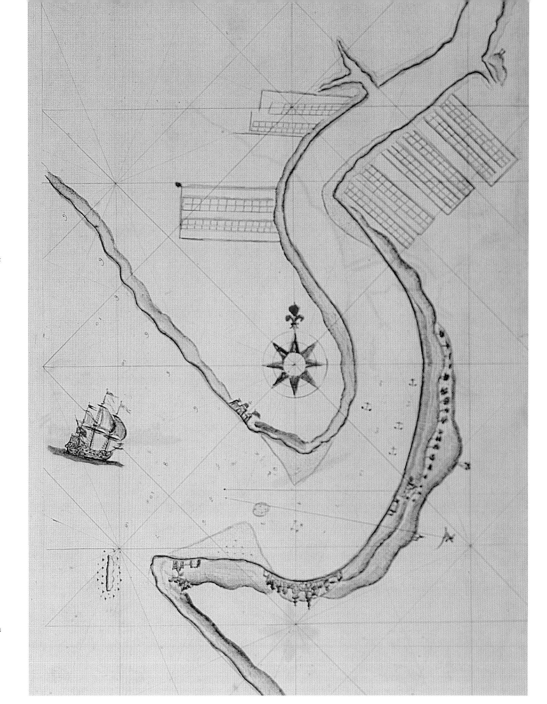

| RIGHT | CAPTAIN JOHN KEMPTHORNE'S VIEW OF SANLÚCAR DE BARRAMEDA, *C.* 1690 | Sanlúcar de Barrameda lies about 10 miles north west along the coast from Cadiz and is flanked by the Guadalquivir Estuary. Columbus set sail from Sanlúcar in 1498 and, a few decades later, the Portuguese explorer Ferdinand Magellan set off to circumnavigate the globe in search of a westerly route to the spice islands of Indonesia. John Kempthorne was the eldest son of one of Charles II's outstanding naval officers, Admiral Sir John Kempthorne. John joined the navy but left, as many did, to join the HEIC (Honorable East India Company) and made four voyages between 1668 and 1690 successively to Surat, the Coromandel coast and Bay of Bengal, to the East Indies and to Bombay. Sanlúcar de Barrameda was surveyed by him during the fourth voyage. It was expected that East India Company captains would make charts and bring them back to London where hydrographic knowledge would be collated and given out to ships. But this was never seriously undertaken until Alexander Dalrymple was appointed Hydrographer of the HEIC in the late eighteenth century. A chart of a port close to the large naval base of Cadiz was useful intelligence and this is one of a number of views now held by the British Library. (By permission of the British Library: Sloane 3665)

| BELOW | CHART OF THE COAST OF MUSCAT BY CAPTAIN FRANCIS STANES, 1703 | While this is a naive attempt to represent the coastline with some sort of perspective before a standard approach to charting was developed by Captain Cook, and showing a similar style to Kempthorne's, Captain Stanes, who commanded the *Rochester* in a voyage to Muscat, the capital of Oman, has drawn a useful chart. Still regarded as confidential intelligence to the HEIC in a competitive trading world that often led to open warfare, attitudes to sharing hydrographic information would only start to change at the end of the Napoleonic War. Oman is a small Arab state strategically placed at the entrance to the Persian Gulf. The town was then the emporium of the western Indian Ocean, and so effective was the rule of law that theft from the valuable cargoes that flowed through the city was unknown. Frankincense was the most valuable commodity traded; some 1400 kilograms each year by ship from southern Arabia to Greece, Rome and the Mediterranean, with Muscat at the centre, and as a result the city had to endure successive sackings. (By permission of the British Library: Sloane 3145)

A New Chart of the Seas,
Surrounding the Island of
CUBA,
with the Soundings, Currents,
Ships Courses &c.
And a Map
of the Island it self
lately made by
an Officer in the Navy.

The Ancien Régime

European, American and Asian War, 1700-93

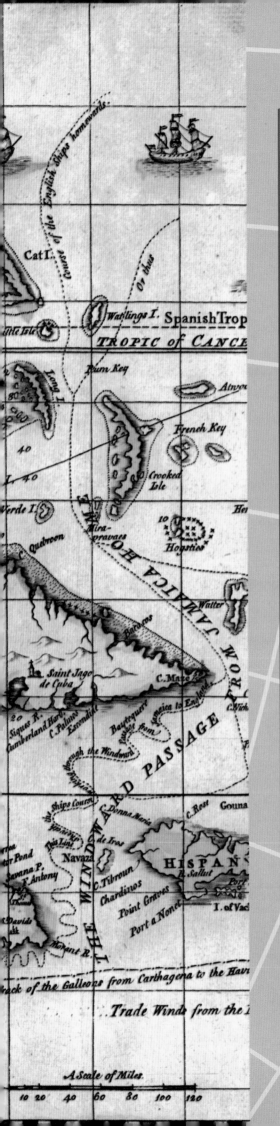

| **CHART OF CUBA WITH SHIPS BY 'AN OFFICER IN THE NAVY', 1760** | This chart is probably copied from a Spanish original with the route taken by the Spanish *flota* clearly marked. It shows the favoured route beating to windward back to England as well. It is constructed with lines of latitude and longitude and one compass rose, and would have been useful as a course-planning chart and a navigational chart for the fleets of the maritime nations, whose primary aim from the sixteenth to the eighteenth centuries was to intercept and capture a Spanish *flota*, although only the Dutch West India Company achieved total success in 1628. From 1540 to 1650 only half a per cent of the *flota* ships were captured or destroyed.

The Spanish system is considered highly efficient. Two convoys sailed a year, the first in the spring with the ships collecting from the Spanish ports in the Caribbean – Vera Cruz, Honduras (Santa Domingo), and a later convoy collecting from Nombre de Dios. The ships would meet up in Havana the following year to sail in advance of the hurricane season (usually June to September) using the Florida current, Gulf Stream, and north-east trade winds to arrive at the Azores, or rendezvous if scattered by a storm, and then make landfall at Cape St Vincent. (Library of Congress)

THE eighteenth century was one of unprecedented competition and rivalry between the two emergent maritime powers, Britain and France: a virtual rehearsal for the final titanic clash that spanned the end of this century and the beginning of the next, of the Revolutionary and Napoleonic Wars. The dominant conflicts that characterize this period are the War of Spanish Succession (1701–1714) and the Seven Years War (1756–63). The War of American Independence and its effect on chartmaking is considered in Chapter 5, while the impact of the French Revolution on European relations in covered in Chapter 6.

As the seventeenth century drew to a close Spain's power was already declining under the Spanish-Habsburg King Charles II's weak rule with internal factions, wars overseas and the exhaustion of the South American silver mines from around 1640. Should his successor be from the Bourbons of France, or from the Austrian branch of the Habsburg family in Germany? Whoever was chosen, it would need to be decided whether he would rule the entire empire of Spain, including her vast overseas territories in America and the East Indies, or some division of this enormous kingdom, to maintain a balance of power in Europe so optimistically established in 1697 by the Peace of Ryswick. In the event, the King's ministers persuaded Charles to sign a will bequeathing all his states to the grandson of Louis XIV, at that time Duke of Anjou and to become Philip V of Spain. This seemed a satisfactory arrangement for Spain as it brought her nearest land neighbour, and one of Europe's most powerful states, into a defensive framework with Spain. This union was to France's advantage, too, but to the perceived disadvantage of other European states. A combined France and Spain would dominate the Mediterranean and in consequence the English Parliament, meeting in February 1701, denounced the treaty. Holland began to arm and the Emperor of Austria placed troops into northern Italy.

England organized what came to be known as the Grand Alliance designed to crush the power of Louis XIV: a coalition with her former trade rival during the seventeenth century, Holland, as well as Austria, Prussia, Denmark and later Portugal. To add French insult to English injury, on the death of James II of England in 1702 (who had been deposed in 1689 by William of Orange to rule jointly with his wife Mary as William III), Louis XIV recognized his son, James Stuart 'the Old Pretender', as King. Parliament immediately voted 50,000 soldiers and 35,000 seamen along with subsidies for the German and Danish auxiliaries. Although William III died in March 1702, his wife's sister Anne, who became Queen, pursued the same policy.

The key to British naval policy in European waters was to prevent, through blockade, any link up of French and Spanish fleets, which would allow them control of the English Channel sufficient to invade Britain. Overseas, Britain wanted to protect trade convoys, and her colonies, which of course were sustaining Britain. While French Atlantic, Channel and North Sea ports could be covered by blockading fleets operating out of the British ports of Chatham, Portsmouth and Plymouth, Mediterranean ports such as Toulon and Barcelona, were covered by fleets using Gibraltar and Minorca. These Mediterranean bases were taken by the British in 1704 and 1707 respectively. The attempt to take Barcelona in 1705 by a combined British and Dutch fleet is enlivened by the chart on page 65, but there was never any intention to keep Barcelona. The measure for a base was its secu-

rity and the choice was for an island such as Minorca, which could be easily defended by ships, a near island such as Gibraltar, or a relatively well-established colony such as Halifax, Nova Scotia. The East India Company's convoys were given naval support and with a tacit *quid pro quo* navy ships could not only replenish en route to India at St Helena (given to the East India Company under Royal Charter by Charles II in 1659) but freely use the only dry-dock facilities overseas at the HEIC naval base at Bombay set up in 1754. The action that shattered the local Mahratta's power at Gheriah Fort by Admiral Watson in 1756, illustrated on page 71, was part of the succession of naval and land battles that lead to British naval supremacy in the Indian Ocean.

When Commodore John Byron, on what was almost a re-enactment of Anson's circumnavigation (1740–4), re-established Britain's claim to the Falkland Islands in 1765 (and charted them, too) the First Sea Lord, the Earl of Egremont, might have overstated the case in telling his Cabinet colleagues that the islands were 'the Key to the whole Pacifick Ocean'. But it sat comfortably with Britain's policy of extending overseas bases, which can be followed during the confrontations in that arena from 1776 to 1815, and it was certainly a useful resting port to replenish before taking on the restless Strait of Magellan.

This was, too, a century of improvement in ship design, navigation and charting in response to the change in political emphasis, and the emergence of amphibious teamwork, the concordance of army and naval operations to conduct the attacks on Barcelona, Toulon and Gibraltar illustrated in this chapter, demonstrate the point.

As the conduct of sea warfare became more professional, so the need for a unified approach to charting became more necessary, but change very often only comes about as a result of profound shock, and one came in 1707 with the demise of Sir Clowdisley Shovell's fleet on the Scillies described on page 66. By the turn of the century the ratio of the loss of warships to shipwreck to those during enemy action averaged eight to one. This stark example of a fleet's destruction due to bad navigation became the catalyst to find a means to measure longitude. The salutary lesson slowly inculcated the British navy, and, by example, other European navies, to look at ways of providing reliable charts that would be distributed to all combatant ships. But it took almost another century of war before it happened. As navies grew in size, and ships grew, too, with more guns and complex equipment, and officers and seamen became highly trained, they were more difficult and expensive to replace. Apart from any humanitarian or ethical considerations, an investment in better charts and navigational aids would lead to better seamanship and reduced ship losses. This would include not just better instruments for fixing, but the numerous and improved provision of lighthouses, lightships and buoyage on harbour approaches and channels, a lead taken by Trinity House for English waters.

It had been known for a long time that a ship's longitude position could be found, as the earth rotates at a steady rate of an hour per 15 degrees of longitude. If the time at a prime meridian (fixed through international agreement at Greenwich today) was known and compared with the time of the ship's current position, then its longitude would be easy to determine. As a direct result of the loss of Shovell's fleet, the British Parliament passed an act in 1714 to offer a prize of £20,000 to whoever could provide a solution. The

CARTE DE L'ISLE DE SAINT DOMINGUE.
Dressée au Dépost des Cartes et Plans de la Marine, Pour le Service des Vaisseaux du Roy.
Par ordre de M. le Duc de Choiseul Colonel General des Suisses et Grisons Ministre de la Guerre et de la Marine
Par le S. Bellin Ingenieur de la Marine.
M.DCC.LXIV.

| FRENCH CHART OF SAN DOMINGO BY J N BELLIN FOR THE MINISTER OF WAR, 1764 | French charts in the eighteenth century were generally acknowledged, and therefore prized, as being of a superior quality to those of the English, Dutch or Spanish, and naval officers' portfolios tended to contain a mixture. The French ascendancy in chart design came about because of the active patronage and support under the absolutist rules of Louis XIII and XIV. Nicolas Sanson set the standard in the early part of the seventeenth century and his family mapmaking business continued for over a century, their work noted for its clarity and accuracy. A few small families, such as Cassini, Jaillot and Delisle, dominated the scene that peaked in the eighteenth century with the sea charts of Mannevillette's *Le Neptune Oriental* (1745) and J N Bellin, the first Ingénieur Hydrographe de la Marine, who produced the much used *Le Neptune François* (1753). (Library of Congress)

most practical answer to transporting time aboard ship was invented by John Harrison. He succeeded in the design a timepiece in 1761 that ran to time, needed no lubrication or cleaning, was impervious to rust, and had moving parts that were perfectly balanced in relation to one another, and were not affected by a ship's movement, changes in magnetic field, humidity, temperature or air pressure. It was given the name 'chronometer' by the hydrographer, Alexander Dalrymple.

While the French had taken over Spain's earlier role as the leading expansionist power, the War of Spanish Succession for England was seen as an opportunity to take Spanish possessions overseas, although in actuality the land war was fought in the Netherlands under the brilliant generalship of ex-naval officer John Churchill, first Duke of Marlborough, commanding a combined Anglo-German-Dutch army. This culminated in a final victory against the French in 1709 at the French village of Malplaquet. The whole emphasis for the *raison de guerre* dramatically shifted when the Austrian Habsburg Holy Roman Emperor Joseph I died in 1711 and his successor Charles VI claimed the Spanish throne as well. A victory over France would result in too powerful an Austria, so Britain dissolved the Grand Alliance and concluded separate peace negotiations, known as the Peace of Utrecht in 1713, which finished the war with France, but isolated Charles VI of Austria who continued the fight against France and Spain. A final peace was not concluded until 1714 after some easy French victories against Austria, who made peace with France, but not Spain, gaining Spain's Dutch territories. The result was that the original Treaty of Ryswick was re-ratified. This wheel of war had taken 17 years to turn full circle and bring the European powers back to the position from whence they had started.

There was still no formal system for producing or distributing charts to ships' officers, with the Royal Navy leaving it largely to the commercial sector, but the Dutch through their East India Company, started to have charts and sea maps made through the company. A further difficulty for British warships was that British charts were still being produced of insufficient accuracy with serious implications for naval objectives. For example in 1710, New England settlers were pressing for an attack on the French in Quebec and Rear-Admiral Sir Hovenden Walker sailed with an amphibious force of 12,000 soldiers embarked. The St Lawrence Seaway is a difficult passage under the best of circumstances, but only the French had charted it with any accuracy. Walker's fleet lost their way and in the dark ran on to the coast losing seven of the transport ships.

Charts, or the lack of them, were a significant cause of the problems that beset a military circumnavigation that nearly ended in disaster but which was ultimately a triumph, but at a huge human cost. By 1740 England was back at war with France and Spain. The Board of Admiralty gave Commodore George Anson, command of a squadron of six ships to circumnavigate the world, attacking Spanish America and taking the annual treasure ship. By the time Anson reached Acapulco in 1742 he was down to two ships, the *Centurion* and *Gloucester*. Anson knew of an account by an Italian, Gemelli Careri, who had made an eastbound crossing in 1697, that the Spanish treasure galleons from Acapulco to Manila turned south from Acapulco in latitude 15°51'N to pick up the north-east trade winds that reliably blow between 14°N and 10°N and usually taking 60 to 65 days to sail to the Ladrones Islands (relatively near to Manila). Anson had with him

the charts and accounts of earlier buccaneer explorers William Dampier and Woodes Rogers. But these voyages had been made at a different time of the year and Anson left the inter-tropical convergence zone, or doldrums, where the wind system meets around the equator, in May, by which time the system shifts north. The voyage to the Philippines tragically took 112 days. Many men died of scurvy and starvation and his only remaining escort, the *Gloucester*, was abandoned and burnt. Anson made it to Canton, although the last few miles were difficult as he only had some Dutch charts on board, but nothing to guide him through the waters around Formosa. Even dangling purses with silver coin failed to tempt any pilot to step aboard. Refitted, he sailed south to lie in wait at the Spanish treasure ship's incoming latitude for Guam and captured the *Nuestra Senora de Covadonga* with half a million pounds worth of treasure after a 90-minute engagement . Anson's subsequent account used the chart of the North Pacific seized from the *Covadonga*, which he published 'as the encouragement of the more important purposes of navigation…stressing the value of accurate charts, global recordings of magnetic variation, and proper surveys taken from naval vessels'. The experience left a strong impression on him, and when he was appointed First Lord of the Admiralty in 1751 he became a determined reformer. During an almost uninterrupted ten years in office he improved the dockyards, created a corps of marines, revised the Articles of War and introduced a naval uniform. He also put many measures in place to increase the professionalism of the navy in general and naval officers in particular. He instructed them to keep a Remark Book in which they were to note hydrographic information in a standardized form and he encouraged them to make surveys of where they cruised. He vociferously endorsed the establishment of a Hydrographic Office, and it is a puzzle as to why it took until 1795 for this to happen.

The Seven Years War, which broke out in 1756, was in reality a struggle between Britain and France for overseas supremacy. It was to involve both countries in a succession of naval battles around the Mediterranean. William Pitt the elder, raised to the peerage as Lord Chatham (distinguishing him from his Prime Minister son of the same name) is acknowledged as the architect of Britain's expansion during this war. Guadeloupe was captured along with Quebec and the fall of French Canada to Britain all took place in 1759, called thereafter the year of victories.

On many occasions naval ships decided to force an action on the enemy without a chart of the area. One of the most impressive and daring victories that succeeded, despite having no chart, was that of Admiral Sir Edward Hawke. Quiberon Bay is a complex intermix of fast-running tidal seaways, rocks and islets, and mariners respect it for its challenging littoral. Hawke's fleet had been driven by storm winds on 9 November 1759 to retire from the blockade of Brest. While the prevailing south-westerly winds blew, no ships could beat up the narrow Goulet and out of Brest harbour. On 19 November, however, the wind dropped, and Admiral le Comte de Conflans took his chance and left.

At Morbihan in Quiberon Bay, a passage of about 100 miles south from Brest, a fleet of transports was waiting to be escorted to land troops in Ireland, so as to support the Catholics against George II. The approach through Quiberon Bay was watched by Captain Robert Duff with a squadron of frigates. Conflans chased them off, until he saw Hawke's fleet. Conflans

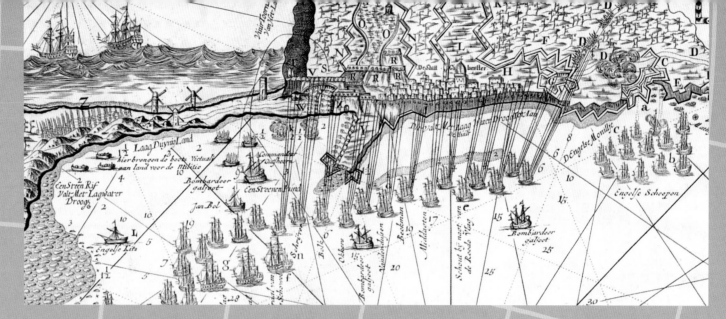

| DETAIL OF THE COMBINED BRITISH AND DUTCH ATTACK ON GIBRALTAR, 1704 | (For the full chart, see page 64.)

had local pilots on board and was confident that if he ran for Quiberon Bay, protected by the bulk of Belle Isle 10 miles to the south west and by the Quiberon peninsula and a series of islands extending seawards, ending at the fearsome rocks 'les Cardinaux' (the Cardinals), he would not be followed. Hawke had seen a copy of the sea maps in *Le Neptune François*, but these were small-scale charts and a large scale was needed for such an intricate area. Hawke put on all sail and followed Conflans. His sailing master anxiously indicated the alarming hazards ahead, but Hawke replied, 'You have done your duty in pointing out to me danger; now lay me alongside the enemy's flagship', and sailed on into the bay effectively using Conflans as his pilot. By 2.30 p.m. action was joined, continuing until dark, by which time out of 21 French ships of the line and four frigates, six were taken, burnt or wrecked, 11 escaped up the River Vilaine well inside the bay, and eight escaped south to La Rochelle. Most of those broke their backs on the bar into the harbour, and the remainder stayed blockaded until the end of the war.

Monsieur le Duc de Choiseul, the great French Minister for War and the Navy under Louis XV put in hand significant efficiency measures but not in time to avert defeat at the end of the Seven Years War. He reconstructed the French navy and incorporated improvements suggested by le Vicomte de Morogues, Sebastien Bigot, who had founded the Académie Marine at Brest to study the art of manoeuvring fleets, navigation, and to make improvements in signalling. His treatise on signalling, published in 1763, was way ahead of the British rudimentary system, which was only improved by Admiral Lord Howe and Rear-Admiral Kempenfelt at the end of the century.

Meanwhile in Britain the phenomenal growth in shipping, doubling by the end of the century, and in colonial trade, from the West Indies, American colonies, India and particularly the East, was creating a demand for charts both for commercial and military purposes. Deficiencies in John Seller's *English Pilot* were self-evident, reliance on Dutch charts resented in official and mercantile circles, and the dominance in London of chartsellers Mount and Page, who held the publishing rights to the *English Pilot* and Greenvile Collins' *Great Britain's Coasting Pilot*, was being diluted by the emergence of a number of independent commercial chart suppliers. Following General Clive's victory at Plassey in 1757, India was effectively ruled by Britain through the East India Company, and its navy the Bombay Marine, which took over the administration of the country, including its defence. It preceded the Admiralty in setting up a hydrographic office in 1779, with the appointment of Alexander Dalrymple as its Hydrographer, and the Company's armed merchant ships, known as East Indiamen,

brought back competent surveys, which were used to compile charts published by the London publishers.

The Admiralty's changing attitude was evidenced when they commissioned the London map publisher Thomas Jeffreys to publish a certain Master James Cook's 'A new chart of the River St Laurence'. Jeffrey's business was built on specializing in North America, and some of the coastlines of France and Spain, which as 'geographer to the King' gave him access to government material for his maps and charts. When Jeffreys died in 1771 his successor, William Faden, continued with the assistance of Aaron Arrowsmith who would in turn start his own chart publishing business in 1790.

The mention of Cook is an appropriate moment to introduce the man who is rightly described as the 'grandfather of naval surveying', for his surveying methods and achievements mark him as one of the outstanding men of all time. He is best remembered for his Pacific voyages but his navigational expertise and invention were honed during the Seven Years War. After the capitulation of Louisburg in 1758, Cook assisted and learned from Samuel Holland, the Army Engineer who supervised the surveys of North America, to make a plan of the city and its fortifications, with such success that Captain Simcoe of the *Pembroke* engaged them both to prepare charts of the River and Gulf St Lawrence, with an eye to the eventual attack on Quebec. So in Halifax, in the winter of 1758–9, Cook studied mathematics and draughtsmanship with Holland and Simcoe, and probably also from Frederick Wallet Des Barres, of whom we will hear more in the next chapter, who was there engaged on similar work from captured French plans.

The British plan to take Canada was three pronged: an attack by one army along Lake Champlain, a second to cross Lake Ontario and go down the St Laurence to join together and attack Montreal, while a third under Vice-Admiral Charles Saunders sailed up the River St Laurence with 20 ships of the line and a number of escorts and transports with an army of 8000 men embarked under the 32-year-old Major-General James Wolfe. As master of the *Mercury*, Cook, in the spring of 1759 brought two small boats at night and took soundings and surveyed the river, including the Traverse and beyond Quebec. The chart he produced enabled ships of the line for the first time to sail past the city, which the French Governor, Louis Joseph Montcalm, had not thought possible. Saunders was able to cover Wolfe's landings upriver of Quebec, in the heart of the French defences, where Montcalm succumbed to Wolfe in the open without the defences of the city.

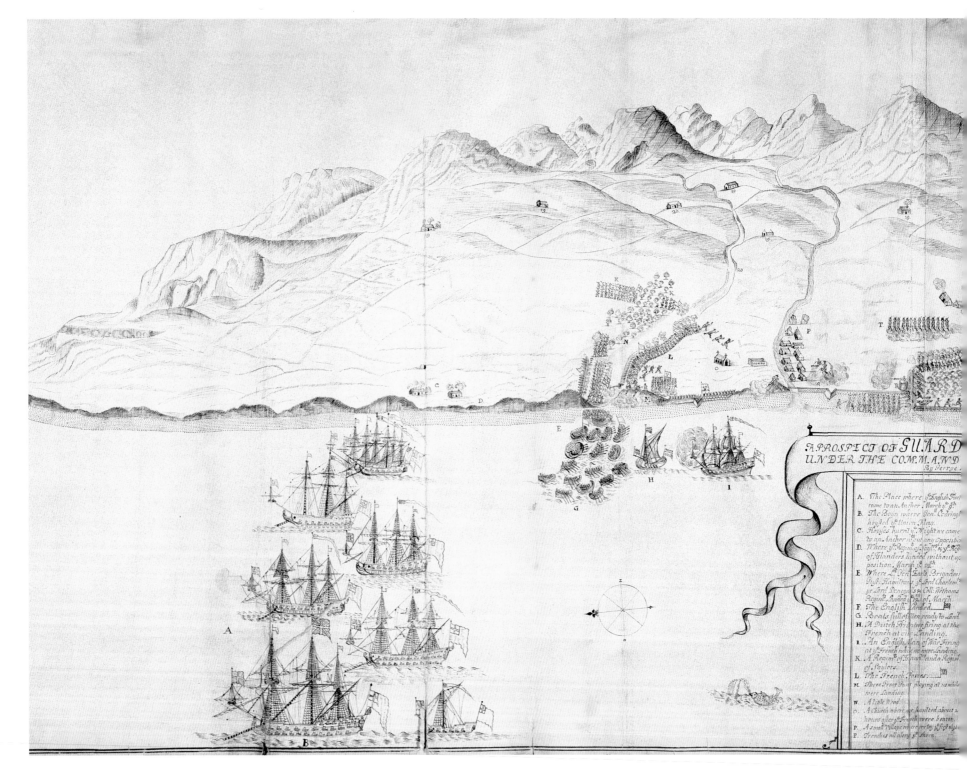

A PROSPECT OF GUARD
UNDER THE COMMAND

| GUADELOUPE BEING ATTACKED BY ENGLISH FORCES BY CAPTAIN GEORGE PARKER, 1703 | An English family, the Codringtons, were to dominate the West Indies' islands of Antigua and Barbuda for some 200 years. These islands were part of the group known as the Leeward Islands, so called because the prevailing winds blow from south to north. Sir Christopher Codrington leased the islands from the Crown and cleared the first sugar plantation there in 1674. His son, also Christopher, in turn took the governorship of the Leeward Islands. The French had taken nearby Martinique and Guadeloupe, and sugar was their main crop. By 1700, with a strengthening market for sugar, competition led to opportunism in the West Indies.

In April 1702 war was declared between France and Britain and in September Captain Hovenden Walker, commanding the *Burford*, a 70-gun third rate, was detached from the Mediterranean with a squadron and some land forces to sail for the Leeward Islands. They arrived at Barbados in January 1703 and Captain Walker organized a home convoy of six richly laden ships. They then joined Codrington, who had previously fought against the Dutch at Flanders, at Antigua and together sailed with an expedition against Guadeloupe at the end of February.

The chart shows how on 12 March the greater part of the troops landed, but they were pinned down by the French until the *Chichester*, a second rate of 80 guns, was sent in to drive the French from their batteries. The next day the remaining troops and 400 seamen were landed and ferociously attacked the north part of the town, forcing the French to retreat into the castle and the fort. The French held out until the 3 April when they blew both up and escaped to the mountains. The British forces burned the town, razed the fortifications and the sugar plantations; the best of the artillery was taken on board and the rest destroyed. They re-embarked with considerable booty without losing a single man.

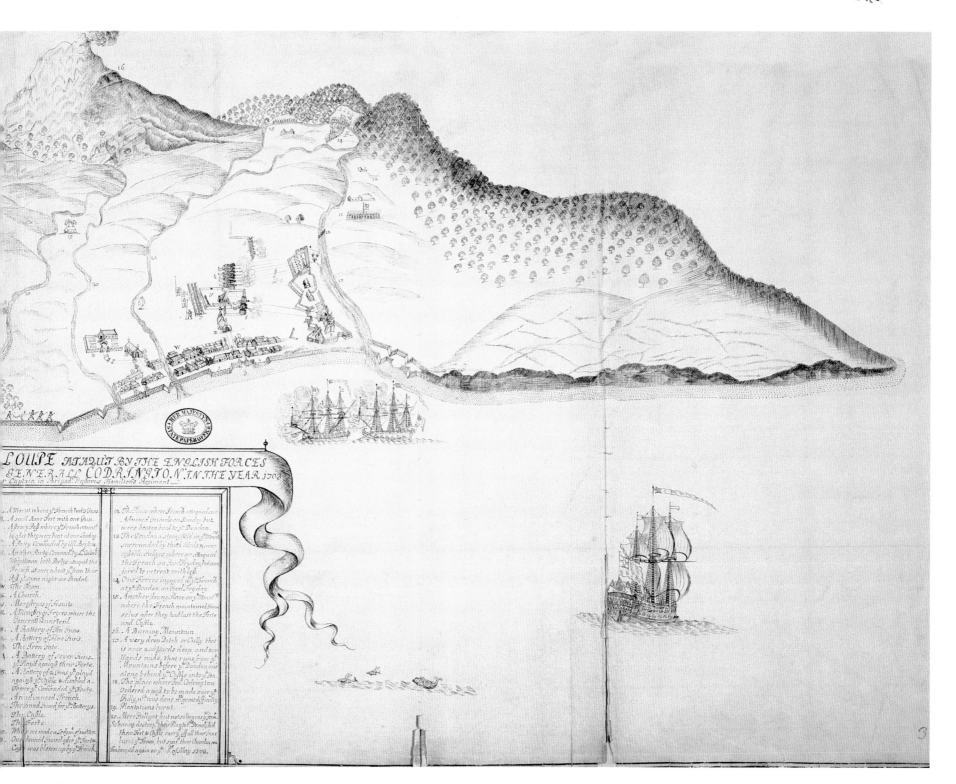

LOUPE *ATAQUT BY THE ENGLISH FORCES*
GENERALL CODRINGTON IN THE YEAR 1703
r Captain in Brigad Brigaruse Hamilton's Regiment

This was a good example of cooperation between army and navy forces working well on an amphibious mission. The chart, foreshortened to bring into perspective the salient aspects of the campaign, shows in some detail the landing of troops and taking of the fortifications. This was a pre-emptive attack to minimize the French opportunity to take British islands. However, the French retaliated by sacking nearby St Kitts and Nevis islands and raiding Montserrat and Antigua, so Parliament authorized the stationing of a regiment on Antigua. (The National Archives {PRO} CO 700)

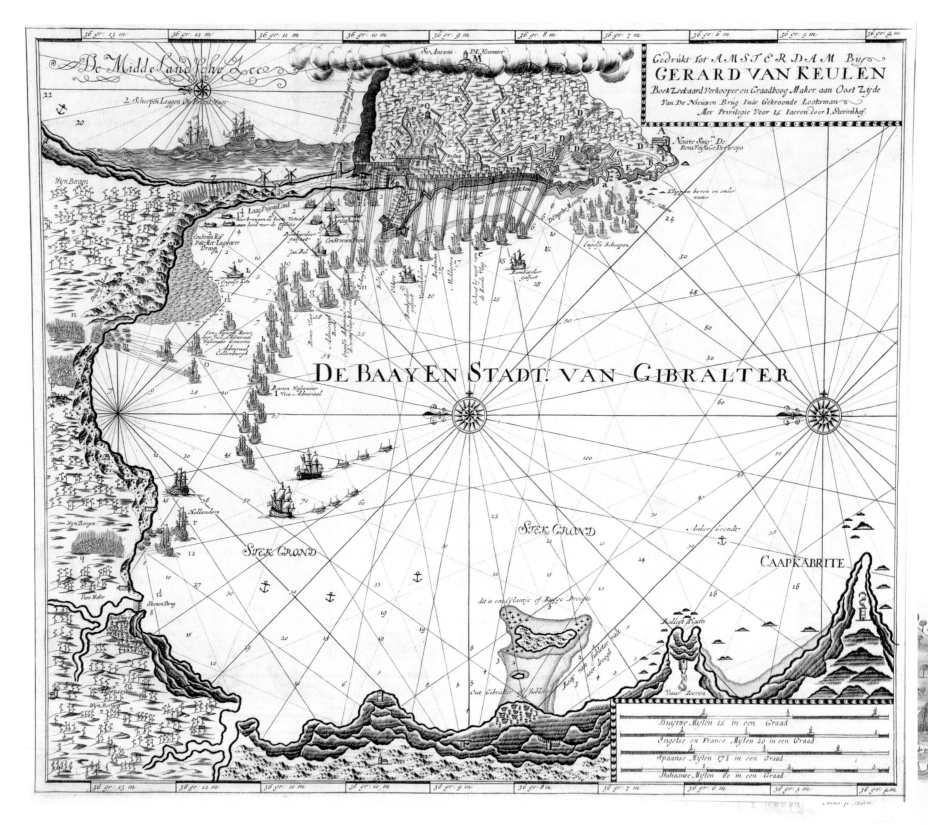

| COMBINED BRITISH AND DUTCH ATTACK ON GIBRALTAR BY GERARD VAN KEULEN, 1704 | This unusual sea chart was made and printed by the Dutch cartographer Gerard Van Keulen. He was from the prolific Van Keulen mapmaking dynasty of Amsterdam and was Hydrographer to the VOC. The chart describes and celebrates the joint Anglo-Dutch capture of the fortress of Gibraltar in 1704. Strategically, Gibraltar has proved a vital asset to British naval operations with its commanding position at the narrow entrance to the Mediterranean. The combined fleet is shown bombarding the town and forts and landing troops, but it is in the detail that the fascination lies. The two Dutch ships from which the troops landed are shown being towed to windward by the ships' boats, supplies are being taken ashore for the invading forces, while bomb ketches fire mortar shells. An 'Algierse Rover' or Barbary pirate ship strayed into the fight and is illustrated being captured by the Dutch commander, Admiral Wassenaar. The entire coastline, typically for an early sea chart, is shown in profile to allow navigation from visual landmarks. Finally, despite the heroic scale of the operations depicted, there is no indication that the semi-ruined fortifications of Gibraltar were, in fact, only being defended by about 150 infantrymen.

The capture of Gibraltar initially gave little advantage to the British, until a proper naval base could be built. In the meantime, the commander-in-chief, Admiral Sir George Rooke, had to improvise using Lisbon as a forward naval base for Mediterranean operations. (By kind permission of The Map House, London)

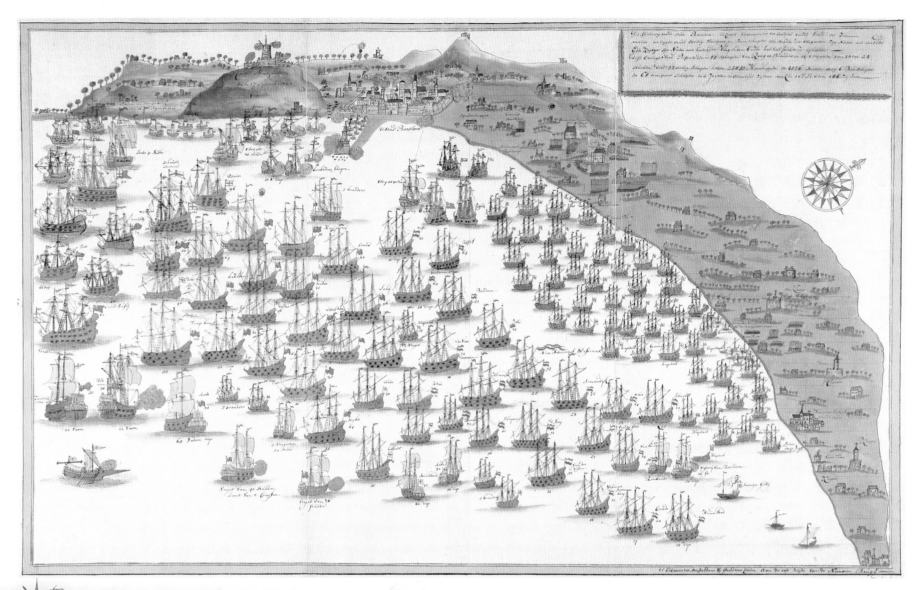

| **COMBINED BRITISH AND DUTCH ATTACK ON BARCELONA BY GERARD VAN KEULEN, 1705** | Gerard Van Keulen's prodigious output established him as the pre-eminent supplier of charts in Europe during the first quarter of the eighteenth century. This exceptional view of the 1705 siege of Barcelona by the British and Dutch navies during the War of the Spanish Succession shows an attempt to establish a critically needed base for Mediterranean operations, and was made with the same meticulous attention to detail of all his charts, not just showing the 156 ships of the combined fleet, but naming them, their captains and the number of guns. Admiral Sir Clowdisley Shovel and Admiral Philip van Almonde had worked together previously at the victory by Admiral Russell over the French Admiral Tourville at Barfleur and La Hogue in 1698, which dashed once and for all any chance of James II regaining the English throne from William III, and now they organized a fleet in Lisbon, which took Barcelona with a straight naval landing and assault in two days, rather than a long army siege. The allies were able to take Cartagena, Alicante, Ibiza and most importantly from a strategic point of view, Majorca, with its ideal base of Port Mahon. (Courtesy of The Hispanic Society of America, New York)

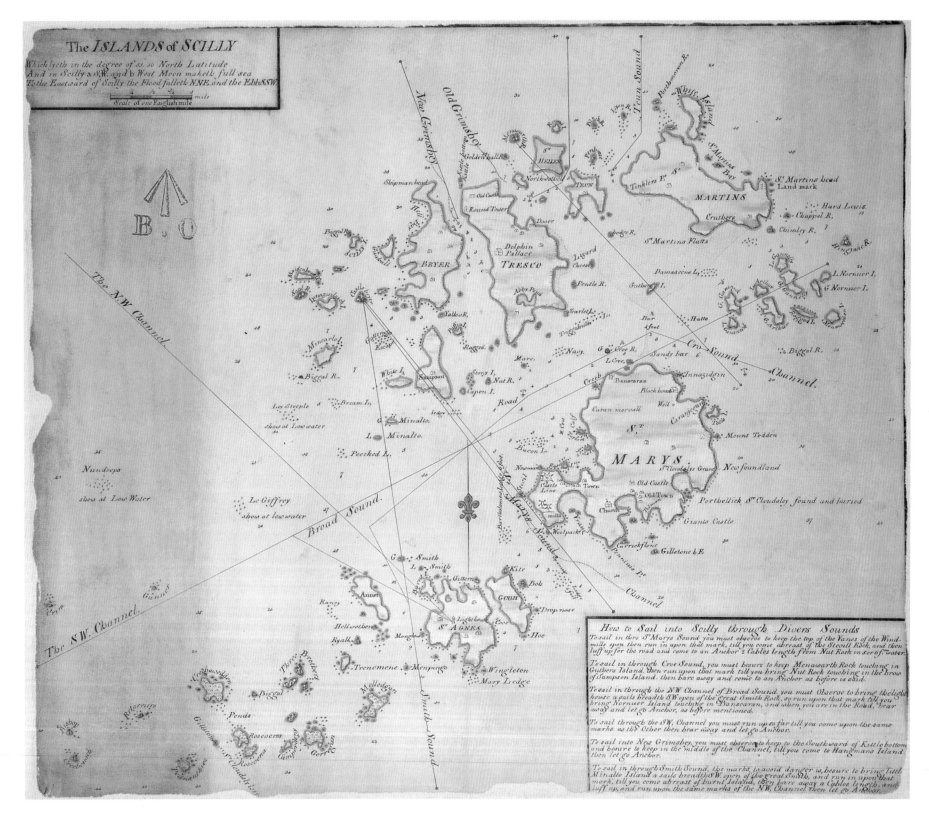

| **CHART OF THE SCILLY ISLES, 1707** | The lack of a Mediterranean base was to be an indirect cause of one of the most serious losses of ships and men by other than enemy action sustained by the Royal Navy. The commander-in-chief of the Mediterranean squadron of 21 ships, Admiral Sir Clowdisley Shovel, could not winter his fleet there and returned home late in the year, when storms and bad visibility in the English Channel latitudes predominate. Ships returning to England had no means of fixing longitude and would usually run down a latitude, then with good visibility a landfall could be recognized and the course adjusted to the follow the coast. Contemporary charts showed the Scilly Isles, low-lying and hard to identify, in a position some 15 miles too far north. As Sir Clowdisley neared the south western approaches to the English

Channel with a hopelessly inaccurate assessment of his position based on dead reckoning, he was unaware of the northerly current sweeping his fleet onto the rocks of the Scilly Isles. The Admiral's flagship, *Association*, and three of his ships of the line, *Eagle*, *Rumney* and *Firebrand*, sank with all hands except one seaman and Sir Clowdisley.

The chart is drawn by an unknown hand shortly after the tragedy and is a copy of another manuscript chart. While noting the place where Sir Clowdisley came ashore, was killed and buried at Porthellick on St Mary's Island, the chart gives soundings and concentrates on sailing directions to give safe courses through the islands. Suggested bearings drawn on the chart are amplified in the notes. (The National Archives {PRO} MPH 1/369

| PLAN OF HARWICH HARBOUR
SHOWING PROPOSED FORTIFI-
CATIONS BY MAJOR JOHN
HANWAY, 1709 | As the only harbour to
offer a safe anchorage between the Thames
Estuary and the River Humber, Harwich
played a vital role in the defence of the east
coast of England, particularly against the
Dutch in the seventeenth and eighteenth
centuries, and against the continuing threat
of a French landing and later in support of
the Scottish Jacobites to the north. This
plan of Harwich harbour was drawn by
Major Hanway, an army engineer in 1709,
and dedicated to John Churchill, Duke of
Marlborough, with proposals for two forts
to defend the harbour, one to be known as
Landguard fort. A later chart drawn in
1754 by Piercy Brett, one of Commodore
Anson's officers in his circumnavigation to
rise to admiral and receive a knighthood,
shows the forts completed. (The National
Archives {PRO} MPH 1/337)

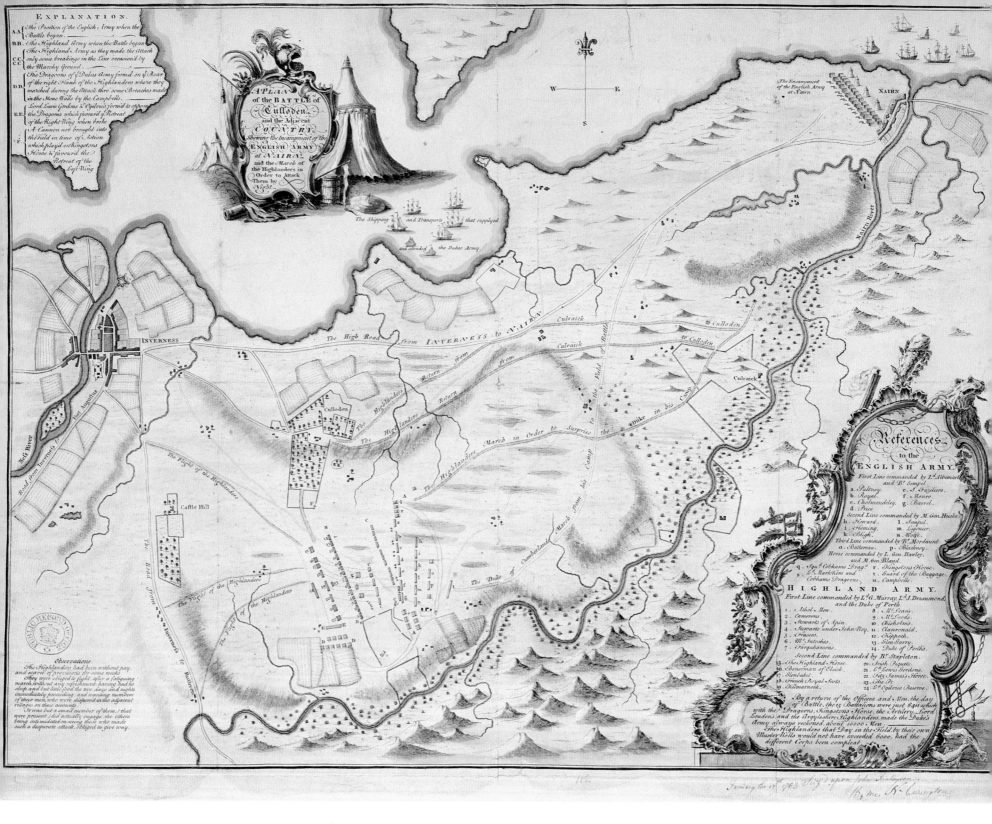

| ABOVE | **THE BATTLE OF CULLODEN, 1746** | This plan of the battle, which brought the Jacobite rebellion to an end, clearly shows the supporting English squadrons in the Moray Firth off Nairn, where they could land troops, ammunition and victuals, and off Fort George, too. The march of the Highlanders, under Charles Edward Stuart, overnight to surprise the English camped at Nairn was a disaster as they approached too close to dawn and decided to march back to Culloden. Hungry and exhausted, the Duke of Cumberland's forces routed them next day. A study of the plan shows the various paths taken by the adversaries. As in so many campaigns control of the sea ensured victory on land. (The National Archives {PRO} MPF 1/1)

| ABOVE RIGHT | **GUANTÁNAMO BAY ON THE ISLAND OF CUBA, 1751** | At the time when this Spanish chart was made, Cuba was the centre of Spanish power in the Caribbean, and Havana was the rendezvous for the Spanish bullion galleons. Dated 7 April 1751, this chart of Guantánamo Bay shows a large natural harbour some 40 miles east of Santiago de Cuba and is an assessment of its suitability as a naval base. The key provides details for its defence, the safest anchorage and, of great importance, details of fresh water. Longitude is based on a prime meridian through Tenerife, as on all Spanish charts. The history of attacks and re-attacks with consequent changes of 'ownership' of the Caribbean islands is bewildering, but Cuba, discovered by Columbus and colonized by Diego Velasquez from 1511, who all but wiped out the indigenous Ciboney tribe, had to 'import' black African slaves. Tough Spanish rule brought a 10-year war in 1868 leading to attempts at independence. The sinking of the US battleship *Maine* was the excuse for America to take over the island until 1909 when Cuba was given independence, except for Guantánamo Bay, which the US, appreciating as the Spanish did its strength, has retained as a sovereign port. (Library of Congress)

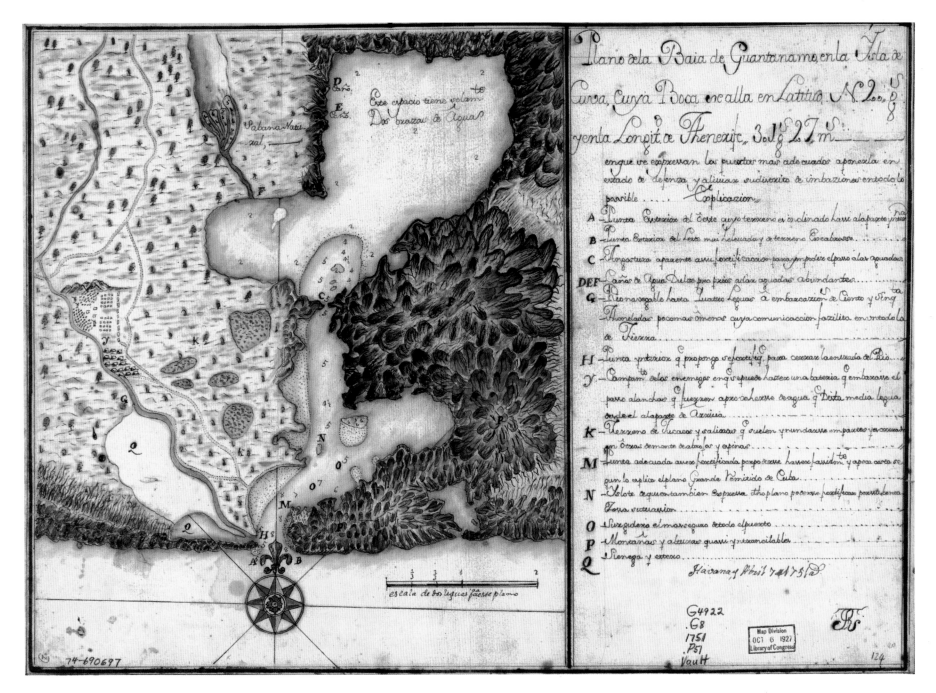

| RIGHT | **BATTLE BETWEEN THE BRITISH AND FRENCH OFF TOULON, 1744** | This is one of a series of seven watercolour schematic representations by the Dutch Admiral Jacob Pieter van Braam of the VOC, who made his name in operations in East Indies waters around Malacca and Selangor in 1784-6, which analyzes the tactics and outcome of the battle near Toulon in 1744.

The War of the Austrian Succession has become a historical catch-all for a number of concurrent wars between various European nations. Britain preferred, as she had mostly done during this warring century, to support her traditional allies, Austria and the Netherlands, by treaty but only committing sea power to the war effort, which was both sustainable and profitable for her, while taking North American and other overseas territory from the French.

One of the important issues at the outbreak of war was to neutralize the Spanish and French fleets, both of which were anchored in Toulon. Admiral Thomas Mathews was appointed commander-in-chief of the Mediterranean fleet in 1742, relieving Rear-Admiral Lestock, who stayed on as his second-in-command. Mathews attacked the combined fleet on 22 February off Toulon. In light winds it was not until the morning that Mathews was close enough in the van to engage the enemy. Lestock was in the rear, claiming afterwards to have been unable to obey two conflicting signals – one to engage the enemy and one to form a line of battle – and did not fire a shot. The allies made it back to Toulon relatively unscathed but at the subsequent court martial, Lestock was acquitted on this technicality and Mathews was dismissed from the service. The verdicts caused great controversy for the next 20 years and the message was that you adhered strictly to the Fighting Instructions or suffered the consequences, stultifying initiative. (Scheepvart Museum, Netherlands)

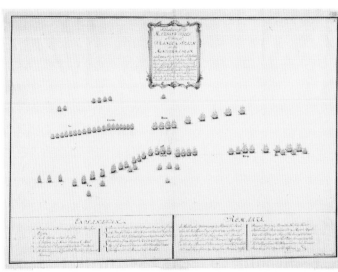

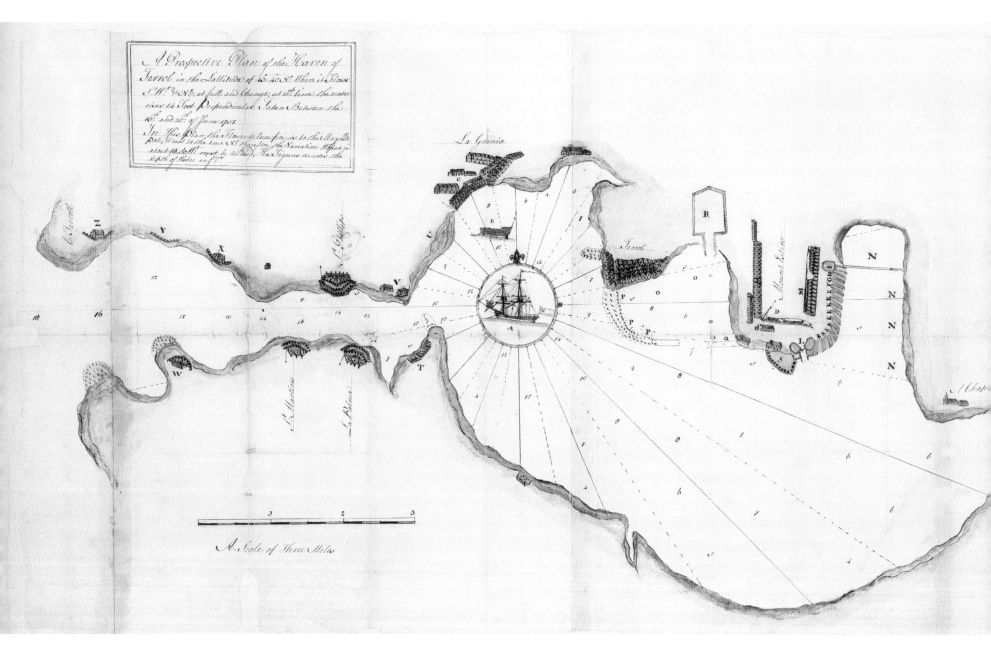

| ABOVE | **PLAN OF FERROL BY CAPTAIN THOMAS FOLEY, WITH SHIP AND FORTIFICATIONS, 1751** | Captain Foley, from a Pembrokeshire family whose nephew, also Thomas Foley, was to fight with Nelson at St Vincent, the Nile and Copenhagen, had gained much experience during Commodore Anson's circumnavigation (1740–4). During a peaceful period with Spain after the War of the Austrian Succession in 1748, as captain of the sloop *Savage*, Foley had taken advantage of a visit to Ferrol, Spain, in 1751 to sound 'the Haven all over on pretence of amusing myself with Fishing and the Fishing Lines were marked for that purpose'. Foley had cleverly marked his fishing line with knots every fathom and quarter fathom. His sailing master actually drew the chart, clearly an intelligence report that showed Spanish ships and port installations, which Foley then forwarded to the Admiralty to provide the latest information that would prove useful in the Seven Years War of 1756. Foley also got hold of a Spanish chart of La Coruña, which he described as a copy of a Spanish plan 'exact enough about the Groin and the Bay to the Southward of Ferrol but the Haven of Ferrol is very incorrect'. (The National Archives {PRO} MPII 1/41)

| RIGHT | **ACTION AT GHERIAH FORT, INDIA, BY JOHN HARDING, 1756** | Rivalry between the various European East India companies inevitably, considering the disparity of time and distance, developed a momentum of its own independent of the wars in Europe. Admiral Charles Watson was perhaps one of Britain's best, although least-known, eighteenth-century admirals, and took the post as Commander-in-Chief East Indies at the main HEIC port of Bombay in 1755. His first task was, in combination with the East India Company Bombay Marine, to take out Gheriah (Vijaydurg today) on the Malabar coast, where the Mahratta, Tulaji Angria, was attacking local trade. With troops under Colonel Robert Clive embarked to take over as Governor of the East India Company Fort St David, at Cuddalore about 100 miles south east of Madras, and thence to take Bengal, Watson sailed into the harbour. He destroyed the Mahratta's fleet while Clive landed and took the fort and town. Watson's success owed much to the accurate surveys his sailing master produced and used to navigate the shoals, 71 so enabling the British ships to bring their guns to bear alongside the fort, reducing it from seaward. John Harding has signed this pictorial account, which shows Watson's fleet anchored and bombarding the fort and shoreline, with details of the ships taking part, including two East Indiamen. (Admiralty Library Manuscript Collection MSS 356)

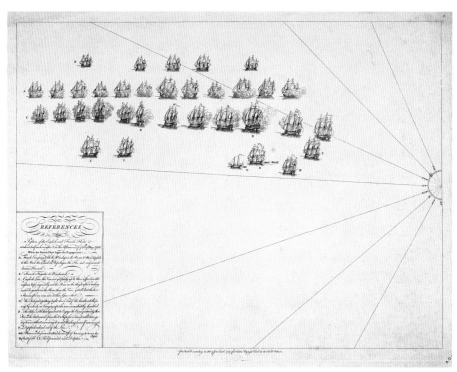

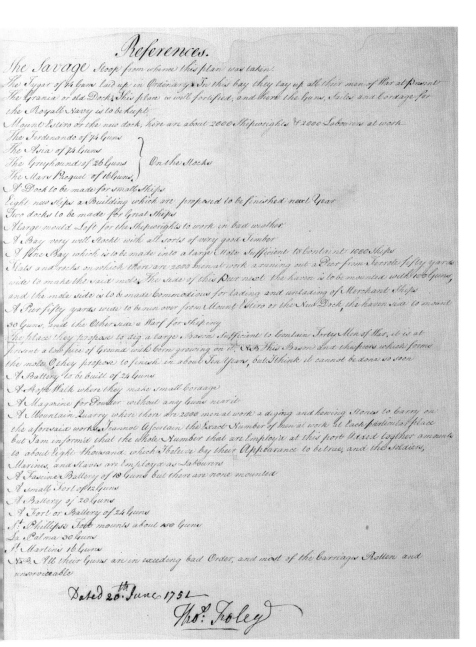

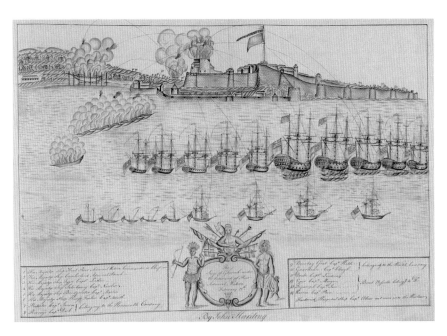

| ABOVE | **MINORCA ACTION, 1756** | Admiral John Byng was the fourth son of Admiral George Byng, Viscount Torrington, who rose to become first Lord of the Admiralty and whose influence facilitated his son's rapid promotion. John Byng was given command of a small fleet of 10 ships of the line in 1756, flying his flag in the *Ramillies*, to relieve Minorca, which was under attack by the French. Upon arrival, he found the island already overrun by French troops, with only the garrison holding out. An indecisive action against the French fleet, where only the van engaged the enemy, was, ironically, a similar situation to that of Admiral Mathews at Toulon in 1744. Byng decided after discussions with his senior officers that the best action was to make for Gibraltar, which was also exposed, as even if they defeated the French fleet at Minorca, they were not strong enough to eject the French from the island. In his absence the garrison capitulated. Byng was recalled and arrested in Portsmouth and charged under Article XII of the 1749 Articles of War for failing 'to do his utmost to take or destroy every Ship which it shall be his Duty to engage'. Although many in the navy supported him, he was found guilty. The Article provided that 'every such Person so offending, and being convicted thereof the Sentence of a Court-Martial, shall suffer Death'.

Clemency, the King's prerogative, was recommended by the court martial but refused, probably on political grounds as the Seven Years War was going badly, and Byng was shot on the quarterdeck of one of the Channel Fleet's ships, *Monarch*, in Portsmouth harbour on 14 March 1757. It inspired Voltaire, the French playwright, to write in *Candide* that in England it was sometimes necessary to shoot an Admiral 'pour encourager les autres'.

A series of five charts, of which this is the second, shows the positions of the French and British fleets on 20 May 1756 at 2 p.m., 2.30 p.m., 3 p.m., 5 p.m. (when all firing stopped) and at 5.30 p.m., and were presented with other papers, accounts of the action, correspondence, minutes and intelligence reports at the trial. (Admiralty Library Manuscript Collection Portfolio A/1-5)

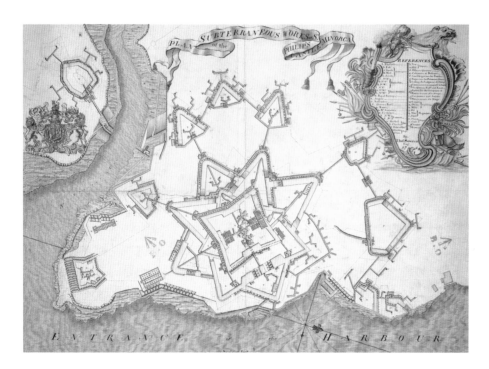

| LEFT | **PLAN OF THE SUBTERRANEOUS WORKS OF ST PHILIP'S CASTLE, MINORCA, BY THOMAS SOWERS, 1754** | Minorca had previously been captured by the Royal Navy in 1708, during the War of the Spanish Succession. The British recognized its strategic value as a deep-water harbour, pivotally positioned in the eastern Mediterranean, and built a naval base and the star fort shown on this chart. The design was state of the art and had developed through the experience of centuries of European wars. Its eight points enabled all walls to be covered by relatively few defenders. The plan is signed by Thomas Sowers, Engineer, in 1754, who re-appears in 1768 in Canada re-designing Fort Niagara for defence against the Native North American Indians. It shows the underground works that enabled the defenders to pass safely from one part of the fort to another. The fort's position at the entrance to the harbour was key to the base's defence. However, the French took the island on 29 June 1756 after a two-month siege, which Admiral Byng failed to lift. The island was restored by the Treaty of Paris in 1763 but captured by a combined French and Spanish fleet in 1782, and recovered by the British in 1798. It was finally ceded to Spain in 1802, but it still retains many British features. (The National Archives {PRO} WO 78/1017)

| RIGHT | **ORAN, CENTRE OF PIRACY IN THE MEDITERRANEAN, BY GEORG MATTHÄUS SEUTTER, C. 1730** | Georg Matthäus Seutter was appointed Geographer to the Imperial Court of the Holy Roman Emperor and published maps and sea views like this one of Oran, Algeria, on the Mediterranean coast of Africa. As the Latin inscription relates Oran was a 'commodious sea port on the sea coast of Barbary, specifically in the kingdom of Tlemcen (Telesin), which the Spaniards held from 1509 and the Moors occupied after 1708, with the Spaniards reclaiming it in 1732. Seutter had engraved this from a collection of contemporary surveys. Quite apart from the rivalries and wars of the European maritime countries, from the sixteenth to nineteenth centuries the Barbary pirates were a continuous source of fear; the Corsairs, such as Barbarossa, were known for the ferocity and skill with which they attacked and harried Christian shipping and ports.

Many European nations sent expeditions to stamp them out, including Robert Blake in 1655, Anglo-Dutch expeditions under Charles II, two French ones in 1682–3, the Americans in 1801–5 and again in 1815, a combined Dutch and British one in 1816 and finally the French conquest and annexation of Algiers in 1830. (© National Maritime Museum, London, F0371)

| LEFT | **PORT MAHON BY THE SPANISH HYDROGRAPHER DON VICENTE TOFIÑO DE SAN MIGUEL, 1786** | Once Minorca was in Spanish hands in 1782 the eminent hydrographer Don Vicente Tofiño carried out a survey to update old charts and this was later published in Madrid in his *Atlas Maritimo de Espana* in 1789. Before joining the Spanish navy he had taught mathematics, useful in his survey work. He was eventually promoted Rear-Admiral and Director of the Spanish Naval Academy. He had developed a style of his own, with very beautiful and effective hatching and contour work, and the strength of the fort's position at the entrance to the well-sheltered harbour can be appreciated from Tofino's detailed survey. (© National Maritime Museum, London, F0028)

Erklärung der Buchstaben.

A. Die Statt Oran
B. Der Marckt.
C. Castell S. Crux.
D. Castell S. Ambrosi.
E. Haus des Frantz
Consuls.
F. Castell S. Andris.
G. Castell Neuve.
H. Cast. S. Hieronymæ
I. Castell Vuste.
K. Cast. Mazalquivir.
L. Stein Klippen.
M. Berg del Santo.
N. Capo Falkon.
O. Hier sind die Spa-
nische Trouppen
angelandt.
P. Hafen von Oran.
Q. Ein paar Fontaine.
R. Capo Ferat.
S. Stein Klippen als
ein Syl e. Schleuse
sich zeigend.
T. Golfo v. Mostagan.
V. Arzeui.
W. Tulgilmac.
X. Tigisni.
Y. Masagran.
Z. Mostagan.

ORAN
munita urbs et comodus port
in Ora maritima Barbariæ
et proprie
in Regno Telensin,
quam Hispani jam A.º 1509. tenuerunt
et postquam A.º 1708. a Mauris occupata
fuit, Hispani A.º 1732. sibi eam denuo vin
dicarunt, Cum Prospectu adjacentium littorum,
juxta recentissimam designationem æri
insculpta per
MATTH. SEUTTER. Sac. Cæs. et Reg. Cath. Maj.
Geographum Augustanum.

DAS

MITTELLÆNDISCHE MEER

Milliaria Gallica 5 Horæ Itineris.

Die Küste von ORAN.

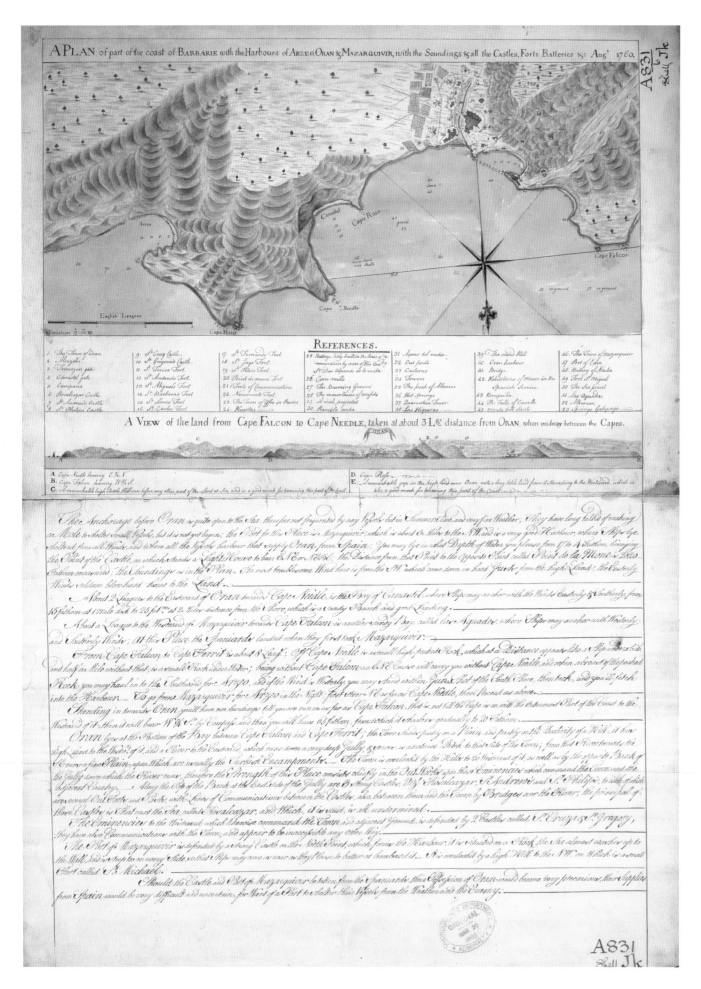

| BARBARY COAST HARBOURS, 1760 |

In 1760 Captain Hugh Palliser was cruising in the Levant and the Mediterranean to gather useful intelligence in the light of Britain's changing relationship with Spain following Charles III's succession to the throne. Part of his portfolio of charts covering the Mediterranean included a plan of Malta (see page 76) and this one of the Barbary coast harbours. The portfolio is put together in book form and also includes charts on Naples, Greece, the coast of Spain and north African harbours. The observations and plans of foreign coasts were made by both Palliser and his master, Robert Christian.

This chart, orientated with North to the bottom of the page, is of the harbour of Oran, then occupied by the Spanish, with Arzeo (Arzew) to the east and Mazarquivir, and includes soundings and shading to lay down the coastline and hills. Beneath the references are comprehensive details of the forts, harbour, walls and gates, with a view of the land from a position 3 leagues (9 miles) north of Oran. As required by the Admiralty, there is a report on the fortifications and descriptions of harbours and anchorages and other sailing directions, all useful for an attack on the harbour. The final notes are unequivocally an assessment of such an attack stating that ships can come very close to the castle at Mazarquivir 'to batter or bombard it', and 'should the castle and port of Mazarquivir be taken from the Spaniards, their possession of Oran would become very precarious, their supplies from Spain would be very difficult and uncertain for want of a port to shelter their vessels from the weather and the enemy'. War broke out with Spain on 4 January 1762. (UKHO © British Crown Copyright)

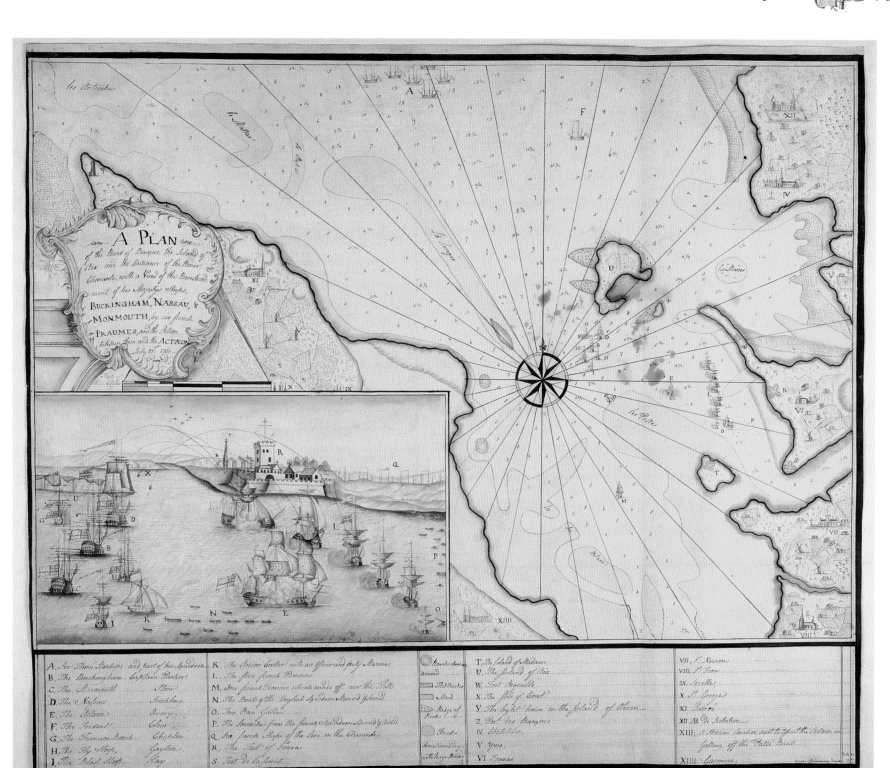

| PLAN AND ATTACK OF THE BASQUE ROADS AND THE ISLAND OF D'AIX, 1761 |

Admiral Hawke's victory in 1759 over the French fleet when he attacked into the dangerous and confined bay of Quiberon in a rising gale and fading light broke the back of French naval power for the rest of the Seven Years War. William Pitt was looking for a 'victorious peace', with a strong negotiating position to keep Britain's gains in Canada, India and the West Indies at the ensuing peace treaty. In April 1761 Commodore Augustus Keppel attacked and took Belle Isle, 22 miles west of St Nazaire giving Pitt a negotiating lever for later. Keppel now had control of most of the French Bay of Biscay seaboard and, to maximize his tactical situation, set out to neutralize the French approaches to the harbour of Rochefort, a port that prospered, as did many, on sugar, Canadian furs and slavery.

The chart shows both the attack and the navigational topography of the channel and approaches, with a key that explains how the attack went. Inside the River Charente, the masts of

six French ships of the line are shown. Trapped, they could be cut out if the forts were silenced. The six French prames (small two- or three-masted ships fitted with 10 to 20 guns for use as floating batteries or gun boats) came out at 7 a.m. on 21 July, together with two 'row gallies' and a lot of small launches with armed solders, and set themselves on the shoals to bombard the British ships. As the strong ebb tide slowed the frigate *Actaeon* was ordered to close the prames but she ran aground on the 'tail of Pall-Bank' and small boats went to warp her off. The bomb vessel *Furnace* lobbed 32 well-directed shells and the prames made off back to the shelter of the cannon on the south point of Ile d'Oleron. The chart is signed by George Dumaresq on 25 July 1761, who is probably from the Jersey Dumaresq family, using the original French chart and superimposing the sketch of the action, to accompany the letter by Keppel reporting the action to John Cleveland, Secretary of the Admiralty. (Admiralty Library Manuscript Collection; A/83)

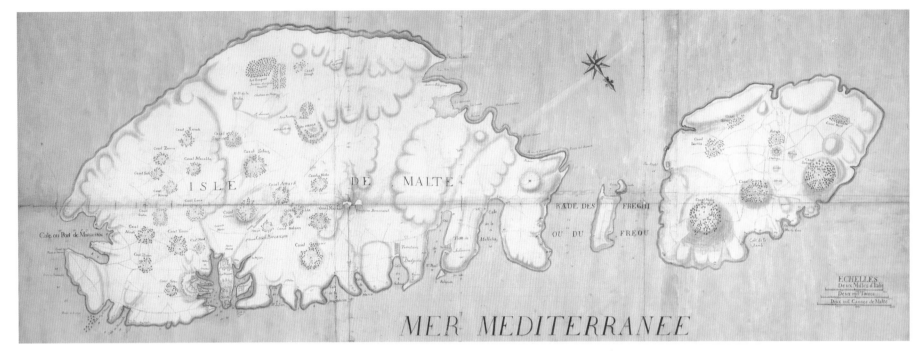

| ABOVE | **PLAN OF MALTA, 1760** | Captain Palliser's chart portfolio also included this French chart of 1760, when the island was still under the control of the Order of the Knights of St John. It confirmed France's continued interest in Malta, describing the harbours and forts and 'where descents can be made' and thus ascents or landings, too. With soundings and rocks shown and the outline of the island with Italian, French and Maltese scales, the description portrays the Maltese as 'hard-working, correct and good Catholics' and goes on to report the number of cannons at the various forts and possible landing places.

The island of Malta, strategically placed in the central Mediterranean to command the relatively narrow channel between the southern European extremity of Italy and the north African coast, has a long history of war and capture. It was variously occupied by the Phoenicians, Carthaginians, a colony of the Romans, then Constantinople, the Normans in 1090, and was a part of Aragon in 1282. By 1530 it was home to the Knights of St John who were driven out of Rhodes, and blockaded by the Turks in 1590 in one of the most famous sieges in history. Napoleon, attempting to secure the route to India, took the island in 1798 and it was then captured by the British in the following year. Its fine deep-water harbour Valetta, named after one the Grand Masters of the Order, was used as the main Mediterranean naval base by the British for 150 years, until soon after Malta's independence in 1963. It still has its own dockyard repair facilites and is a fuelling base for NATO. (UKHO © British Crown Copyright)

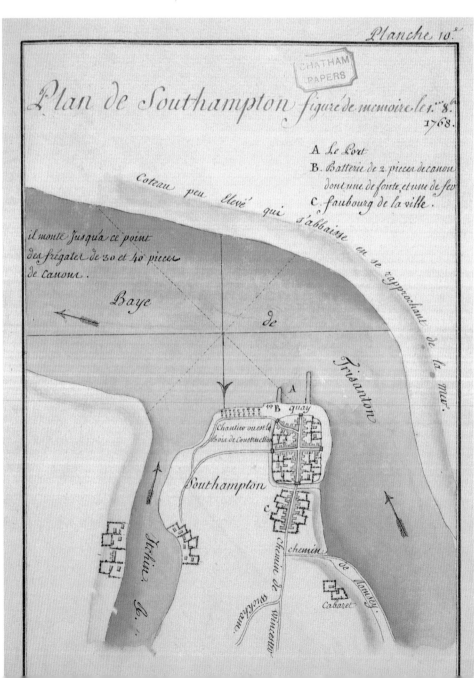

| RIGHT | **FRENCH CHART OF SOUTHAMPTON, 1768** | William Pitt, the first Earl of Chatham and Prime Minister of Britain during the Seven Years War, obtained copies of French charts of two dozen possible landing places in England from Harwich to Milford Haven made by order of the great Minister for War under Louis XV, the Duc de Choiseul, Colonel General de Suisses et Grisons, remembered for his reconstruction of the French navy. De Choiseul was keen to avenge the loss of Canada and other territories such as parts of India and islands in the Caribbean and plotted without the King's knowledge with Spain. He organized spies to make charts of all potential landing places in England. Surprisingly accurate, one wonders at how they were made unnoticed and with such insouciance, for the coastal outlines and details of fortifications are good. (The National Archives [PRO] MR 1/1111)

| PLAN OF SPANISH AMERICA CARTHAGENA HARBOUR AND CITY BY CAPTAIN JOSEPH SMITH SPEER OF THE 49TH REGIMENT OF FOOT, 1771 | The Army produced some very good cartographers: Captain Cook himself was taught much by Samuel Holland, an army surveyor under General Wolfe at the attack on Quebec, where he learned the use of the plane table, and trigonometry applicable to cartography. After his time in the army, Captain Speer became an active pilot and hydrographer in the West Indies and Caribbean, specializing in charts of the region. In 1766 he published his West India Pilot of various small charts of Caribbean harbours. His map of Carthagena in Spanish America (Colombia today) along with his other charts were designed to give merchants safe guidance, but were of value to naval officers, too, showing important points on the fortifications and the harbour, and produced in a clear, easily assimilated style. Naval officers had to put together their own portfolio of charts, purchased commercially in London, before the centralization of charts issued from the British Hydrographic Office, and this one of Caragena by Speer was included in an atlas of 20 littoral maps and charts by him relating to Spain and Portugal and some of their overseas possessions. Cartagena was an important Spanish harbour, but well guarded as Admiral Vernon discovered when he failed to take the city after a five-day siege in 1741 against an unexpectedly virile defence from the Spanish Governor Vice-Admiral Don Blas de Lazo. (The National Archives {PRO} SP 112/101)

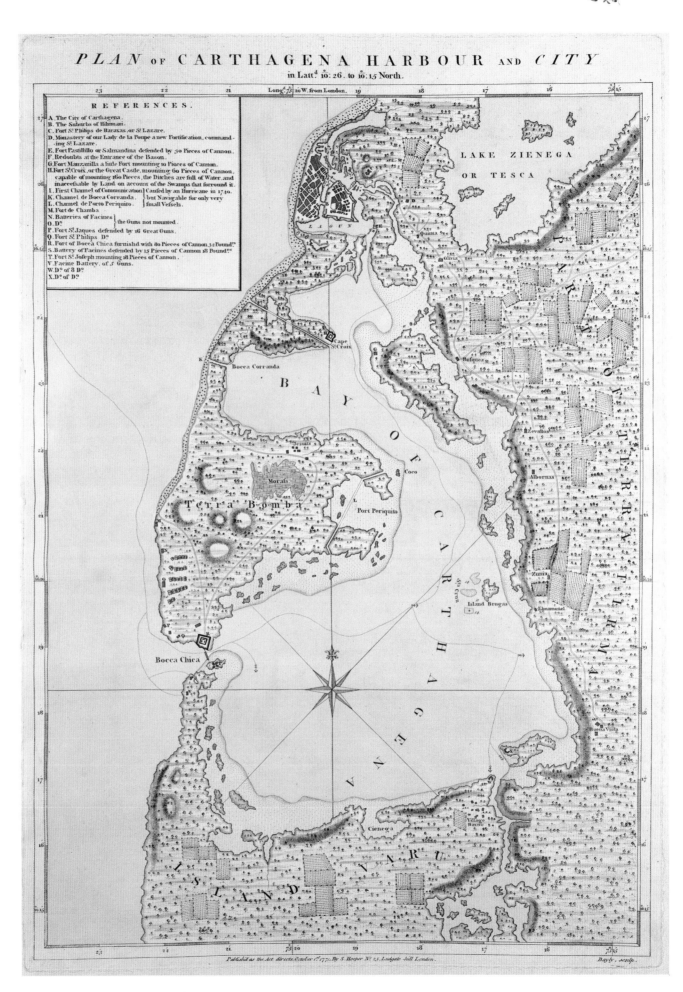

PLAN OF CARTHAGENA HARBOUR AND CITY
in Latt⁴ 10: 26. to 10: 15 North.

REFERENCES.

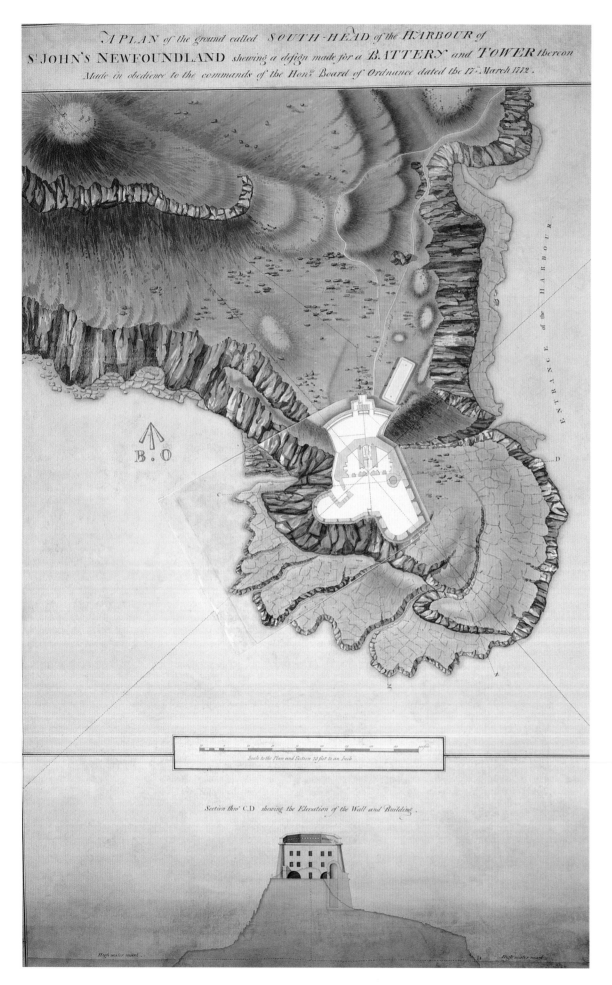

A PLAN of the ground called SOUTH-HEAD of the HARBOUR of St JOHN'S NEWFOUNDLAND shewing a design made for a BATTERY and TOWER thereon Made in obedience to the commands of the Hon.ble Board of Ordnance dated the 17.th March 1772.

Scale to the Plan and Section 23 feet to an Inch

Section thro' C.D showing the Elevation of the Wall and Building.

| PLAN OF THE BATTERY AND TOWER, ST JOHN'S HARBOUR, 1772 | The final action of the Seven Years War in Newfoundland in 1762 with the French surrender to Colonel William Amherst was formalized by the Peace of Paris in 1763, from which Britain gained Canada, Nova Scotia, Cape Breton, Florida, Senegal, St Vincent, Tobago, Dominica, Grenada and the huge triangular slab of land that is Newfoundland with ports and access to the cod-rich fishing grounds adjacent. Rivalry over these fishing grounds was always going to be a potential flash point and strong harbour defences were vital, but the existing works at St John's were incapable of providing it and a careful study during the 1760s resulted in the construction during the 1770s of new fortifications. This was judged the harbour most suited for the defence of the fishery, because of its central location and the ease with which it could be defended. Fort Amherst was built first, to defend the entrance to the Narrows, then Fort Townshend overlooking the harbour, to guard against any attack from the rear and designed to repulse any attack up to the strength the French could muster in 1762.

The defences were first tested and succeeded by default when in 1796 during the Revolutionary War a French fleet under Admiral de Richerry sailed on without attempting a fight. (The National Archives {PRO} MPHH 1/273)

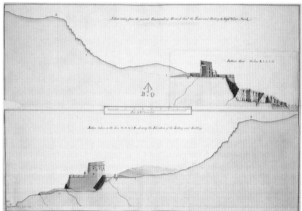

| ABOVE | Profiles of the fort viewed from the east and west.

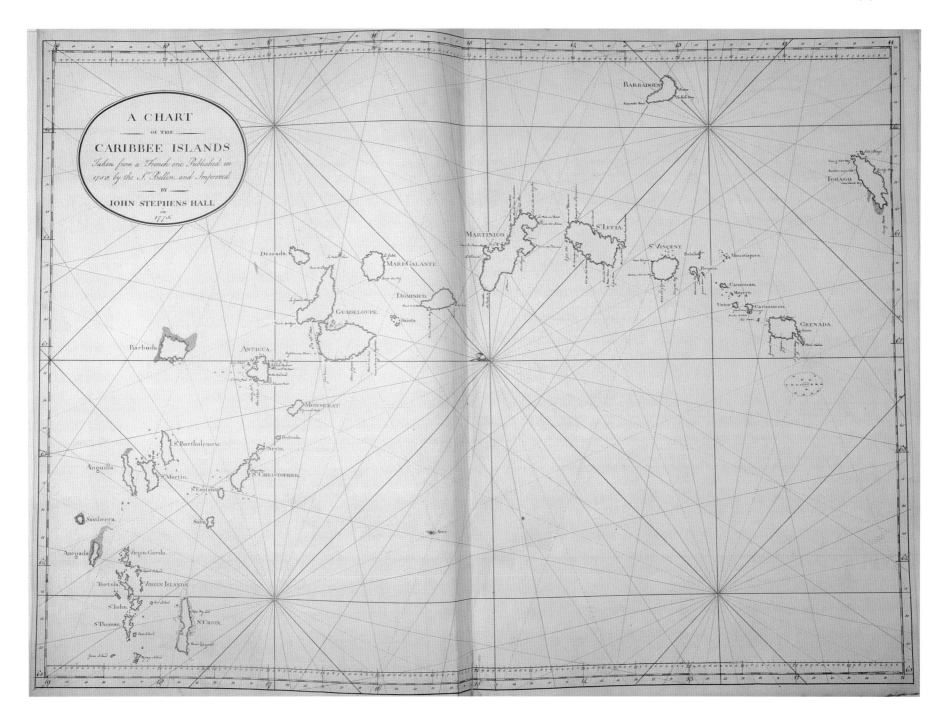

| CHART OF THE CARIBBEAN FROM THE VIRGIN ISLANDS TO TOBAGO, TAKEN FROM A FRENCH CHART PUBLISHED IN 1775 | This chart is part of a volume of seven bound charts, harbour plans and sailing directions for the Windward and Leeward Islands, so named because of the prevailing south westerly wind; it could take just a few days to sail to the north west to the Leeward Islands, but sometimes weeks to beat back to the Windward Islands, an important factor in naval strategy during the age of sail. The cartouche shows this printed chart, encompassing the Windward and Leeward Islands in the Caribbean from the Virgin Islands to Tobago, including Barbados, was published in 1775 with 'improvements' added by John Stephens Hall about whom little is known, but he was probably a Royal Navy sailing master. The 'improvements' seem to be added names of bays and headlands to certain islands and the addition of a reef with soundings off Grenada, which typically would have been taken on a cruise or naval patrol. The original French chart, which was extensively copied by the British and other navies, is from the 1758 version of *L'Hydrographie Française* by J N Bellin. (Admiralty Library Manuscript Collection: MSS 370)

Marais Impraticables innondés pendant une partie de l'Année

Marais

Marais

isle gardée par des Sauvages anglais nommés Cheroquais

la Fluite la Truite Com. par M. DuRumin on y avoit mis des Canons de 18. elle Bloquoit par sa Position le Port de Savannah et Canonoit la Ville

Batiment Anglais qui a Tiré du Canon pendant l'attaque

Batimens Anglais qui se sont brûlés aux approches des B.s François

K

Port et Mauillage des Batimens Anglais

Galeres Américaines

Galere anglaise Echouée

Batiment anglais Echoué

Chemin d'Augusta

SAVANNAH

Redoute de Spring-Hill.

O.

Brewton-Hill.

Marais

Retranchement en Abatis

Cimetiere des Juifs.

Fausse Attaque.

Fausse Attaque.

B.

Poste Evacué par M. Des François

Premiere Position des Troupes Françaises en Retraite

Chemin de Vaugusta

A.

Ouverture de la Tranchée

D. C.

Depôt de la Tranchée

Ambulance

Troupe des Chasseurs Mulatres

Colonne Américaine

Camp des Américains

Ordre de Marche des Troupes le Jour de l'attaque

Avant-Garde. Col. de Droite. Col. de Gauche. C.ce de Retour

Chemin de Biowlay

Quartier Général du General Lincoln

Camp des Troupes Françaises

Quartier Général de M.l c. D'Estaing

Chemin de Biowlay

Chemin de S.t Augustin

Maisons servant d'hopital

Echelle de 1200. Toises ou d'½ lieue de France

100 200 300 400 500 600 1200

Thunder Bloff.

Birth of a Nation

The American War of Independence,
1776-82

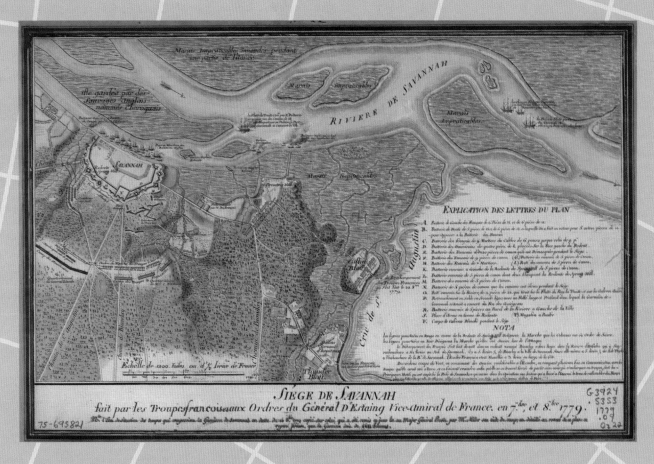

| SIEGE OF SAVANNAH BY THE FRENCH FLEET BY PIERRE OZANNE, 1779 |

The Battle of Savannah was notable as the first significant help the Americans received from the French navy. Admiral le Comte d'Estaing was asked by Major-General Benjamin Lincoln to help re-take the Georgia port of Savannah, held by the British. With 22 ships, 10 support vessels and 4000 men, d'Estaing sailed up the River Savannah and bombarded the town, but delayed an infantry assault allowing the British to consolidate their defences. Pierre Ozanne, who drew this chart, was well known for his charts and elegant drawings of naval battles. He accompanied d'Estaing and drew this exquisite chart showing the position of the French ships. The approach to Savannah from seaward is relatively narrow and the ships were warped or towed into suitable bombarding positions shown abreast of the fort. The advantage of the ships' mobility in bringing heavy firepower to force a breech is apparent from this chart, and the tracks of the attacking forces are marked, too. (Library of Congress)

THE parameters of this chapter encapsulate the struggle by the American colonies to achieve independence from Britain. What was intended as a protest by the Colonists to obtain greater autonomy over local government and taxation by the 13 states escalated into a six-year conflict that forged the United States of America, and extended to other arenas as other European countries tried to exploit the situation to their advantage forcing Britain to fight a war on several fronts. The American War of Independence, which is so much more than just that, merits a chapter to itself, and the selection of charts are focussed accordingly.

From the outset of the war, British naval policy against America, similar to that used later by the Unionists against the Confederates during the American Civil War, was to encircle the colonies by blockade along 3000 miles of coast and use of the inland 'waterway' of the Hudson north to Lake Champlain. This forced the Americans into a maritime war of cruising and privateering, beginning with a fleet of just eight schooners – the embryonic US Navy. They harried the British supply line and disrupted merchant shipping with panache taking some 1000 British merchant ships by 1778.

The First Lord of the Admiralty stated that 18,000 Royal Navy seamen were lost to desertion to the Americans, a serious loss for any maritime nation but nevertheless encouraging for an emergent one. France came to America's aid with money, and in 1778 the French entry on the American side with 80 ships of the line and Spain's 67 in 1779 tipped the balance for the Colonists against Britain. The French involvement at the Battle of Chesapeake in 1781 during which Admiral Graves was defeated by Admiral de Grasse, led directly to General Cornwallis's surrender at the siege of Yorktown. The chart illustrated on page 95 shows the general situation at Chesapeake where Graves had delayed his attack while forming his ships, in accordance with the Fighting Instructions, into a line of battle on the approach to Chesapeake Bay and de Grasse outmanoeuvred him. General Cornwallis, at Yorktown, could not be relieved, and capitulated. This was the de facto end of the war, although peace was not signed until 1783.

While the British kept an overall parity in ship numbers with the Bourbon combination of France and Spain, she had to divide her ships between defending the English Channel, blockading French and Spanish ports, giving support in India and fighting the American Continentals. This meant that she spared only the smaller ships, the third rates of 74 guns and less, to the American war.

Before the outbreak of the conflict the popular navigational guide for American waters was the fourth volume of *The English Pilot* published by John Seller, but it lacked essential information such as tides, currents, channels, soundings, landmarks and underwater hazards in the form of rocks, reefs, shoals and sunken ships. Seller updated it in 1775 to include some 45-year-old charts by a Boston sea captain, Cyprian Southack, who had compiled numerous charts of the north-eastern seaboard of America from his own observations after a lifetime at sea, and included them in his *New England Coasting Pilot*, published 1729–34. Incidentally, this was the first marine atlas published in America and Southack's *New Chart of the British Empire in North America* was the earliest printed in America showing all the colonies. All the protagonist fleets involved in the war would have had Seller's and Southack's charts available. But with inadequate charts covering the more remote islands such as Sable Island and the Bermudas, these areas became virtual ship graveyards during this time and some vessels drifted around the approaches for weeks until a local pilot could be found to guide them in. The Admiralty rectified the situation at the end of the war by appointing Thomas Hurd (who later became Hydrographer to the Navy), after active service in the war, to begin a nine-year survey of the Bermudas, which was to solve these problems and benefited Britain and America during the French Revolutionary War.

Thomas Jeffreys' wide range of American charts were acquired by the London chartseller Robert Sayer in 1766 and he published *A General Topography of North America and the West Indies*. The prestigious sailing directions and charts of North America by James Cook and Michael Lane were published as the *Newfoundland Pilot and Collection of Charts* in 1769. Navigators and sailing masters were getting a rapidly increasing choice of charts and neptunes with the *West India Atlas* 1775, the *North American Pilot* and the *Western Neptune* in 1778. At the peak of his career in 1787 Robert Sayer published the *Catalogue of Pilots, Neptunes and Charts, both general and particular for the Navigation of all the seas and coasts of the Universe*, somewhat grandly as the planet was yet to be fully charted, with 49 pages and details of 25 pilots and 123 loose charts.

The quality of a chart could affect the outcome of a naval encounter. In 1778 Admiral Lord Howe skilfully laid his small fleet of seven 64-gun ships of the line, two 50-gun and a few frigates across the entrance to New York, so blocking Admiral d'Estaing, although with firepower odds of two to one in favour of the French, from any attempt to make an assault. D'Estaing's American pilots were uncertain if there was enough water over the bar for the larger French ships, and his charts were unsufficiently detailed to show him. After 11 days' hesitation, d'Estaing withdrew.

Of the charts that reflect the American War of Independence some of the best came from the hands of French engineers of which an outstanding example is Pierre Ozanne's vivid portrayal of the Siege of Savannah that opens this chapter. During the war British charts were copied by the French, such as Jean de Beaurain's chart of Boston on page 87, or used as a briefing chart, such as the Comte de Rochambeau's chart of the attack at New Hampshire on page 85. By this time, however, with the eclipse of the Dutch East India Company (finally wound up in 1798) following the invasion of Holland by

| RIGHT | **SURVEY OF FROG'S NECK WITH THE BRITISH ARMY LANDINGS AND ROUTE AGAINST THE AMERICANS UNDER GENERAL HOWE BY CHARLES BLASKOWITZ, 1776** | Charles Blaskowitz was a skilled British military surveyor. His surveys combined beauty, accuracy, and clarity and this manuscript survey of Frog's Neck (as it was written down by Washington, but spelt today Throg's Neck, or Throggs Neck, after John Throckmorton was allowed to farm there by the Dutch in 1642) was used to plan and record progress. Without soundings or shoals marked, because he had no naval assistance, Blaskowitz shows the narrow channel between Harlem and Queens where Admiral Richard Howe, with British command of the sea, brought troops to land them at Frog's Neck on 12 October 1776 and for his brother General Sir William Howe to outflank Washington's American troops who were making a stand at Harlem Heights. After the 'Battle of Harlem' Washington then withdrew north to the White Plains; the road is marked. Admiral Howe was free to transport the General's army north again by sea to land at Hunter's Neck using the brig *Halifax* and the sloops *George* and *Kingfisher*. Tardiness in following up the advantage allowed Washington to escape to reconsolidate. This was to be the pattern for the war, with the British navy doing all it was asked, but the army being too cautious and losing the advantage. (Library of Congress)

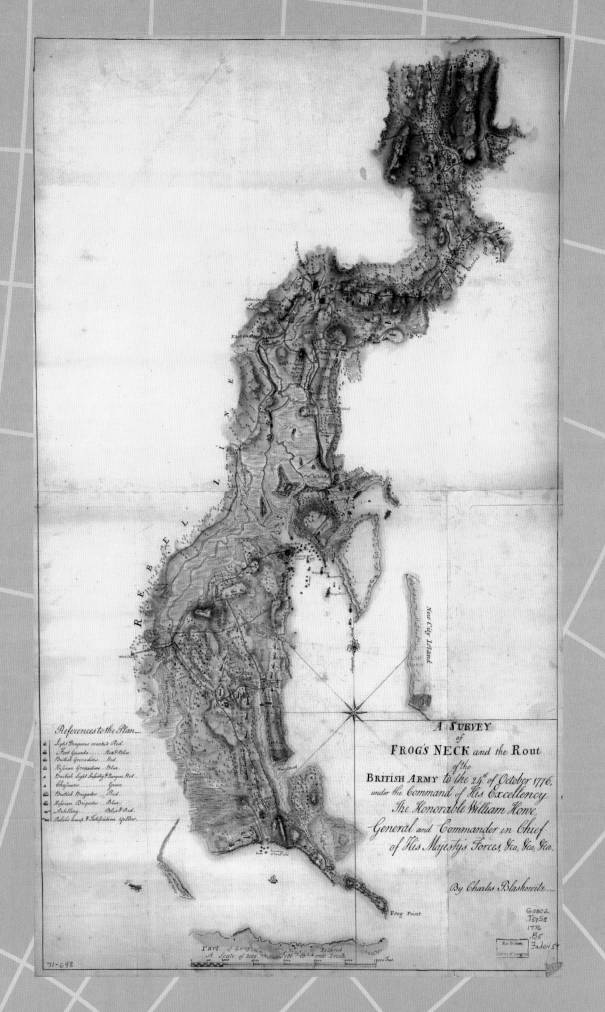

References to the Plan.

A SURVEY
of
FROG'S NECK and the Rout
of the
BRITISH ARMY to the 24ᵗʰ of October 1776,
under the Command of His Excellency
The Honorable William Howe,
General and Commander in Chief
of His Majesty's Forces, &ca, &ca, &ca.

By Charles Blaskowitz

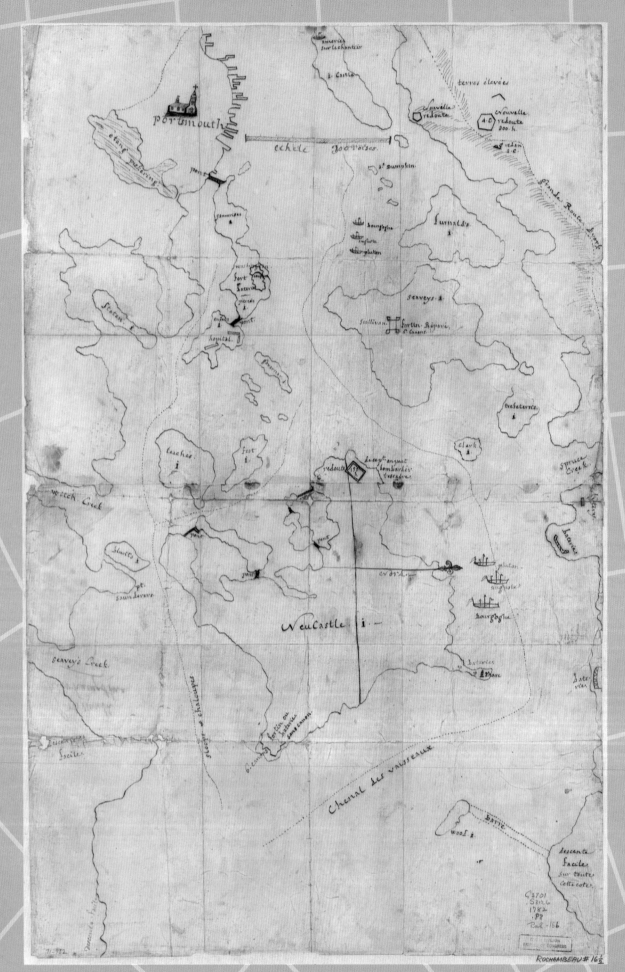

| LEFT | **FRENCH CHART OF PORTSMOUTH, NEW HAMPSHIRE, 1781** | To give maximum assistance to the Americans the French expeditionary leader, General Jean Baptiste Donatien de Vimeur, Comte de Rochambeau, Commander-in-Chief of the naval and land forces needed as complete a portfolio of charts of the American East Coast as soon as possible. This hasty sketch of Portsmouth, New Hampshire, is one of the complete set donated to the US at the end of the war. The plan gives hydrographic information of a port that was used by the French navy to refit, recoup, or as a temporary shelter, and shows fortifications on shore and the positions of three French ships *Pluton* (74 guns), *Auguste* (80 guns) and *Bourgogne* (74 guns), all of which were at the Battle of Virginia Capes (1781) and the Battle of the Saintes (1782).

The Comte de Rochambeau's personal cartographic collection, now known as the *Rochambeau Map Collection*, of 40 manuscripts charts and maps, 26 printed maps, and a manuscript atlas containing cartographic items covering much of eastern North America, and dating from 1717 to 1795, was purchased by an act of Congress in 1883. The maps show military and naval actions, some of which were published in Britain and France. Many of the items in this extraordinary group underline the importance of cartographic material in the campaigns of the American War of Independence. (Library of Congress)

French forces, the centre of chartmaking shifted to London. And the Royal Navy would gain the cartographic advantage over the French with the publication of charts by Joseph Frederick Wallet Des Barres.

Des Barres was Swiss-born and had emigrated to England in 1752, studying at the Royal Military Academy at Woolwich near London, and gained a commission in the Royal American Regiment in 1756. In 1763 he was appointed to carry out and oversee the coastal survey of the eastern seaboard of the United States and Canada. Ten years later, Admiral Lord Howe, responding to the needs of the navy in meeting the threatening revolt by the American colonists, ordered des Barres back to England to engrave and publish his surveys. The resulting portfolio of charts compiled as the *Atlantic Neptune* is one of the gems of the cartographer's art comprising exquisitely painted landfalls and approaches by des Barres with sophisticated charts by him and a number of other British surveyors. The opening pages of the *Atlantic Neptune* – a copy of which was presented to George III who took great interest in maritime matters – cite example after example of ships and squadrons that avoided disaster through the use of des Barres' charts and plans.

Des Barres was one of the first chartmakers to standardize navigational symbols. While hitherto, symbols had been used by convention starting with the early portolans, and spread by Wagenaer's *Spiegel der Zeevaerdt* discussed in Chapter 2, des Barres' symbols became the basis for later standardization published by the British Hydrographic Office in 1835 as a sheet showing 'Abbreviations used in Admiralty Charts'. The sophistication, for example, in the use of hatching shows not just hills and cliffs, banks and shallows, but rocky iron-bound shores, cliffs of red earth, fresh water rivers, creeks and meadows; shoals with depths in fathoms and feet, flood tide directions, sunken rocks, rocks visible at low tide and rocks always above water with standard symbols for each, and anchoring places, the best channels into harbours and deep channels 'fit for the King's ships' and finally abbreviations for the nature of the sea bed, so important to assess the anchor holding properties, such as mud, sand, shells, gravel, stones and rocks.

As the American War of Independence overtook the progress of the production of the surveys so records of the actions between the sea and land forces of the British and Americans were included, and the result was not just a first-class piece of maritime surveying, but a historical snapshot too.

Des Barres' surveys were able to make use of the latest surveying techniques using a theodolite, improved by the Yorkshireman Jesse Ramsden, to give greater precision in measuring vertical and horizontal angles. Its use for 'coastlining', the practice of accurately delineating the coastline as part of the maritime survey, had built up from Murdoch Mackenzie Senior's triangulation survey of the Orkney Islands followed by his 20-year survey commissioned by the Admiralty of Ireland and the British coast as far as Pembroke, finished in 1770. His nephew, also named Murdoch Mackenzie and a lieutenant in the Royal Navy, continued the survey to the Thames, and with his assistant Graeme Spence, used the quadrant invented by John Hadley, an English mathematician and scientist, to take the all-important horizontal angles. Captain John Campbell improved it in 1757, and, named it the sextant. It measured angles up to 120 degrees, enabling better surveying and measurements of the altitude of sun and stars for celestial navigation.

The *Atlantic Neptune* is not made up solely of the work of des Barres. Major Samuel Holland was appointed Surveyor-General of the Northern District of North America, and an example of his survey, and one utilized by Lieutenant John Hills to show the plan of attack on Forts Clinton and Montgomery on the Hudson River under Sir Henry Clinton 1777, is featured on page 91. With prodding from the Admiralty, Holland, Charles Blaskowitz (whose chart of the landings at Frogs Neck near New York is shown on page 83) and other surveyors who had worked for the Board of Trade and Plantations, handed over their work to des Barres.

However, des Barres was reluctant to attribute the other charts that were combined into the *Neptune* to those who made them. The sequence seems to have been as follows: Holland worked on the mainland from the town of Quebec down the St Lawrence river and along the western shore of the Gulf to the Strait of Canso; he also charted the islands of St Jean, Cape Breton and the Magdalenes. Des Barres surveyed Sable Island, his greatest undertaking in the field; it was a task of two years with ever-present danger of shipwreck. He also traversed the coast of Nova Scotia from the Strait of Canso to the Bay of Fundy, and as far as the Saint John River, on the south coast of New Brunswick. From the Saint John River to Passamaquoddy Bay the survey was conducted by Thomas Wright and then Lieutenant Thomas Hurd, acting under Holland. Southwards at least as far as New York, Holland and his deputies George Sproule, Charles Blaskowitz, James Grant and J Wheeler surveyed the coast. Further south still George Gauld was responsible for the charts around Florida, Louisiana and Jamaica.

When hostilities ceased the emphasis in charting shifted to surveying the areas shown up as inadequately covered and the fishing grounds with newly agreed rights. Charts and maps have played an important role in laying down newly defined territorial boundaries and the map illustrated on page 97 reflects those agreed at the Peace of Paris of 1783 on the American Continent, and within what was now the United States.

For many decades after the war the United States Navy and merchant navy had only Admiralty charts to work from and the Depot of Charts and Instruments wasn't set up, by order of the Secretary of the Navy within the Department of the Navy, until 1830. Similarly the Americans had to rely on British charts on the west coast of North America until the westward expansion across the continent had matured a populous infrastructure that wanted and could sustain their own surveys along that coast.

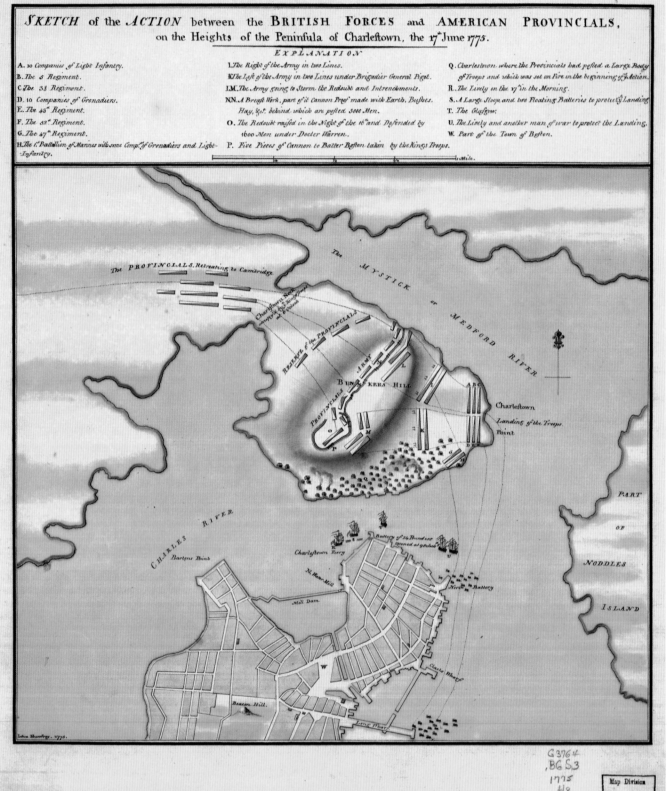

SKETCH of the ACTION between the BRITISH FORCES and AMERICAN PROVINCIALS, on the Heights of the Peninfula of Charleftown, the 17th June 1775.

EXPLANATION

A. 10 Companies of Light Infantry.
B. The 5 Regiment.
C. The 38 Regiment.
D. 10 Companies of Grenadiers.
E. The 43th Regiment.
F. The 52th Regiment.
G. The 47th Regiment.
H. The 1st Battalion of Marines with some Compy. of Grenadiers and Light Infantry.

I. The Right of the Army in two Lines.
K. The Left of the Army in two Lines under Brigadier General Pigot.
I.M. The Army going to Storm the Redoubt and Intrenchments.
NN. A Breaft Work, part of it Cannon Proof made with Earth, Bufhes, Hay, &c. behind which are pofted 5000 Men.
O. The Redoubt raifed in the Night of the 16th and Defended by 1600 Men under Docter Warren.
P. Five Pieces of Cannon to Batter Bofton taken by the Kings Troops.

Q. Charleftown where the Provincials had pofted a Large Body of Troops and which was set on Fire in the beginning of the Action.
R. The Lively on the 17 in the Morning.
S. A Large Sloop, and two Floating Batteries to protect the Landing.
T. The Glafgow.
U. The Lively and another man of war to protect the Landing.
W. Part of the Town of Bofton.

| THE BATTLE OF BUNKER HILL BY JOHN HUMFREY, 1775 | Following the American colonialists' objection, dramatically stated by the Boston Tea Party of 1773, to British taxes levied on them towards the costs of the Seven Years War, fighting between British and American soldiers broke out in April 1775, and by June the British Commander-in-Chief in America, General Thomas Gage, had retreated to Boston. The American forces occupied the hills to the west of Boston and Gage planned to take the Charleston peninsula across the harbour. However, the Americans pre-empted his move during the night of 16 June by occupying Breed's Hill and Bunker Hill on the peninsula, digging defensive redoubts so that by the morning fortifications were complete.

The British had a small fleet in harbour comprising the ships *Glasgow*, *Somerset*, *Falcon* and *Lively*. General Howe put together a force, which was landed by ships' boats, their tracks shown on the chart along with the disembarkation point, but this gave the Americans time to reinforce and consolidate to prevent any flank attack. Howe made three assaults with the British fleet firing their guns in support, heavier than the light guns that the army landed, which in the event had 12-pounder balls for 6-pounder cannon. The first two frontal attacks were repelled with heavy casualties, and the third, concentrating on the redoubt and centre of the American line, broke through and the Americans retreated from the peninsula. However, British casualties were serious with over 1000 men killed, wounded or taken prisoner, while American casualties amounted to 400, and this gave a huge boost to their morale. (Library of Congress)

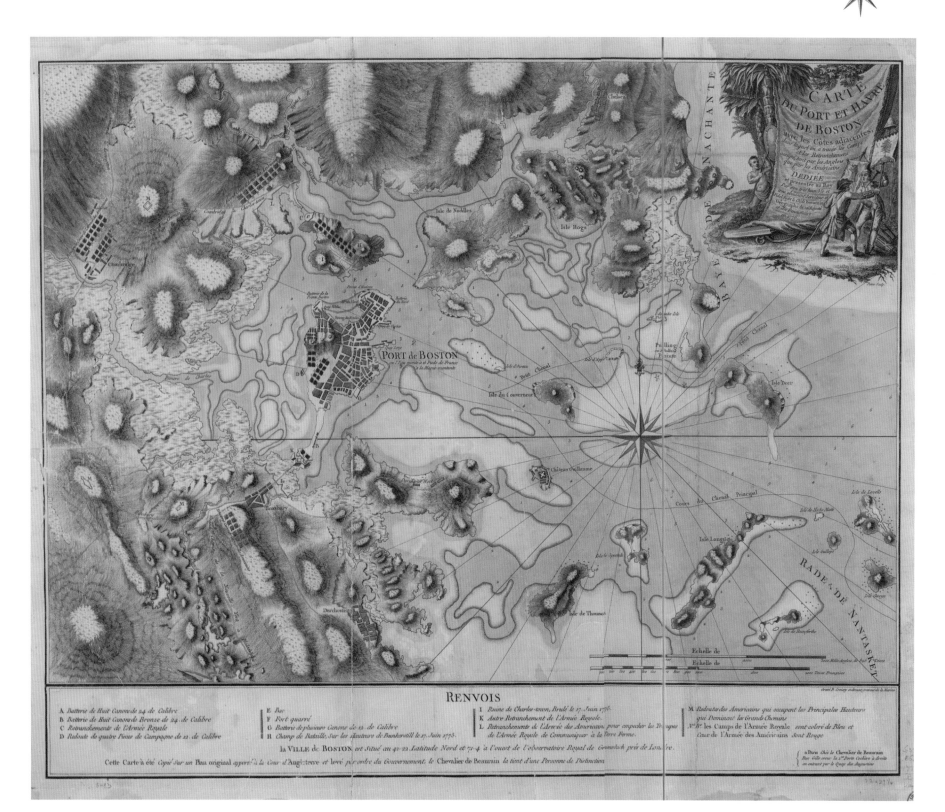

| FRENCH CHART OF BOSTON BY CHEVALIER JEAN DE BEAURAIN, 1776 |

As described in the title at its base, this is a French chart 'lifted' (*levé* – a euphemism, in British eyes, for illegally copied) from an original British plan drawn and taken 'to the English court'. Dedicated to the King of France by Chevalier de Beaurain, Geographer and Cartographer to the King in Paris, it has useful information for the French whose leading Minister, the Comte de Vergennes, had secretly decided in May 1776 that it was in France's interest to exploit the war in America with the assumption that Britain relied almost exclusively on those colonies for trade and seamen to man her ships. France was still smarting over her losses resulting from the Seven Years War and the young Louis XVI's avowed aim was indicated in instructions to his ministers: 'To meddle adroitly in the affairs of the British colonies…at the first serious fear of rupture, to assemble numerous troops upon the shore of Brittany and Normandy and get everything ready for an invasion of England…'.

The first real French involvement in the American war was only when Admiral d'Estaing sailed for America in April 1778, the French involvement at the Battle of Chesapeake in 1781 led directly to Cornwallis's surrender at the siege of Yorktown and the ultimate recognition of US independence by Britain.

In copying the chart, which gives the main and secondary channel into the harbour, positions of British and 'rebel' redoubts and soldiers, the French cartographers have made interesting errors of transcription such as 'Bunkerstill' and 'Grunwhich' (Greenwich). French *toises* (equivalent to just under 2 metres before 1799) have been added to the scale. (Library of Congress)

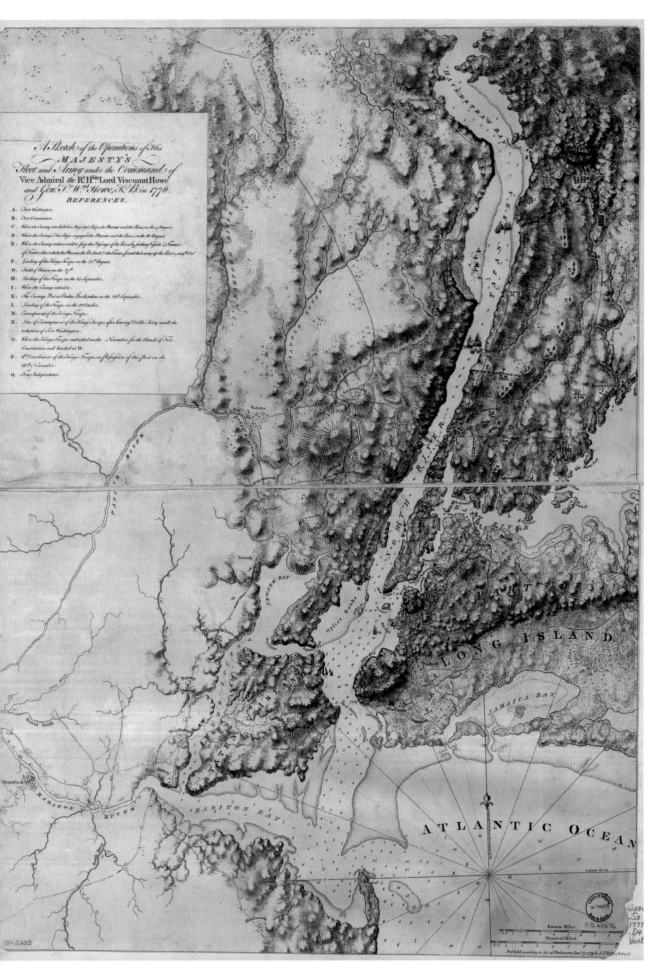

| LEFT | **A SKETCH OF BRITISH ARMY AND NAVY OPERATIONS UNDER VICE-ADMIRAL LORD HOWE AND GENERAL SIR WILLIAM HOWE AROUND NEW YORK IN 1776, 1778** | Lieutenant Joseph Frederick Wallet des Barres, who carried out the survey used as basis for this chart, is most respected for producing the folio of charts known as the *Atlantic Neptune* published in 1777, in time for use by the Royal Navy during the American War of Independence.

This published chart was available both as a working chart, with its accurate coast outline, sophisticated hatching, and fascinating topographical features, and for sale to an eager audience in Britain. Lord Sandwich, First Lord of the Admiralty, retained the navy's first, second and third rate ships to counter the French invasion threat and allotted only 44- or 55-gun two-deckers for what was then judged at the outset of the American war as a minor campaign that would be resolved quickly. The chart shows in detail the combined operations around New York in 1776 by the Howe brothers, Admiral and General, including the small fleet beating off the American fireships attack at 'D' and 'rebels' sinking fishing boats and pre-constructed frames to block access along the North (Hudson) River at 'E', as well as landing troops to take the key forts which resulted in the retreat of General Washington and the 'rebels'. With the loss of Boston to the British, New York became the main naval base and was held throughout the war, only handed over to the Americans at the peace treaty signed in Paris in 1783. (Library of Congress)

| RIGHT | **THE ENGAGEMENT BETWEEN THE KING'S FORCES AND THE AMERICANS, LEADING UP TO THE BATTLE OF HARLEM, BY MAJOR SAMUEL HOLLAND, 1776** | The coast of the Atlantic seaboard of North America was surveyed by the Royal Navy from Passamaquoddy Bay southwards to at least as far as New York under Samuel Holland, Surveyor-General of the Northern District of North America, and his deputies Thomas Wright, George Sproule, Charles Blaskowitz, James Grant and Thomas Wheeler. Their surveys were handed over to des Barres in 1776 to add to the *Atlantic Neptune*. Holland's survey of New York was used to place the positions of the British fleet, who then had free access to conduct warfare against the Americans and to hold the Narrows between Staten Island and Long Island for an unopposed landing of British and hired Hessian (German) troops on 26 August to outflank the American army, and to show the positions of the British and American forces the following day. (Library of Congress)

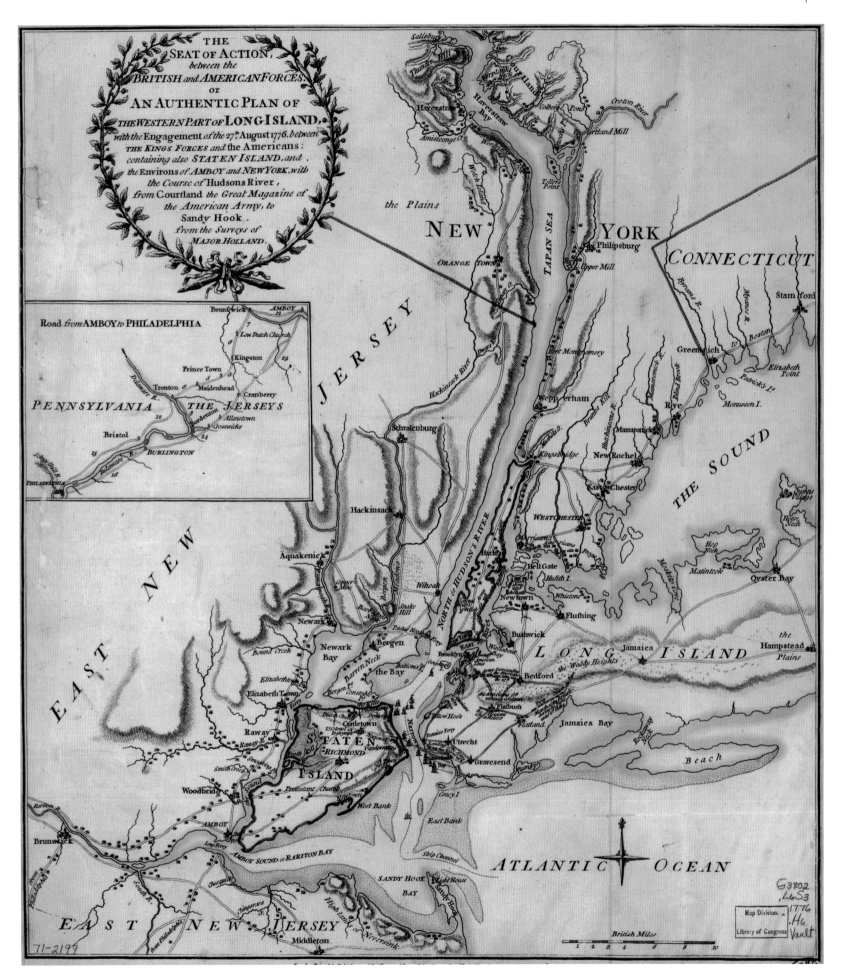

THE
SEAT of ACTION,
between the
BRITISH and AMERICAN FORCES,
or
AN AUTHENTIC PLAN of
THE WESTERN PART of LONG ISLAND,
with the Engagement of the 27th August 1776. between
THE KINGS FORCES and the Americans:
containing also STATEN ISLAND, and
the Environs of AMBOY and NEW YORK, with
the Course of Hudsons River,
from Courtland the Great Magazine of
the American Army, to
Sandy Hook.
from the Surveys of
MAJOR HOLLAND.

Road from AMBOY to PHILADELPHIA

PENNSYLVANIA   THE JERSEYS

BURLINGTON

PHILADELPHIA
Bristol

Trenton
Prince Town
Maidenhead
Kingston
Cranbery
Allentown
Crosswicks
Bordentown

Brunswick
AMBOY
Low Dutch Church

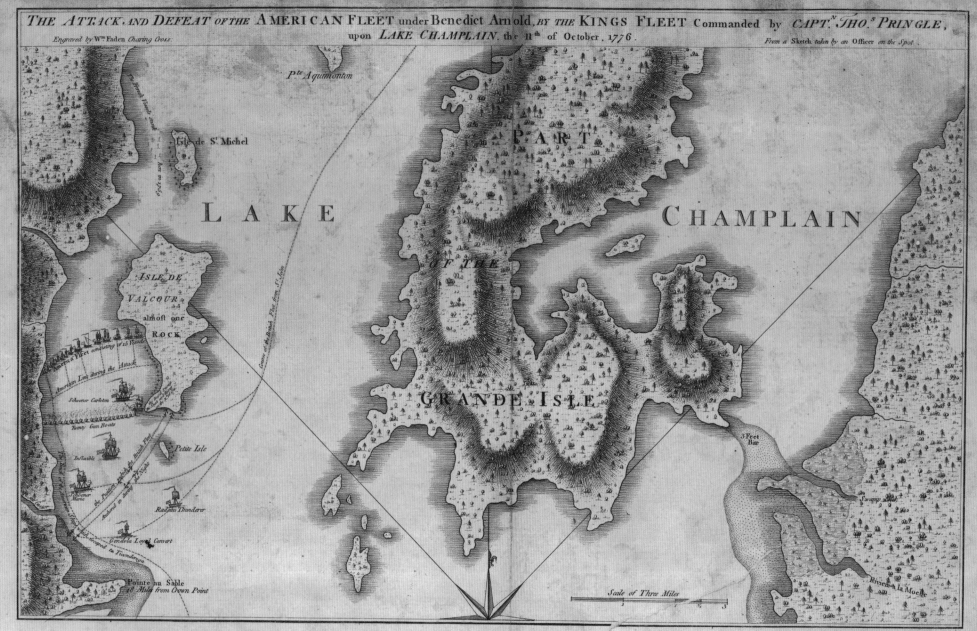

THE ATTACK AND DEFEAT OF THE AMERICAN FLEET under Benedict Arnold, BY THE KINGS FLEET Commanded by CAPT.N THO.S PRINGLE, upon LAKE CHAMPLAIN, the 11th of October, 1776.

Engraved by Wm. Faden Charing Cross.

From a Sketch taken by an Officer on the Spot.

London, Publish'd according to Act of Parliament, Dec.r 3.d 1776; by Wm. Faden (Successor to the late Mr. Jefferys Geographer to the King) Charing Cross.

An ACCOUNT of the Expedition of the British Fleet on LAKE CHAMPLAIN, under the Command of Captain THOMAS PRINGLE, and of the Defeat of the REBEL FLEET, commanded by BENEDICT ARNOLD, on the 11th and 13th of October, 1776.

Taken from the Letters of Sir Guy Carleton, Captains Douglas and Pringle, dated off Crown Point, 15th October, 1776.

LIST of His Majesty's Naval Force on Lake Champlain.

Vessels.	Guns.	Commanders.
Ship Inflexible,	18 Twelve pounders,	Lieut. Schank.
Schooner Maria,	14 Six pounders,	Capt. Tho. Pringle, Commander of the Fleet, Lieut. Starke.
Schooner Carleton,	12 Six pounders,	Lieut. Dacres.
Radeau Thunderer,	6 Twenty-four pounders 6 Twelve ditto 2 Howitzers,	Lieut. Scott.
Gondola Loyal Convert,	7 Nine pounders,	Lieut. Langcroft.

24 Gun boats, 1 brass field piece each, from 24 to 9 pounders, some with howitzers;

4 Long boats, 1 carriage gun each, serving as armed tenders;

44 Long boats with provisions.

670 Seamen were detached from his Majesty's ships and vessels in the river St. Lawrence to serve in the above fleet.

LIST of the Rebel Fleet on Lake Champlain under the Command of Benedict Arnold.

Vessels.	Guns.	
Schooner Royal Savage,	8 Six pounders, 4 Four ditto,	Burnt the 11th, at Valcour.
Schooner Revenge,	4 Six and four pounders,	Escaped, the 13th.
Sloop,	10 Four pounders,	Escaped, the 13th.
Cutter Lee,	1 Nine pounder in her bow, 1 Twelve ditto in her stern, 2 Six ditto in her sides,	Abandoned, the 13th.
Galley Congress,	2 Eighteen ditto in her bow, 2 Twelve ditto in her stern, 6 Six ditto in her sides,	Benedict Arnold, Commander of the Fleet, run on shore and burnt the 13th.
Galley Washington,	1 Eighteen ditto in her bow, 2 Twelve ditto in her stern, 6 Six ditto in her sides,	Taken the 13th.
Galley Trumble,	the same force,	Escaped the 13th.

Eight gondolas, carrying 1 eight pounder in the bow, and 2 nine ditto in the sides —some of them had 4 guns in the sides—of which 1 was sunk the 11th, 1 taken the 12th, 4 burnt the 13th, one escaped, and one missing.

Schooner ——, 8 four pounders, taken from Major Skeene, was gone for provisions.

Galley Gates, said to be of greater force than any those mentioned above, was fitting out at Ticonderago, and expected to join the fleet in a few days.

AFTER attending, for the space of six weeks, the naval equipment for the important expedition on Lake Champlain, was seen, with unspeakable joy, the reconstructed ship, now called the Inflexible, commanded by Lieutenant Schank, her rebuilder, sailed from St. John's, 28 days after her keel was laid, and taking in her 18 twelve pounders beyond the shoal, which is on this side the Isle aux Noix, in her way up.——The labours which were effected after the rebels were driven out of Canada, in constructing and equipping a fleet of above thirty fighting vessels, of different sorts and sizes, all carrying cannon, since the beginning of July; and afterwards dragging up the two rapids of St. Teresa and St. John's, 30 long boats, the flat-bottom'd boats, a gondola weighing about 30 tons, and above 400 battoes, almost exceed belief, the sailors of his Majesty's ships and transports having exerted themselves to the utmost on this occasion: Above two hundred prime seamen of the transports voluntarily engaged themselves to serve in the armed vessels during the expedition.

On the 11th of October the royal fleet came up with that of the rebels, which was at anchor under the Island Valcour, and formed a strong line, extending from the Island to the west side of the continent. The wind was so unfavourable that for a considerable time nothing could be brought into action with them, but the gun boats, and the Carleton schooner, commanded by Mr. Dacres, by much perseverance at last got to their assistance : but as none of the other vessels of the fleet could then get up, it was thought not adviseable by any means to continue so unequal an engagement; Captain Pringle, the commander of the fleet, therefore, with the approbation of his Excellency General Carleton (who was on board the Maria) called off the Carleton Schooner and gun boats, and brought the whole fleet to anchor in a line as near as possible to that of the rebels, in order to cut off their retreat; which purpose was frustrated by the extreme obscurity of the night, as by the morning the rebels had got a considerable distance from them up the Lake, consisting of eleven sail.

Upon the 13th the rebel fleet were again discovered making off towards Crown Point, when after a chace of seven hours, Capt. Pringle in the Maria, came up with them, having the Carleton and Inflexible a small distance a-stern, the rest of the fleet were almost out of sight. The action began at twelve o'clock, and lasted two hours,

at which time Arnold, in the Congress galley, and five gondolas ran on shore, and were directly abandoned and blown up by the enemy, a circumstance they were greatly favoured in by the wind being off shore, and the narrowness of the Lake; the Washington-galley struck during the action, and the rest made their escape to Ticonderoga.

The number of the killed and wounded in his Majesty's fleet, including the artillery in the gun boats, does not amount to 40; but from every information yet received, the loss on the side of the rebels must have been very considerable.

The rebels upon receiving the news of the defeat of their naval force, set fire to all the buildings and houses in and near Crown Point, and retired to Ticonderoga.

Engraved by W. Faden, (Successor to the late Mr. Jefferys, Geographer to the King) the Corner of St. Martin's-Lane, Charing-Cross, and to be had of Messrs. Wallis and Stonehouse, Booksellers, Ludgate-Street.

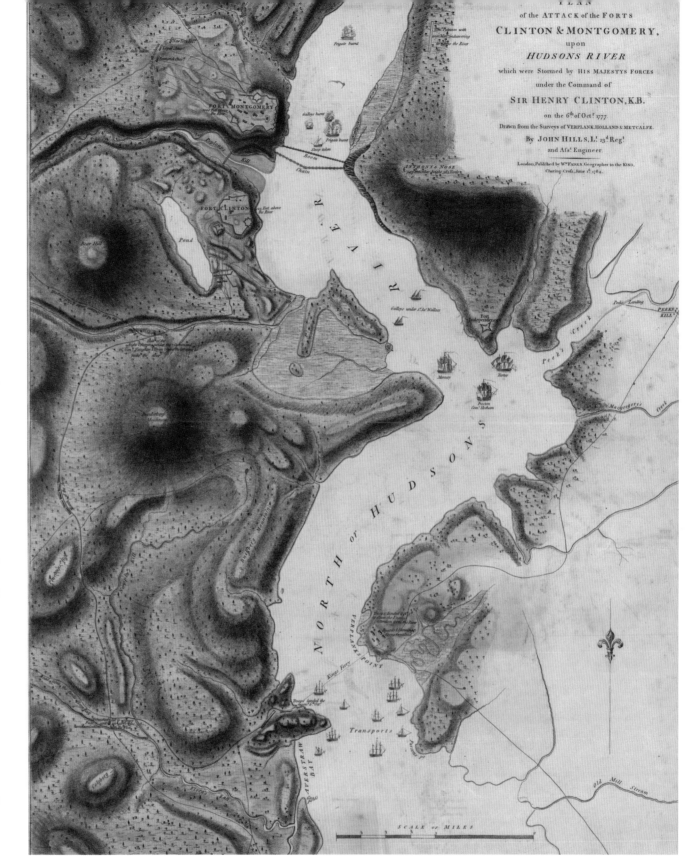

| LEFT | ATTACK AND DEFEAT OF THE AMERICAN FLEET BY THE KING'S FLEET ON LAKE CHAMPLAIN, 1776 |

This chart, published by William Faden in London and engraved from the drawing of 'an officer on the spot', encapsulates the action between the British, under the direction of General Sir Guy Carleton, and the Americans under Benedict Arnold – the very first engagement between British and American fleets, albeit on Lake Champlain.

A study of a map of North America shows Montreal and New York to be almost exactly on the same longitude, and joined by water, but for 10 miles. After the American attempt to take Canada, Carleton was keen to attack from the north towards New York to secure Mohawk and the upper reaches of the Hudson River and knew of the almost continuous waterway to join the two cities. Lake Champlain, 90 miles long but only 15 miles across its widest point, joins Lake George, and drains into the River Hudson flowing south for 150 miles to Manhattan and New York, a superb natural watercourse to transport troops rapidly south or north again. The southern end was controlled by Forts George and Ticonderoga, located in Essex County, 95 miles north of Albany, New York, on a neck of land between Lake George and Lake Champlain. The name Ticonderoga comes from the Iroquois Indian word '*cheonderoga*' meaning 'place between two waters'.

Carleton got three large vessels from England that sailed up the St Lawrence to Lachine rapids near Montreal, where they were disassembled and carried to St John's and reassembled. Thirty gunboats and 200 flat-bottomed transports were built at Montreal while Carleton's opponent, Arnold, spent the summer assembling a small fleet of three schooners, two sloops, three galleys and eight gondolas fitted with 70 guns, with which he could only hope to delay Carleton from reaching Fort Ticonderoga before the winter. As can be seen on the chart, he placed his flotilla across the water from Isle de Valcour to the mainland. After seven hours of heavy fighting, Arnold slipped away in the night to the fort. Carleton decided it was too heavily defended and retired for the winter – a puzzling decision for the British and a strategic victory for the Americans; one that delayed General Burgoyne's intended attack against Washington until after the winter. (Library of Congress)

| PLAN OF ATTACK ON FORTS CLINTON AND MONTGOMERY ON THE HUDSON RIVER UNDER SIR HENRY CLINTON, 1777 |

Control of the Hudson River and, as such, control of the approach to New York could be maintained through the forts built along its banks. James Clinton, whose brother George became Vice-President of the fledgling United States, as a Colonel in 1776 reconnoitred a suitable position to build the fort named after him. It became apparent that a second fort to complete command of the river would be needed and Fort Montgomery was built opposite on the west bank. The original site for the fort, named Fort Independence down-river on the corner with Peek's Creek was abandoned as building was too difficult. With a boom stretched across the river the British knew they had to attack and General Sir Henry Clinton took both forts in 1777. But in attacking Fort Clinton, defended by General George Clinton, Henry Clinton delayed the reinforcements that General Burgoyne, who had travelled down from Montreal to attack Washington at Saratoga, needed, and this was a direct cause of Burgoyne's defeat. There is a historical irony in a Clinton attack and defence of Fort Clinton.

This Faden chart, held in the Library of Congress archives, was published to portray the action and the earlier survey of Verplank, Holland and Metcalfe was overdrawn with a graphic account of the battle by one of the army engineers, Lieutenant John Hills. (Library of Congress)

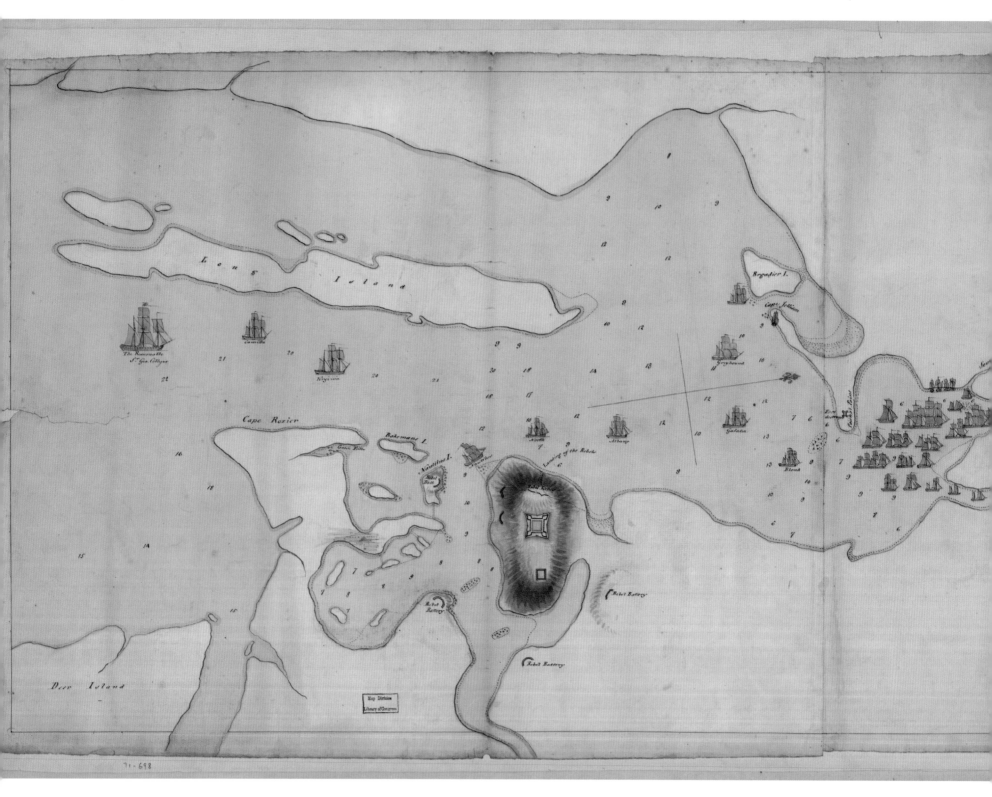

| **CHART OF THE BATTLE FOR FORT CASTINE BETWEEN THE BRITISH AND MASSACHUSETTS FLEETS IN PENOBSCOT RIVER AND BAY, 1779** | The Penobscot Expedition is detailed in this manuscript chart, which is part of the William Faden Map Collection in the Library of Congress. Executed in pen and ink with watercolour it has river depths with 'full soundings' almost to Bangor, along with the positions of the American and British fleets.

In early July of 1779, a naval and military force under the command of General Francis McLean sailed into the Penobscot settlement's ample harbour, a region abundant in fish and timber to supply the Royal Navy, landed troops, and took control of the village, and began erecting a fort on one of the highest points of the peninsula, to become Fort Castine. The Massachusetts legislature despatched a fleet of 19 armed vessels and 24 transports, carrying 344 guns, under Dudley Saltonstall, and a land force of about 1200 men, under General Samuel Lovell. Though badly outnumbered, the British managed to repel American attacks for nearly three weeks. In mid-August, British reinforcements appeared at the head of the bay, under Sir George Collyer. The Americans abandoned the fight and retreated to the west side of the Penobscot, destroying their entire fleet to keep it out of British hands. The failed Penobscot Expedition proved to be the greatest American naval defeat in terms of ship losses until Pearl Harbor in December 1941. (Library of Congress)

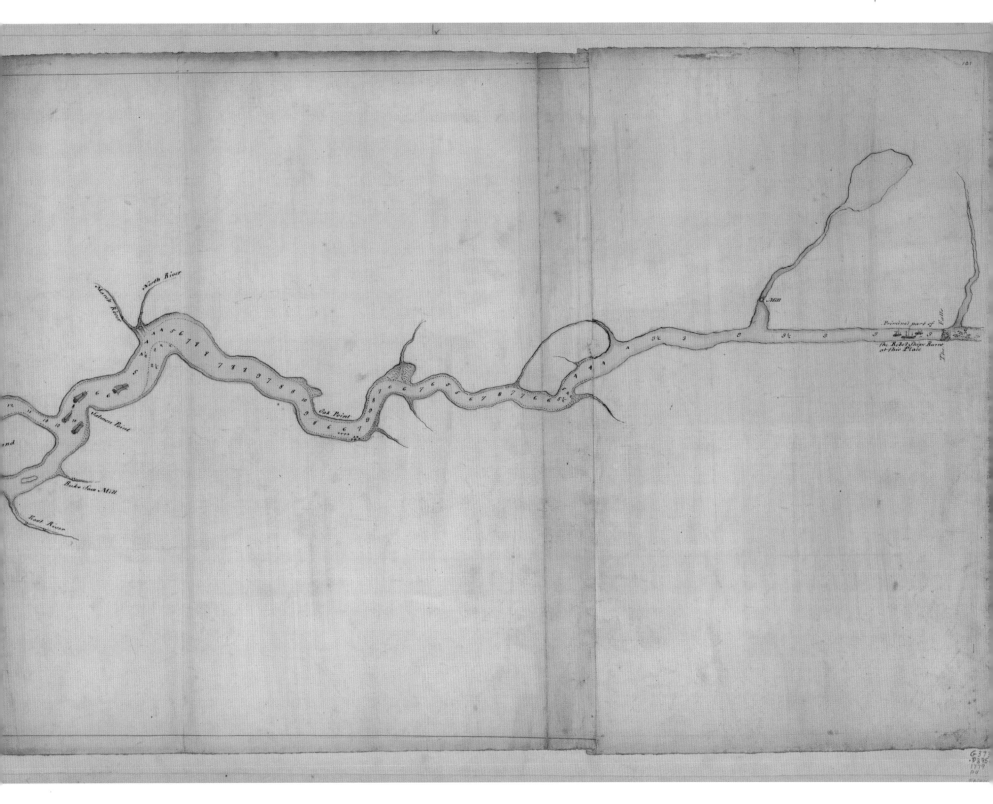

PLAN DE LA VILLE, PORT ET RADE DE NEWPORT, AVEC UNE PARTIE DE RHODE ISLAND OCCUPÉE PAR L'ARMÉE FRANÇAISE AUX ORDRES DE Mᴿ LE COMTE DE ROCHAMBEAU ET DE L'ESCADRE FRANÇAISE COMMANDÉE PAR Mᴿ LE CHᴿ DESTOUCHES.

| **PLAN OF THE TOWN AND PORT OF NEWPORT, RHODE ISLAND, *C.* 1781** | The British had withdrawn from Newport, Rhode Island to New York, which allowed the French Admiral Ternay to deliver the expeditionary forces on 10 July 1780, where they established a base camp while awaiting the arrival of one-third of their troops who had been left behind in Brest due to lack of troop transports. In January 1781 the British sent a naval squadron to blockade Newport. In spite of bad weather, the 64-gun *Eville* and two French frigates mauled the British ships.

This chart of the town and port, and Newport Roads with Rhode Island, shows the defensive line of named ships positioned across the entrance with their arcs of fire drawn on together with those of the two forts to prevent any attacking ships getting into the harbour. From Newport the French were able to threaten New York and land the troops that the Comte de Rochambeau marched south to Yorktown to assist in Washington's defeat of Lord Cornwallis. (Library of Congress)

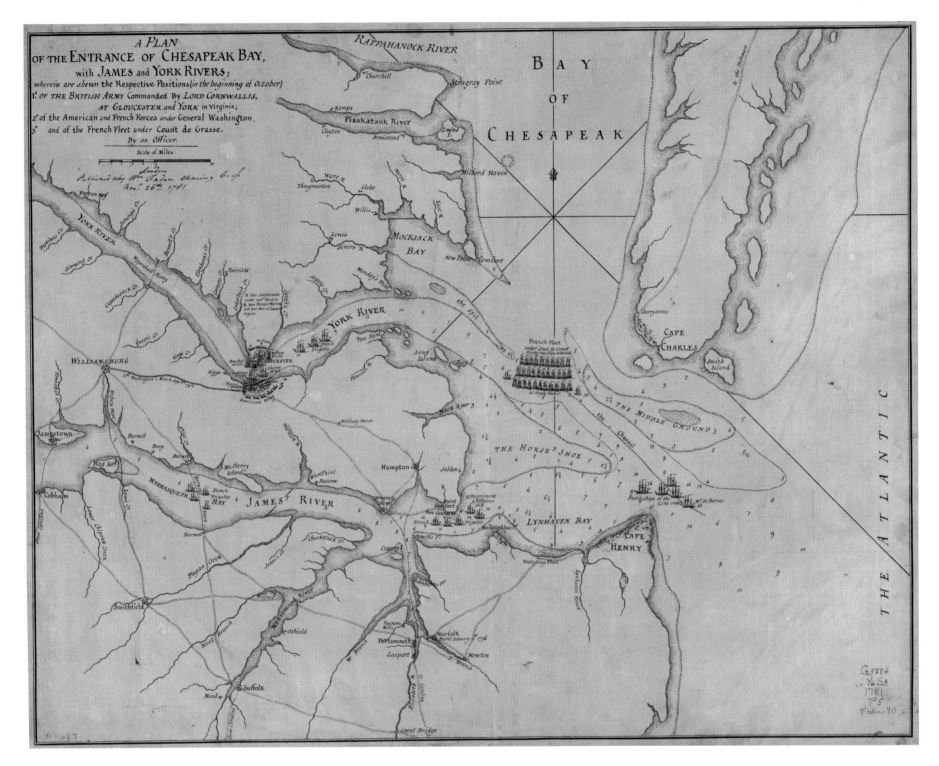

| PLAN OF CHESAPEAKE BAY WITH THE ATTACK BY THE FRENCH ADMIRAL DE GRASSE IN SUPPORT OF GENERAL WASHINGTON ON THE BRITISH GENERAL LORD CORNWALLIS AT YORKTOWN, 1781 | The British had hoped to win the war by gaining the support of the Southern States, but after a successful start to this strategy in 1778 it collapsed in Virginia and Lord Cornwallis moved to Yorktown to consolidate his army, close to reinforcements or evacuation by sea at Chesapeake Bay. However, the French Admiral François Joseph Paul, Comte de Grasse, sailed from the West Indies where he had been fighting the British over sugar islands such as St Lucia, to assist Washington, strengthened by Rochambeau's troops from Newport and joined with the French squadron also from Newport under Rear-Admiral Comte Barras de Laurent to blockade Yorktown. By September

1781 a further contingent of soldiers under the French volunteer general le Marquis de Lafayette swelled Washington's forces to 16,000 against Cornwallis's 7000. The British were slow to respond. A fleet of 10 ships of the line under Admiral Samuel Hood joined Admiral Thomas Graves with nine ships and met de Grasse to fight an unsatisfactory battle with Hood disengaged in the rear. Hood and Graves retreated to New York to repair the damage. A second relief fleet sailed on 19 October but arrived too late to challenge de Grasse and evacuate Cornwallis. He had surrendered the previous day.

This contemporary pen and ink manuscript plan shows the unassailable position of the French warships blockading Cornwallis. Used strategically by de Grasse, it was later the basis by which William Faden prepared and published his chart account of the battle. (Library of Congress)

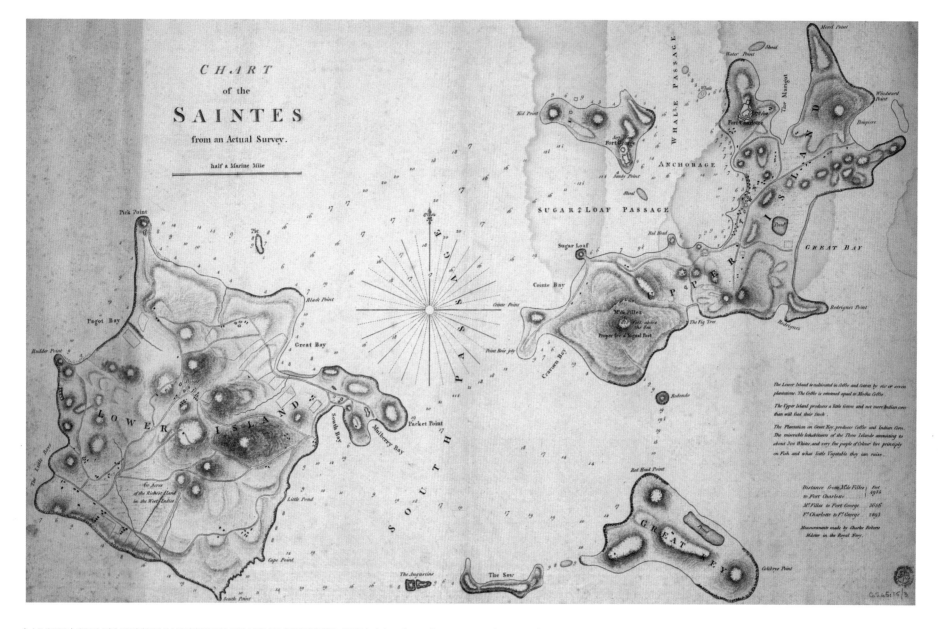

| ABOVE | **CHART OF THE SAINTES BY CHARLES ROBERTS, 1782** | After the nadir of the Royal Navy's performance at Chesapeake, a victory was sorely needed to raise morale in the fleet and Britain. The American War of Independence was in reality part of a world war. Spain and Holland, as well as France, were already at war with Britain. There was continuous action in the Indian Ocean, the Spice Islands and, of course, in America, while in northern Europe, the League of Armed Neutrality was formed in the Baltic States to counter random British impressments of neutral seamen. France's strategic intention was to capture much of the West Indies as well as assisting the American colonies. Admiral de Grasse, in charge of a Franco-Spanish squadron encountered Admiral Rodney and Rear-Admiral Hood with a combined fleet of 34 ships of the line. The British correctly surmised that they were aiming for Jamaica. The two sides met by a group of three islets known as Les Saintes, lying about 10 miles south of Guadeloupe (French), close to Dominica (British). An advantageous shift in the wind enabled Rodney to break through the French line, followed by Hood, commanding the rear, and engage them with overwhelming force, concentrating on clusters of French ships, while others tried to beat upwind to engage in the mêlée. Five French ships of the line were captured including the admiral in *Ville de Paris*, and the attempt to take Jamaica was abandoned.

This chart, published by Aaron Arrowsmith, was based on an actual survey by one of the navy's masters, Charles Roberts, who served in the West Indies at the time of the battle. His original work is an example of the charts that the British fleet had available during the battle, which were slowly superseding the Spanish and French charts of the area. (© National Maritime Museum, London F0335)

| RIGHT | **USA, BRITISH POSSESSIONS OF CANADA, NOVA SCOTIA AND NEWFOUNDLAND, DIVIDED WITH THE FRENCH AND SPANISH TERRITORIES, 1783** | US independence was provisionally ratified at the Treaty of Versailles on 20 January 1783, but Britain secretly negotiated with the Americans to recognize the USA in return for retaining Canada. France and Spain were still trying to eke out territorial advantage by taking Gibraltar and islands in the West Indies. The boundaries of North America were finally settled at the Peace of Versailles on 3 September along with a working agreement as to who could fish how much from where around the Grand Banks of Newfoundland and Nova Scotia. As it transpired, this was no more than a break in hostilities for the powers to gain strength and reshuffle alliances before the next conflicts engulfed that the world – the Revolutionary and Napoleonic Wars.

R Sayer and J Bennett, based in Fleet Street, London, very quickly produced this map which shows the agreed division between Canada and the United States, while recognizing Spain's claim to Florida and Mexico, and France's to Louisiana, and reprinting the part of the treaty relating to the fishing rights. (Library of Congress)

THE UNITED STATES
OF AMERICA
with *THE BRITISH POSSESSIONS OF*
CANADA, NOVA SCOTIA, & of NEWFOUNDLAND,
Divided with *THE FRENCH;*
and *THE SPANISH TERRITORIES OF*
LOUISIANA *and* FLORIDA
according to the Preliminary Articles of Peace
Signed at Versailles the 20.th of Jan.r 1783.
LONDON.
Printed for R. Sayer and J. Bennett, Map and Printsellers. N.º 53, Fleet Street,
as the Act directs, 8.th February, 1783.

Art. III. It is agreed, that the People of the United
States shall continue to enjoy unmolested the Right
to take Fish of every kind on the Grand Bank and on
all other Banks of Newfoundland, also in the Gulf of
St. Laurence, and at all other places in the Sea where
the Inhabitants of both Countries used at any time
heretofore to Fish; and also that the Inhabitants of the
United States shall have liberty to take Fish of every
kind on such part of the Coast of Newfoundland as
British Fishermen shall use (but not to Dry or Cure the same
on that Island) and also on the Coasts, Bays and
Creeks, of all other of his Britannic Majesties Dominions in
America, and that the American Fishermen shall have
liberty to Dry and Cure Fish in any of the unsettled Bays,
Harbours and Creeks of Nova Scotia, Magdalen Islands,
and Labrador so long as the same shall remain unsettled, but so soon as the same, or either of them, shall be
settled; it shall not be lawful for the said Fishermen
to Dry or Cure Fish at such Settlement, without a previous Agreement for that purpose with the Inhabitants,
Proprietors, or Possessors of the Ground.

English Miles 69 ½ to a Degree

ATLANTIC OF WESTERN OCEAN

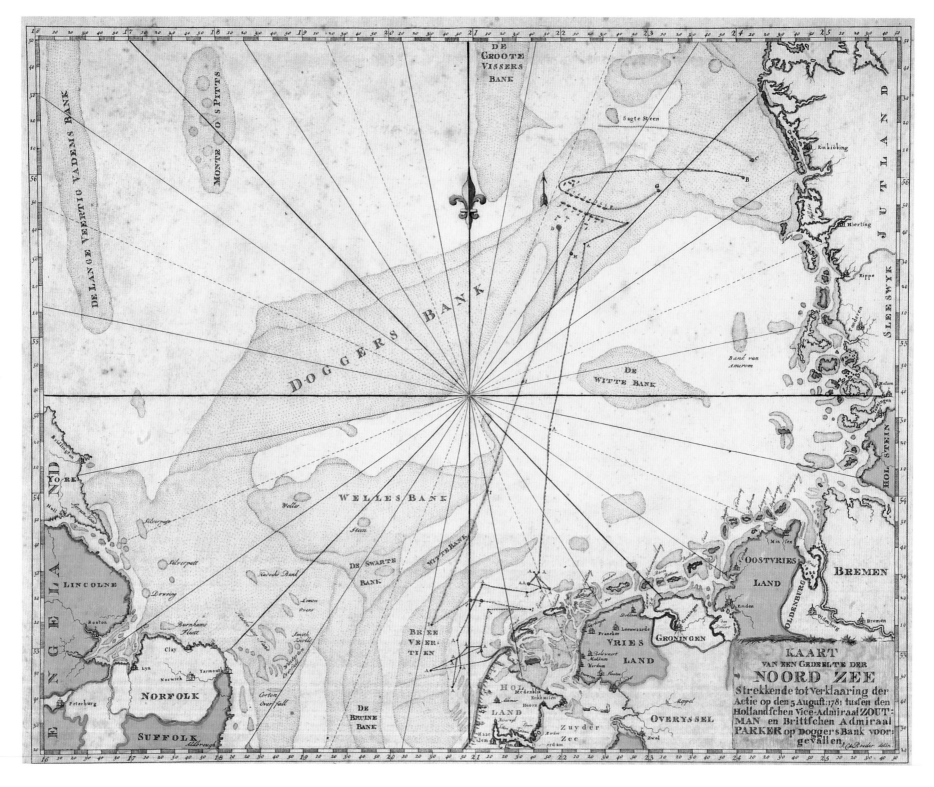

| **BATTLE OF DOGGER BANK, 1781** | The British policy of stopping neutral ships to search out deserting British seamen, weapons and contraband caused great offence amongst the neutral European maritime nations. The Russians formed the League of Armed Neutrality with the Danes and Swedes to put pressure on Britain. The Netherlands had watched their East Indies empire slip away from its seventeenth-century peak and saw an opportunity to redress this by joining the neutrality. Britain learned of this, and relations were further soured when the Dutch allowed the American, John Paul Jones, to operate out of Holland. He had brought the American War of Independence to British home waters with a number of audacious attacks, including one on Sutherland. Britain declared war and diverted some much needed ships of the line to cover convoys to the North Sea. Admiral Sir Hyde Parker, flying his flag in the *Fortitude* (74 guns), while escorting a convoy met with the Dutch Admiral Johan Zoutman in *Admiraal de Ruijter* (68

guns) carrying out the same task, and the fight off the Dogger Bank on 5 August ensued.

Although this battle, part of the fourth Anglo-Dutch War (1780–4), was acclaimed as a victory for the Dutch, the net effect was that their fleet remained in harbour and their trade ships were kept off the seas by British privateers and cruisers – an economic disaster for Holland. The Dutch Republic joined a ceasefire between Britain and France in January 1783. The Peace of Paris made Negapatnam, in India, a British colony. Ceylon remained with Holland, while the British gained the right of free trade with part of the Dutch East Indies.

This Dutch chart shows the sophisticated state of Dutch cartography with latitude and longitude scales, shoals, and the tracks of the Dutch and British fleets and the escape of the convoy into Texel. (Scheepvart Museum, Netherlands, by courtesy of Vaderlandsch Fonds ter Aanmoeiging van's Lands Zeedienst)

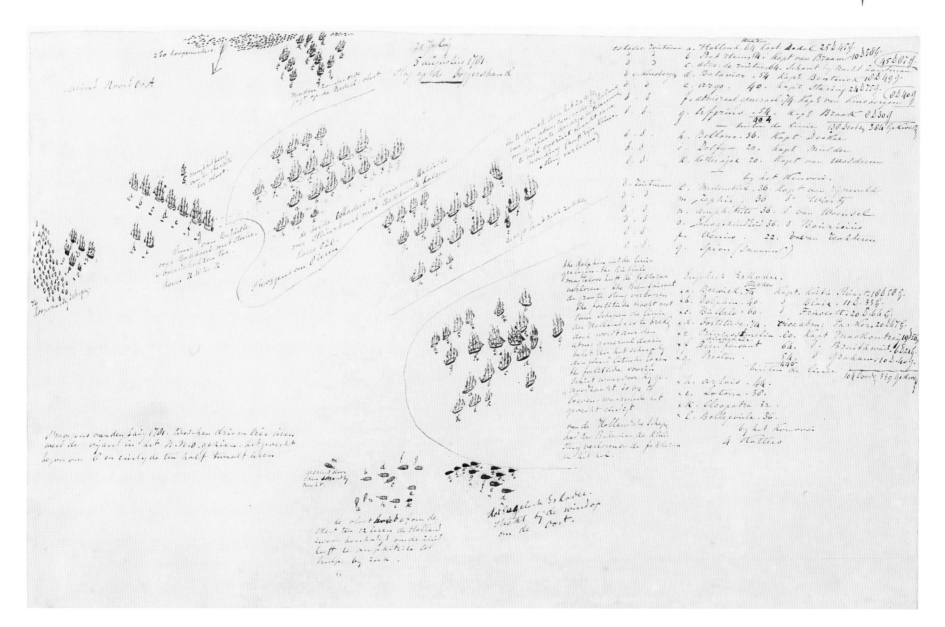

| SKETCH OF THE BATTLE OF DOGGER BANK, 1781 | This sketch of the Battle of Dogger Bank, held in the Scheepvart Museum, is actually a nineteenth-century copy of the original. It shows, with detailed notes, the movement of the fleets and convoys involved, with a succession of status quo positions of the combatant ships. Admiral Parker went head on into the Dutch line exposing his ships to their broadsides and positioning his flagship opposite the Dutch flagship. But as fourth in line to the enemy's fifth, Parker left the British van outnumbered three to two and the rear ship with no opponent. Realizing his mistake, Parker signalled for General Action to bring all of his ships into battle, and the scirmish turned into a four-hour close range cannonade. Midway through the action, the Dutch convoy returned from the lee of the Dutch line to the safety of the Texel.

The key on the right of the sketch names the ships of each fleet, their captains and number of guns with a total for each fleet, always important for those weighing up the results. (Scheepvart Museum, Netherlands)

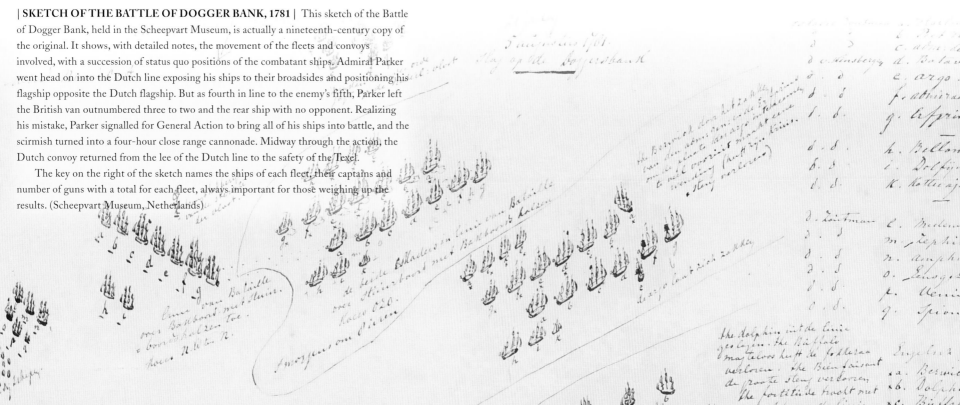

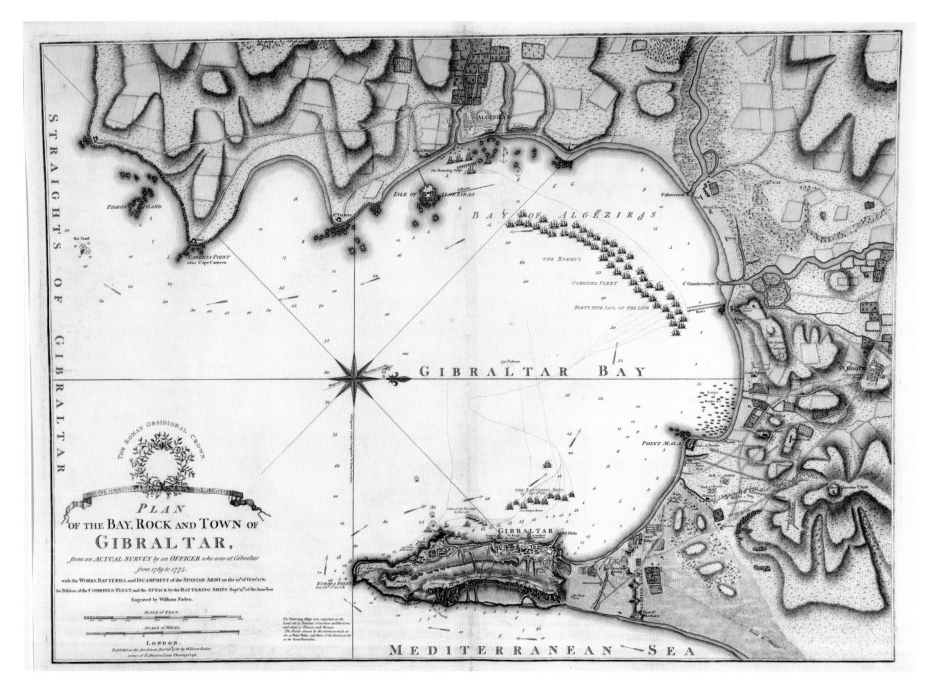

| PLAN OF THE BAY, ROCK AND TOWN OF GIBRALTAR, BY 'AN OFFICER', 1782 |

Following Spain's declaration of war in 1779, a Spanish force began a siege of Gibraltar in an attempt to starve out the British, with a garrison of 5000 led by General George Elliot, over three and a half years. The spirit of the defendants might be summed up by Elliot's laconic letter, dated 21 September 1779, to the Misses Fuller: 'Nothing new G. A. E.'. The besieged garrison managed to survive through the shelter given by the honeycomb of tunnels they built, and the siting of guns at the entrance of some of these high up in the rock that gave them a good angle of fire against their attackers.

On 13 September 1782, the French and Spanish made one final all-out attack on the Rock with 49 ships, 450 cannon and 100,000 men, continuing the assault with a squadron of floating batteries of innovative design. The moment of greatest danger occurred when these floating batteries were moored at point-blank range in the bay. Their destruction, with red-hot shot from the defenders' guns high up in the caves, broke the attackers' resolve.

Published in 1783 by William Faden as a copper-engraved map, the year that the siege was finally broken, this superbly detailed plan shows the climactic moment, with the failure of the French floating gun batteries. Leaving the English Channel exposed with some risk to Britain, Admiral Howe had sailed with the Channel Fleet of 35 ships of the line and a convoy of store-ships on 11 September 1782 to relieve the garrison. Although he expected to encounter the Spanish admiral, Don Luis de Córdoba, with 50 ships of the line in Gibraltar Bay, he got the convoy into Gibraltar, then met Córdoba with 45 ships in an indecisive action off Cape Spartel near Tangier on 20 October. The American War of Independence and hostilities with Spain ended five months later. (By courtesy of The Map House, London)

| **ENGLISH HARBOUR, ANTIGUA, BY JOHN BROWN, 1782** | John Brown's sophisticated plan of English Harbour, Antigua, combines elegance with detail. While he was stationed in Antigua with the British Army he produced this useful navigation plan including soundings and a scale in chains and yards (1 chain is 66 feet or 4 rods {22 yards} long and an acre was exactly 1 chain wide by 10 chains long, i.e. 660 square feet, which made mental surveying calculations easy).

English Harbour is a beautiful natural harbour with a dockyard built in 1725 and surrounding mountains that give protection against hurricanes. It was an ideal headquarters for the fleet tasked to protect the Leeward Islands. Between 1672 and 1815 some 40 coastal forts were built to protect the sugar industry. In 1784 Nelson arrived as a young captain commanding the *Boreas* with the Duke of Clarence, the future King William IV, as one of his officers, zealously determined to enforce the Navigation Act's no-trade rules between the colonies and the Americans. This was highly unpopular with the colonists whose governors had hitherto been turning a blind eye, and it caused political problems in London. (© National Maritime Museum, London, F0219)

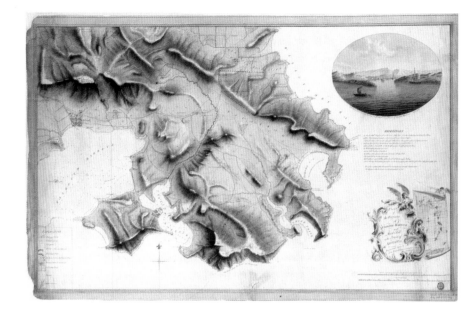

| RIGHT | **SPANISH CHART OF HAVANA, 1783** | By the middle of the eighteenth century one third of Spain's ships were built in Havana. Made of South American hardwoods such as mahogany they were much more durable than European oak-built ships. Havana was to remain the key Spanish port in the West Indies until independence. It was fortified over the centuries but was attacked on several occasions. It was taken in 1762 by a British fleet under Admiral Sir George Pocock, who caught the Spaniards by surprise by taking the old Bahamas channel to the north of Cuba which, although acccurately sounded by the Spanish, was thought by them to be impassible to sail. John Elphinstone, captain of the *Richmond,* made an astounding running survey of the channel, marking the safe passage with beacons for the fleet to follow and allowing an attack on the unprepared Spanish from the north. However Cuba was formally returned to Spain in exchange for Florida at the peace made in 1763. The chart is a copy made in 1790 by the Spanish fleet pilot of the original of 1783, an up-to-date survey of the harbour, with detailed soundings, and showing fortifications and key buildings. (Library of Congress)

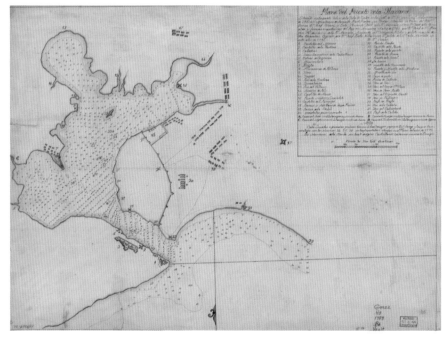

| BELOW | **THE BATTLE OF HAVANA, 1762** | Although the action portrayed in this attractive watercolour of a British attack on Havana harbour dates 1762, it gives an interesting view of the harbour that would have looked substantially the same as at the time of the survey shown above it. As such, the painting visually enlivens the Spanish chart. (By courtesy of the Museu de Barcelona)

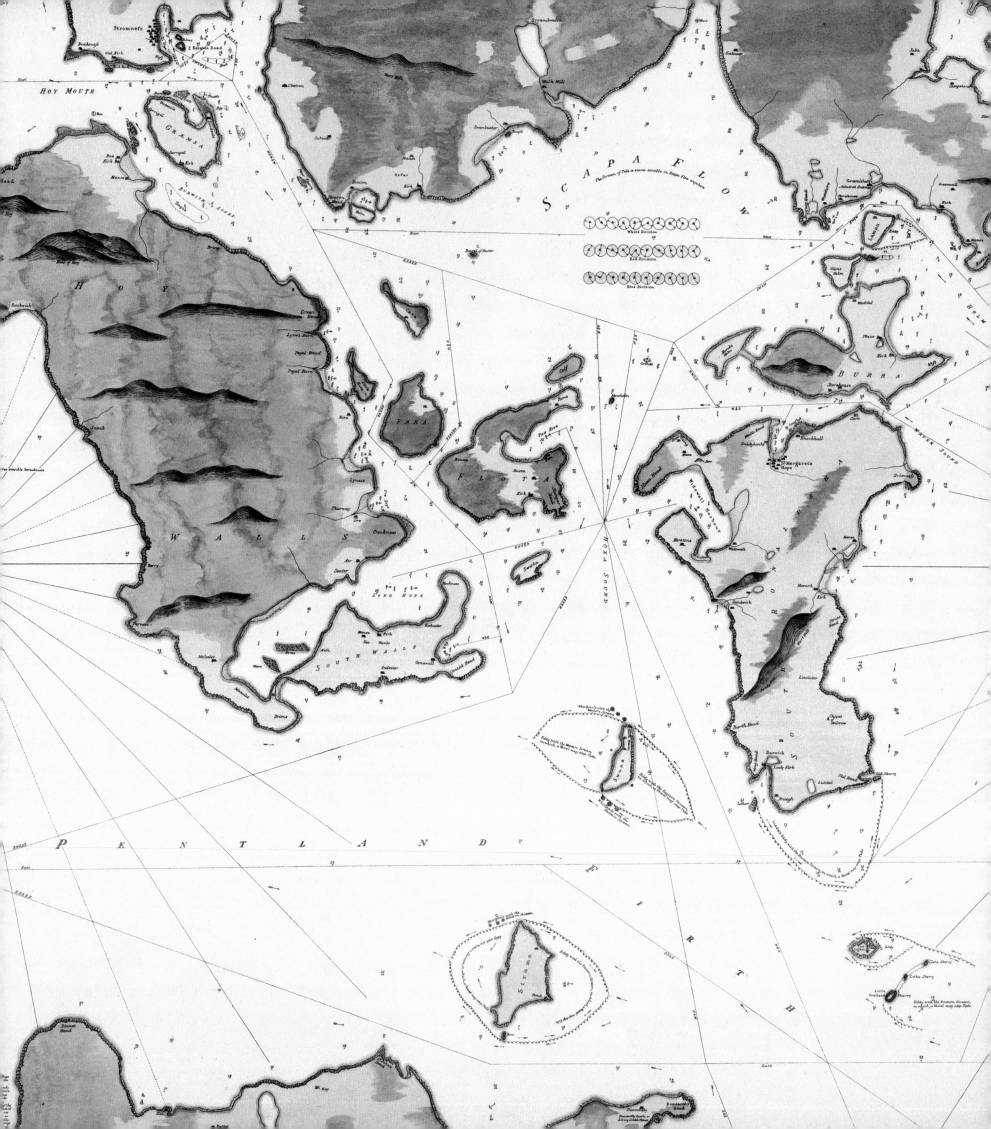

CHAPTER 6

Charts of Global War

The Revolutionary and Napoleonic Wars, 1793-1815

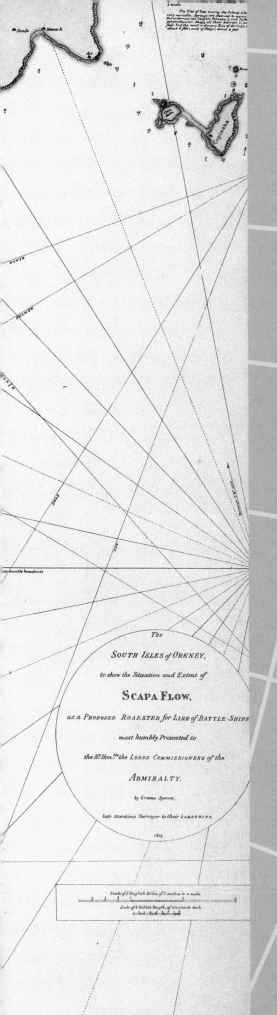

| **SURVEY OF SCAPA FLOW, ORKNEY ISLANDS, BY LIEUTENANT GRAEME SPENCE, 1812** | Lieutenant Spence had worked with Lieutenant Murdoch Mackenzie and completed the important surveys of the Thames Estuary from Margate to Beachy Head. He had taken over from Mackenzie as Chief Surveyor to the Admiralty in 1788 and his invention of the station pointer for resection fixes to make ever more accurate charts was adopted for the next 130 years. He retired from the navy in 1803 to write up his sailing directions at the Admiralty as Head Maritime Surveyor until 1811. One of his last enterprises was this chart of the southern isles of Orkney in which he highlighted the position and extent of Scapa Flow as a potential roadstead for ships of the line, including details of how three divisions of 10 battleships could be anchored with sufficient sea room, and with the pithy observation that if the British did not use it, then the French could. It was to become the northern naval base for the Home Fleet during the First and Second World Wars. The chart is rich in navigational information together with tides, eddies and whirlpools, and suggested bearings for passage through the islands. (© National Maritime Museum, London, F0107)

THE campaigns that characterize this era were set in motion by a cataclysmic event that shook the monarchical status quo across Europe. The French Revolution of 1789 was in great part a result of the financial burden imposed on the French people through her support of America during the War of Independence. A pivotal moment in history, when the Bastille in Paris fell on 14 July 1789, brought in the virtually inevitable declaration of war by the Revolutionary government against almost all of Europe, and ushered in a period of almost continual warfare beginning in 1792, when the Revolutionaries declared war on Austria, and ended in 1815 after the final defeat of Napoleon at the Battle of Waterloo. This period is divided into the French Revolutionary War (1792–1802) and the Napoleonic War (1803–15).

This was the zenith of the age of the sailing warship, the design of which reached a peak of efficiency in its endurance, sailing qualities and armament. French ships were well designed and built to a laid down standard set by one of the best ship designers of the age, the French engineer Jacques-Noel Sané, controlled by the Ministre de la Marine et des Colonies, and became a role model for British designs: captured ones were copied.

The British developed the use of copper sheathing, which allowed for longer time at sea between refits and bottom cleaning, and the carronade (named after the Carron Company in Scotland). Known as the smasher it was highly effective for the British tactic of closing alongside the enemy ship of the line and firing rapidly into the hull, whereas the French tended to aim high at the sails, so diminishing sailing abilities, and avoidance of pursuit if tactics dictated.

Between 1794 and 1805, six major British fleet actions knocked out the Spanish (Cape St Vincent), French (Glorious First of June, Nile and Trafalgar), Dutch (Camperdown) and Danish (Copenhagen) navies, so that after Trafalgar in 1805 there was no real threat of invasion and British naval activity became more focussed on blockading, convoy escort, assisting the army with naval gunfire support, amphibious operations and ship-to-ship duels. In this latter regard, the frigate was pre-eminent. Built for speed, frigates could sail closer to the wind than a ship of the line, and were lightly armed with typically thirty-two, thirty-six or thirty-eight 18-pounder guns on a single gun deck, although these were upgraded to 24 pounders after a number of British frigate defeats by the USA during the War of 1812 that was fought in North America between the two countries. They were highly useful as the 'eyes of the fleet', such as Captain Blackwood in the *Euryalus*, who kept watch on the combined French and Spanish fleet before Trafalgar; scouting ahead of ships of the line; and as repeating ships to fly the Admiral's battle signals or watching close in to a blockading port for signs of the enemy getting under way. Besides escorting convoys, the frigate cruised in search of privateers or blockade runners under daring and resourceful captains such as Lord Thomas Cochrane and Philip Broke.

By the end of the American War of Independence in 1783 the French navy had restored its image, but discipline was bad and the state of training and standards of seamanship and navigation were low. Reforming Ministers Gabriel de Sartine and then the Marquis de Castries tried to modernize these aspects while the Spanish navy, although performing well in the war, was herself concentrating on these aspects. France, however, would continue to think that over-running the countries of Europe, then imposing a policy of economic isolation by blocking all British trade with Europe would weaken Britain and facilitate an invasion.

The guillotining of a high proportion of experienced French officers, and the exodus of many more, who were by definition aristocrats, decimated naval efficiency, and it took some years to replace their lost experience. In the British system of patronage, gentlemen were sponsored and moulded from a typically tender age of 12, and would literally learn the ropes and everything else in seamanship, including navigation and surveying, from practical experience to rise up the ranks of the officer class. British gunnery was practised during continuous sea-time and could achieve firing rates four times higher, while the French and Spanish fleets, blockaded in home ports, grew stale.

British naval strategy, evolved through experience from over eight major maritime wars with France between 1689 and 1815, put the prevention of invasion of the British Isles (including Ireland) first. Apart from the Duke of Wellington's campaign from Spain into France in 1814, and some half-hearted landings in support of the Royalists after the French Revolution, the British never contemplated an invasion of France, while invasion of Britain was a continuous cornerstone of French policy.

The blockade was key to prevention, and was the routine (and boring) lot of the British ship of the line. Admiral Lord Anson had advocated close blockade of the key French and Spanish ports during the Seven Years War, while Admiral Lord Howe advocated open blockade during his time as Commander-in-Chief of the Channel Fleet and First Lord of the Admiralty. Admiral Lord St Vincent during his tenure as First Lord of the Admiralty reverted to the close blockade – better for keeping the fleet on its toes – while coastal blockades were established from time to time, such as Lord Keith's in the North Sea in 1803. The chart on page 117 emphasizes the significance of blockade work in the war strategy of the Admiralty when they sent one of their top navigators, Captain William Bligh, to survey the approaches to the River Scheldt, specifically to help the navigation of the blockading squadron boxing in the Dutch and French ships.

British trade with her colonies and other accommodating states overseas, off-setting any reliance on European trade which Napoleon tried to deny through the 'Continental system', grew exponentially during this period and overseas naval bases were key to this. From four in 1793 the number grew to 15, including store depots at Barbados, Minorca, Martinique, Lisbon and San Domingo. Gibraltar remained a British base, despite repeated intrepid Spanish attempts to take it. Further south en route to the Orient, the island of St Helena was held by the Honourable East India Company. Surveys were encouraged to identify potential bases in Diego Garcia in the Chagos Archipelago, conveniently on the sailing route from the Cape of Good Hope to India, and the Andaman Islands. Bombay and Madras, administered by the East India Company, 'serviced' the Indian Ocean and beyond. Later, at the entrance to the Malacca Strait, the East India Company set up a base at Penang in 1802.

The need for better charts and an improved system to get these charts out to the fleets was vital. French charts were still considered superior and were carried on British ships. For example, a French chart was used in the highly successful planning of the British attack on the French fleet during the Battle of the Nile in 1798, illustrated on pages 112 and 113. Page 109 shows the French chart that was used on board the *Leviathan* during the Glorious First of June in 1794, when a British fleet under Admiral Howe was sent to intercept the French fleet under Admiral Villaret de Joyeuse escorting a vital convoy of grain from America following the failure of the French harvest. The charts on pages 110 and 111 portray Howe's brilliant tactics in breaking through the French line to win the battle, although the grain convoy got through to France.

In 1796 the Spanish declared war on England, but their fleet was effectively suppressed by Admiral Sir John Jervis's victory at Cape St Vincent in 1797, during which a rising star in naval warfare, Horatio Nelson, played a decisive part. In October that year Admiral Duncan achieved total victory over the Dutch at the Battle of Camperdown, denying the French the use of the Dutch fleet. These two British successes were all the more surprising as they sandwiched the mutinies of the Royal Navy at Spithead and the Nore, and although a French invasion at Fishguard in Pembrokeshire turned into fiasco, it made for a dark time in Britain. In the West Indies a long campaign between France and Britain from 1793 to 1796 established a set of island bases with the capture of Martinique and St Lucia. But this was offset by the French capture of Guadeloupe and Corsica. Continuing a strategy of establishing naval bases around the world, Trincomalee in Ceylon and the Cape of Good Hope were captured from the Dutch in quick succession in 1795.

Even as late as the Battle of Trafalgar sea surveys made by naval officers and masters were sold to private publishers whose civilian cartographic skills constructed charts in a well-established and formalized commercial arrangement. They were then sold through private publishers in the City of London or by the docks to Royal Navy masters and commanding officers as well as merchant masters. During this period the Secretary of the Admiralty superintended the job of purchasing the requisite charts from private publishers, such as William Faden and James Imray, and distributing them to the fleets. But this system was clearly inadequate and following pressure from the First Lord of the Admiralty and one of the Sea Lords, Admiral Sir Charles Middleton (later Lord Barham), a British Hydrographical Office was formed by an Order in Council in 1795 – 75 years after the French. This was signed by George III, and the new office had direct responsibility for, initially finding and distributing charts around the fleet, and then organizing surveys to improve on existing charts, and to chart areas that had not been surveyed at all. Alexander Dalrymple, who had been serving as Hydrographer to the East India Company, was appointed.

Advances in the printing press were utilized by the Admiralty, which installed its first press in 1800, and in the next year published the first Admiralty chart. But results under Dalrymple, while he is to be admired for his meticulous approach, were slow. In 1807, therefore, impatient for results, the Admiralty set up the 'Chart Committee of the Admiralty' to accelerate good charts into the fleet. The three members appointed were senior and experienced naval officers: Captains Thomas Hurd, Sir Home Popham (whose chart of the Red Sea is shown on page 114) and Edward Columbine. Popham was appointed in spite of various brushes with senior officers including Admiral Lord St Vincent, who accused him of shady dealings with his ship repair bills in Calcutta after his Red Sea operations. Popham petitioned Parliament and not only proved his innocence but showed Admiralty maladministration. On another occasion he commanded the attack in 1806 to seize the Cape of Good Hope from the Dutch, but then went on to attack Buenos Aires, which was totally beyond his orders and for this he was court-martialled. Nevertheless, the Admiralty was prepared to forgive a firebrand if his talents warranted it and his appointment on the Committee, recognizing his surveying credentials, went ahead. The Committee chose 100 charts from commercial sources and, after rejecting the majority as unsafe, marked the rest with the approbation, 'Approved by the Chart Committee of the Admiralty'. This mark of approval can be seen on the chart of Nelson's chase of Villeneuve to the West Indies on pages 118–119. By 1808 the Committee was achieving results with the organized distribution of charts to the fleet. The captain of a ship was issued with a box of charts for the area of his service. For the North Sea, for example, he would have 28 charts with four for the Baltic, and a tour in the North Atlantic would include a general chart of the West Indies, Tortuga and the Florida Keys, the west end of Cuba and Grand Cayman, coasts of West Florida and Louisiana, along with a book of smaller charts of various islands.

By the late eighteenth century hydrographers were required to produce navigational and coastal views to complement the flat chart, giving the navigator a good idea of how the coast would look on the approach, and where important leading marks that give a safe course to steer could be expected. They were trained to draw both for intelligence purposes and as part of a coastal survey, but some of the best exponents of the navigational view, such as W H Smyth and John Thomas Serres, showed artistic merit above the expected standard, as collectors today will aver.

Navigation at this time was at a point where it would remain unchanged for a century. Campbell's sextant was widely used for sun and star sights, along with the now fully available *Nautical Almanac*, which had the tables to do the maths. Improvement in navigation went in hand with ship improvement. In the Napoleonic War two compasses, of a 'dry card' magnetic type, were placed on a binnacle near the wheel but course inaccuracies persisted. As accurate a bearing as possible in relation to a course across the sea and of visible landmarks for plotting position on a chart are vital and considerable investigation and advances were made at this time. While magnetic variation, the change in magnetic strength and direction on a compass, was understood, and the local effect noted on the chart, to become customarily noted on the compass rose on Admiralty charts, the understanding of magnetic deviation caused by a ship's own metallic construction was poor until investigated by the surveyor of much of Australia, Captain Matthew Flinders. Named after him, Flinders Bars made of iron are still placed around the magnetic compass to offset a ship's magnetic effect. Important too was the addition of a prism, invented by Schmalcalder in 1812, and later improved on by Lord Kelvin in 1876, that involved one person to take a compass bearing. Experience showed that to get as accurate a fix as possible to plot a ship's position on the chart, three bearings were best, using visible landmarks (but buoys with caution as they shift) ideally intersecting each other at one point, although in practice a triangle of error, known as a 'cocked hat' (named after the naval officer's tricorn hat) is often formed. The old type of chip log, used to measure a ship's speed through the water, which was essentially a float attached to a line that was cast over the side, was being replaced by technologically improved types. The first development used a rotator and speed was recorded on dials within a casement towed behind the ship. Invented by Edward Massey in 1802 it was

|RIGHT | **NAVIGATIONAL VIEW OF THE APPROACHES TO FERROL BY J T SERRES, 1800 |** About a month after Serres had made this watercolour view of the approach to the Spanish port of Ferrol in 1800, an unopposed landing was made to seize the dockyard. Inexplicably, within sight of their objective, the British general withdrew and re-embarked.

Ferrol, unlike most other European ports was virtually impossible to blockade because the prevailing westerly winds would drive a squadron northwards along Spain's hazardous and rocky coast. Furthermore, there was no safe shelter or anchorage readily to hand, unlike, for example, Brest with nearby Douarnenez Bay, or from a real blow to Torbay off Devon; and for a blockade of Cadiz, a squadron could soon make the shelter of Gibraltar; similarly from Toulon to shelter by Sardinia or Port Mahon in Majorca. When the weather eased a quick return to blockade Brest kept the French fleet in harbour before it had time to navigate the narrow channels and leave. The topography of Ferrol, however, allowed a whole fleet to slip out on a single tide. (UKHO © British Crown Copyright)

surprisingly accurate. Massey's nephew, Thomas Walker, designed an improvement that could be read inboard and something like a modern ship's log was now in use. In 1876 Lord Kelvin also invented the sounding machine, which could record depths under way at up to 16 knots. This transformed the navigator's dead reckoning accuracy.

The sailing master was to 'represent to the Captain every possible danger in or near the Ship's course, and the way to avoid it'. The master's responsibility to the captain for navigation was often defined by disaster, to the extent that when HMS *Impregnable* was wrecked on the Poles Shoal off Chichester Harbour in 1799 her captain was acquitted by the court martial but her master was found negligent. But such responsibility needed compensation and the master was the best paid of the officers and warrant officers after the captain, and the best accommodated after the captain and first lieutenant. Thomas Atkinson had been Nelson's master during all of his actions from Santa Cruz, including the Nile and Copenhagen, and he provided the data for the Nile chart illustrated on page 112. On board the *Victory* he had his cabin, which was also his office, on the starboard side of the quarterdeck appropriately close to the wheel, and near to the ship's captain and the flag officer.

The master continued, as in previous centuries, to be responsible for training midshipmen and master's mates in navigation and he had to ensure that the ship, and in Atkinson's case as the Admiral's master, the fleet, was adequately equipped with 'such charts, nautical books [i.e. tables and pilots] and instruments as are necessary for astronomical observation and all other purposes of navigation'. He would, as we have seen, take surveys and send them back to the Admiralty where they would be the basis and raw material for charts.

Masters worked their way up from the lower deck, rated as master's mates or quartermasters, or joined from the Merchant Navy. Others volunteered or were midshipmen, who had waited years without promotion to lieutenant and took a master's rate. They were examined by a senior post captain, three

senior masters and by Trinity House, who employed them from time to time to make surveys of the Thames and important seaports and to help with the siting of lightships and buoys. Courses steered and log readings (speed) were recorded during the watch on the traverse board and transferred by the master to his log, which would also be sent to the Admiralty at the end a voyage, or could be pored over by any Board of Inquiry. The captain had to keep a log, too, and many of these logs are now held in the British National Archives. Some have historically significant entries, such as 'ship's boats away taking soundings', recorded the day prior to the Battle of Copenhagen in 1801 in Captain Bligh's ship *Glatton* (see the charts on 115), while the log of the *Victory* interestingly shows her noon position on 21 October 1805 relative to Cadiz N 39° E 9½ leagues, Cape St Mary N 49° W 26½ leagues, prior to the Battle of Trafalgar. It goes on to report, 'cleared for action, standing towards the enemy van – at 11.40 the *Royal Sovereign* commenced firing upon the enemy', and, 'Lord Nelson wounded in the shoulder'. During a battle the master still had to make sure to bring the ship into line of battle station, or as the captain wished.

The British response to Nelson's outstanding role in the war against Napoleon stimulated the production of the celebratory chart. The chart depicting the Battle of the Nile on page 113 was put together with a montage to eulogize the man who was by 1798 not just a leader that seamen loved and would follow anywhere, but a national hero, too. His reputation was assured by a public who needed a national figure to adore at a time of low morale, as French armies swept across Europe. The piece on Nelson's Nile victory was originally printed in the *Illustrated London News* and adapted by Faden, who published and sold this example.

At the end of the Napoleonic War Britain preferred trade rather than territory for her economic power and she wanted to prevent any new Napoleon, or a Louis XIV, taking the Dutch lowlands and building a channel fleet that could threaten invasion from Antwerp. Holland was therefore created as a powerful central European country and to keep her strong, Dutch territory

won by Britain was returned to this new country that combined the former Dutch Republic with the Austrian Netherlands, Liege and Luxembourg. The Dutch chart on page 124 gives a vivid example of recapturing Sumatra as part of this policy. Martinique and Guadeloupe were similarly returned to France so that she would be commercially independent, but without the wish or need for military conquest. Britain, in contrast to Napoleon's reliance on European soldiery for his worldwide ambitions, had India, self-supporting and with a large land army available 'on site'.

The conclusion of the Napoleonic War ushered in almost a century of relative peace when Admiralty charts slowly replaced the commercial chart-makers, who then found their niche in supplying merchant ships with the 'Blueback' charts. These were far preferred by merchant captains as their small-scale focus on a typical passage enabled a merchant shipmaster to draw a course between his first and last port of call on one, or just a few, charts. Sailing directions were printed on the chart itself, rather than as a separate pilot. Suggested courses drawn on the chart cut across bays and steered clear of rocky, intricate coasts, and a harbour pilot would guide the master into port on arrival. The naval chart, however, was the antithesis of this: as a warship had to be able to go anywhere and be prepared to call into seemingly obscure bays or harbours, perhaps to secretly land troops or to carry out other military operations, assist with relief in the wake of natural disasters or take unscheduled shelter from storms. All charts were on the Mercator Projection, but charts for passage planning used a Gnomonic Projection that facilitated great circle passage planning, for example from New York to London.

Navies could concentrate on the suppression of piracy and the slave trade. The chart on page 123 shows Admiral Lord Exmouth's attack on Algiers to wipe out the Corsair pirates and free the Christian slaves that the local Dey had refused to release.

Where war did breakout during the rest of the nineteenth century it was more localized, rather than dragging in all the European powers. Turkey,

then described as the sick man of Europe, was seen as the aggressor over territory with Greece and the Battle of Navarino highlighted by the chart on page 125 where her fleet was destroyed, weakened her further. When Russia tried to take her lands in the Balkans, Turkey was propped up by France and Britain during the Crimean War, and the charts on page 127 show naval aspects of this war. Attempts to force China to trade are demonstrated by the chart on page 129 illustrating the attack on Canton in the First Opium War.

The century also witnessed one of the most fundamental changes in ship design initiated by, as is so often the case, the needs of war. Influenced by the destruction of the wooden Turkish fleet at Sinope by Russian high explosive shells in 1853 and the duels between ironclads during the American Civil War, which is looked at in Chapter 7, warships were given armour protection and adopted steam propulsion. Naval bases became coaling stations, too. The world's first true ironclad warship was the French *Gloire* launched in 1859, followed closely in 1860 by Britain's *Warrior*, the world's first iron-hulled battleship. Armed with the rifled gun mounted in a turret that could be turned towards the enemy, the Dreadnought class of battleship of 1906 fired a broadside in any direction independent of the ship's course and, able to steam with complete freedom of action regardless of the wind, rendered the old wooden ship of the line obsolete. The next major war at sea would involve these gargantuan ships, quite unrecognizable to Nelson and his band of brothers, but using navigational techniques and charts that would be.

The peace dividend of the nineteenth century gave the Royal Navy the opportunity to concentrate on surveying all the coasts of the world. This was initiated by the British Hydrographer Rear-Admiral Sir Francis Beaufort with the difference that now the results were almost all published and sold worldwide. The meticulous standard as set down by Cook had been kept and 'as safe as an Admiralty chart' was a simile of respect for a trusted product.

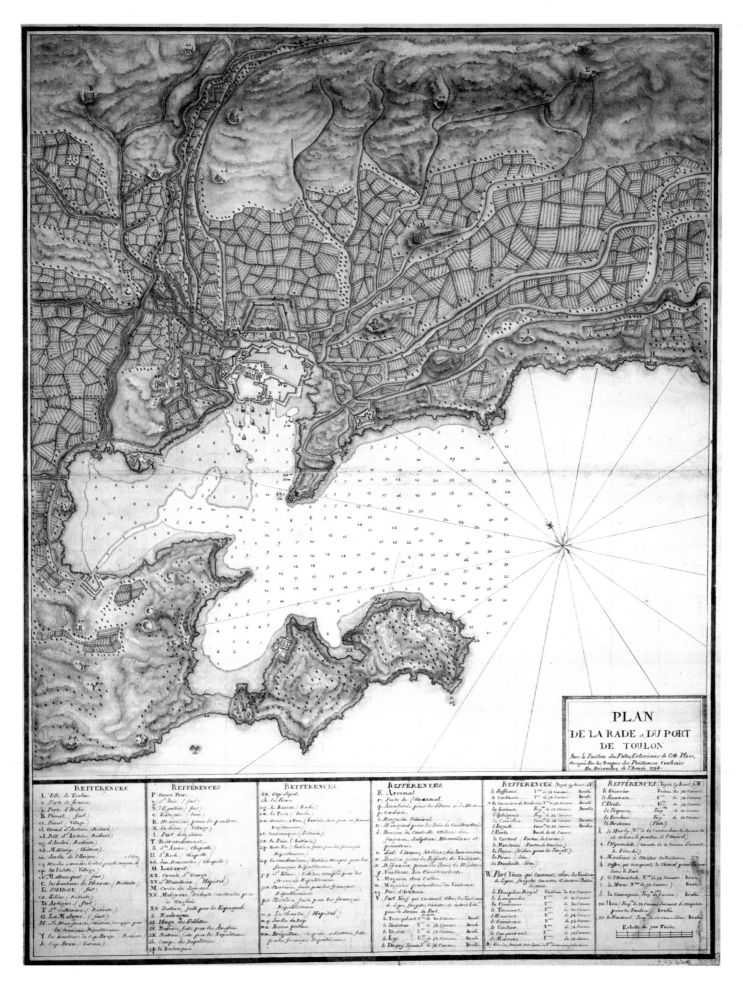

| CHART OF THE ROADS AND PORT OF TOULON, 1793 | With the French Revolution came a call for all European countries to overthrow their monarchies. France was already at war with Prussia and Austria when they invaded the Austrian Netherlands in September 1792, followed by a declaration of war against Britain on 1 February 1793. A Royalist revolt in the Vendeé in western France and an appeal by the Royalists in Toulon to Admiral Hood, commanding the blockading Mediterranean Fleet, to help them, captured at a stroke half the French navy and opened up a second front against the French. However, a young artillery officer called Napoleon Bonaparte was advancing on Toulon and with Spanish help uncertain and William Pitt's government committing a large force to attacking French West Indies islands, Hood decided to vacate Toulon. As Bonaparte overran Toulon, Hood managed to escape overnight, taking three French ships, but only destroying 9 of the 22 ships of the line.

The anonymous French manuscript chart of Toulon approaches and harbour dates to December 1793 and shows the fleet, with those ships burnt, and fortifications, naming them in the key. Drawn on a squared pencil grid, with soundings but no graduations, the scale is in French *toises* and the fort, L'Eguillette, that Bonaparte took is marked 'N'.
(© National Maritime Museum, London, F0012)

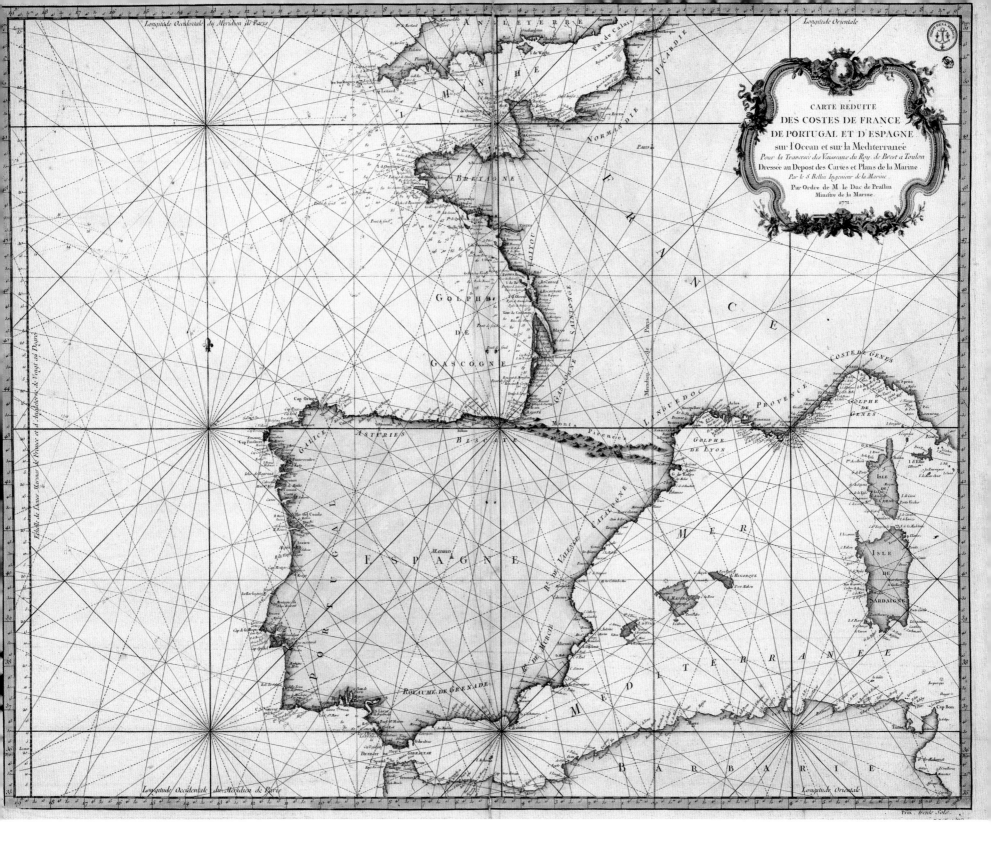

|FRENCH CHART BY J N BELLIN SHOWING THE TRACKS OF THE *LEVIATHAN*
IN 1794–5 | The ruthless suppression of mutiny at Brest by the Jacobin government in Paris brought the French fleet into sufficient discipline to sail out in May 1794 to escort a large grain convoy sailing from Chesapeake Bay urgently needed to replenish the failed French harvest. Admiral Lord Howe sailed to the most likely latitude around 47°N to intercept the convoy. He met Admiral Villaret de Joyeuse about 400 miles off Ushant in what was the first naval battle of the French Revolutionary Wars, and during four days of skirmishing through fog managed to take the weather gage. Most sea battles have been fought within sight of land, and named after the nearest point accordingly. In consequence, charts anchor the action to the land, but the charts of the action of what came to be called the Glorious First of June by the British and 'le Bataille du 13 prairial an 2' in the French Revolutionary calendar, reflect the relative movement of the ships involved.

The French chart, produced in 1771 by Jacques Nicholas Bellin, a key figure in French charting as Hydrographer to Louis XV and producing sea charts of the known coasts of the world to a very

high standard, was made for the use of the French King's ships to navigate from Brest to Toulon. A copy was later used on board one of the ships in Howe's fleet, the *Leviathan*, a third rate with 74 guns commanded by Lord Hugh Seymour, and the tracks she took leading up to and during the Battle of the Glorious First of June are marked on. Red ink shows her track from 11 to 23 January 1794 from Cadiz to the Lizard on blockading duty. In early May Howe had sailed from Portsmouth to check on the Brest fleet, and brown dots mark the dead reckoning course between 5 May and 20 June, from the Lizard to where the French were first encountered, and shows the course of the *Leviathan* during the battle. The continuous brown line marks the track from 5 to 20 February the following year on a cruise. This chart has French and English marine leagues (a league is 3 nautical miles) and, with a price of 'trente sols', was probably purchased as part of the ship's chart portfolio. During the battle, *Leviathan* was, with Howe's flagship, *Queen Charlotte*, and the *Bellerophon*, to break through the French rear and cut off three French two-deckers. (© National Maritime Museum, London, F0125)

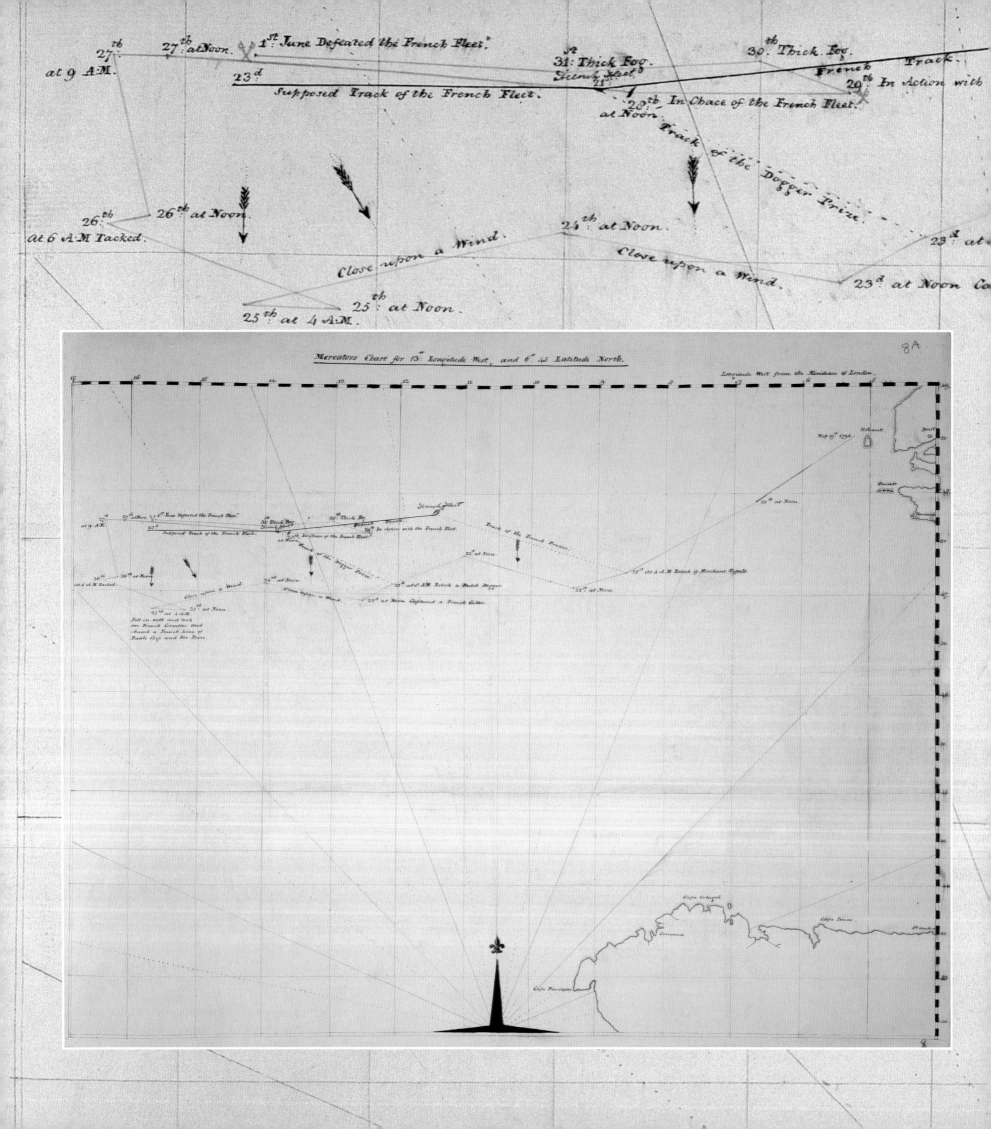

...Track of the French Prizes...

...Fleet

...at Noon.

13

1ˢᵗ of June. A the British fleet. The dotted lines shewing their track in bearing down upon the Enemy and breaking their line.

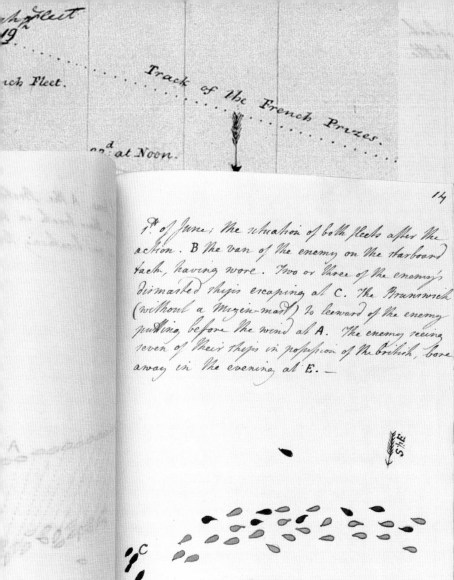

14

1ˢᵗ of June; the situation of both fleets after the action. B the van of the enemy on the starboard tack, having wore. Two or three of the enemy's dismasted ships escaping at C. The Brunswick (without a Mizin-mast) to leeward of the enemy putting before the wind at A. The enemy seeing seven of their ships in possession of the British, bore away in the evening at E. —

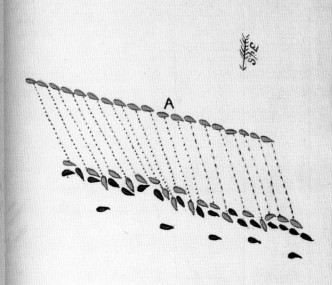

12

31ˢᵗ of May at seven o'clock in the evening, both fleets in order of battle. —

| PAGES FROM THE ADMIRALTY REPORT PROCEEDINGS |
Three pages from the Admiralty Report of Proceedings now held at the Admiralty Library, Portsmouth, clearly show the ships' positions of both fleets at three stages during the battle, and how the French wore away to make Brest harbour. (Admiralty Library Manuscript Collection, 1988.500)

| LEFT | **TRACK CHART OF THE *QUEEN CHARLOTTE* DURING THE GLORIOUS FIRST OF JUNE BY JAMES BOWEN, 1794** | James Bowen was the sailing master on the *Queen Charlotte* and thus responsible for the safe and timely navigation of the ship. At least during this battle he would have been able to breathe easily as they were well out in open water, away from any coastal hazards. He drew this chart which, summarized, shows the *Queen Charlotte*'s track from Ushant on 19 May; on the 21st re-taking nine French-prize Dutch merchant vessels; on the 23rd taking a Dutch Dogger (trawler) and French Cutter; on the 25th taking two French cutters and chasing a French line-of-battle ship and her prize, then tacking north heading east. The tracks show the action on the 29th with the French, the 30th and 31st in thick fog, and on 1 June at the location of the main engagement against the French fleet. The daily noon sun sight positions, a must for all ships out of sight of land, are marked. (The National Archives {PRO} MPI 1/324)

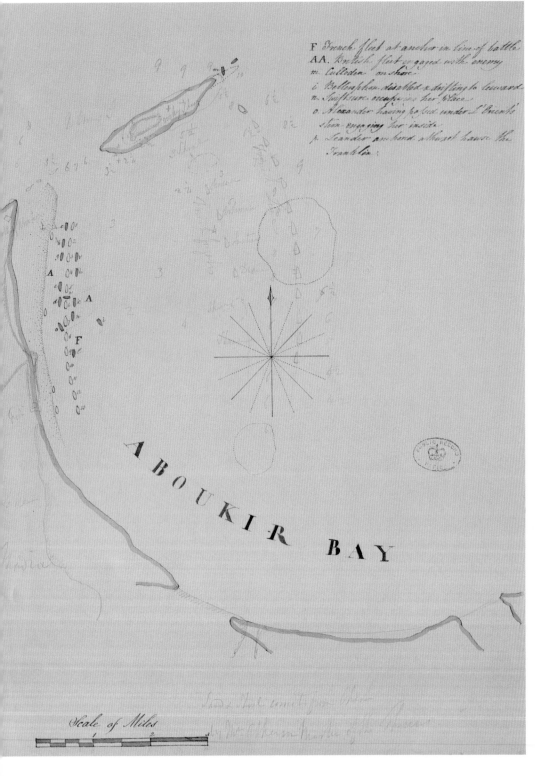

F *French fleet at anchor in line of battle.*
AA. *British fleet engaged with enemy.*
m. *Culloden on shore.*

i *Bellerophon disabled a drifting to leeward.*
n. *Swiftsure occupies her place.*
o *Alexander having hauled under L'Orient's stern engaging her inside.*

p *Leander on hand athwart hawse the Franklin.*

A B O U K I R   B A Y

Scale of Miles

| LEFT | **CHART OF ABOUKIR BAY, 1798** | Napoleon Bonaparte was putting together a large army and embarking them at Toulon: this much was known, but not their destination. Admiral Lord St Vincent appointed a relatively young and inexperienced admiral, Horatio Nelson, to seek out the French. His flagship, *Vanguard,* dismasted in a violent storm – whether by bad luck or shiphandling is conjectural – had to put into Sardinia for repairs, losing precious days. The French fleet, meanwhile, ransacked Malta, before heading south – Bonaparte's plan was to conquer Egypt before proceeding overland to take India. Nelson, working on instinct, headed for Alexandria but arrived before the French, passing within 60 miles of them as he left to begin scouring the Mediterranean. Finally, after capturing a French brig, he discovered their destination was indeed Egypt and found the fleet anchored in Aboukir Bay, 15 miles east of Alexandria.

The French ships were moored across the bay. Captain Thomas Foley in the *Goliath* had a French chart that showed there was enough room to sail to the west and round the lead French ship between their line and the shore. With other British ships following, Nelson was able to double up on the French and working down the line throughout the night of 1 August 1798, he annihilated them in an action known as the Battle of the Nile.

This detailed chart shows the situation of the fleets in the early evening and has been drawn using data prepared by Thomas Atkinson, master of the *Vanguard,* who had first worked under Nelson in the *Theseus* in 1797. Nelson so valued the professional abilities of his sailing master that he took Atkinson with him from ship to ship, a relationship that would last for eight years. He was regarded as the best in the navy and was with Nelson in the *Victory* at Trafalgar. (The National Archives {PRO} MPI 1/536)

|RIGHT | **CHART OF BATTLE OF THE NILE, 1798** | The jingoistic account published by Laurie and Whittle is an example of the adaption of the chart for celebratory purposes and popular consumption. It was drawn up from sketches similar to that shown adjacent with notes by one of the sailing masters. Typically masters would sell their sketches to chart publishers who compiled the information to sell on as a navigational chart to ships' captains. It has a full acount of the battle and, with extracts from the *London Gazette,* gives interesting details of the ships, captains and casualties. (The National Archives {PRO} MPI 1/536)

| BELOW | **NAVIGATIONAL VIEW OF BREST BY J T SERRES, 1800** | In 1800 John Thomas Serres was appointed Marine Draughtsman to the Admiralty and embarked in HMS *Clyde* under the command of Captain Charles Cunningham, with the British fleet engaged in blockading French, Spanish and Portuguese ports during the Napoleonic Wars. He made spectacular paintings and drawings of their coasts in the form of elevation views, to be adapted on copper engravings for inclusion as navigational views on charts, and for coastal interpretation and intelligence at the Admiralty. The views were also published with sailing directions in a specially produced book whose listed subscribers included the Board of Admiralty, the East India Company, the Right Honourable Commissioners for the Affairs of India, Trinity House, Earl St Vincent (First Lord of the Admiralty) and Vice-Admiral Nelson, Duke of Bronte.

Serres painted this navigational view of Brest with Pointe de Grande Minout to the left, Pointe Camaret to the right and the Goulet. Look between the headlands along the Goulet, and you can see the dramatic view that *Triton, La Nymphe* and the cutter *Joseph* saw on 10 June 1800 of 46 French and Spanish ships of the line anchored in the harbour. This is the blockade in action. (UKHO © British Crown Copyright)

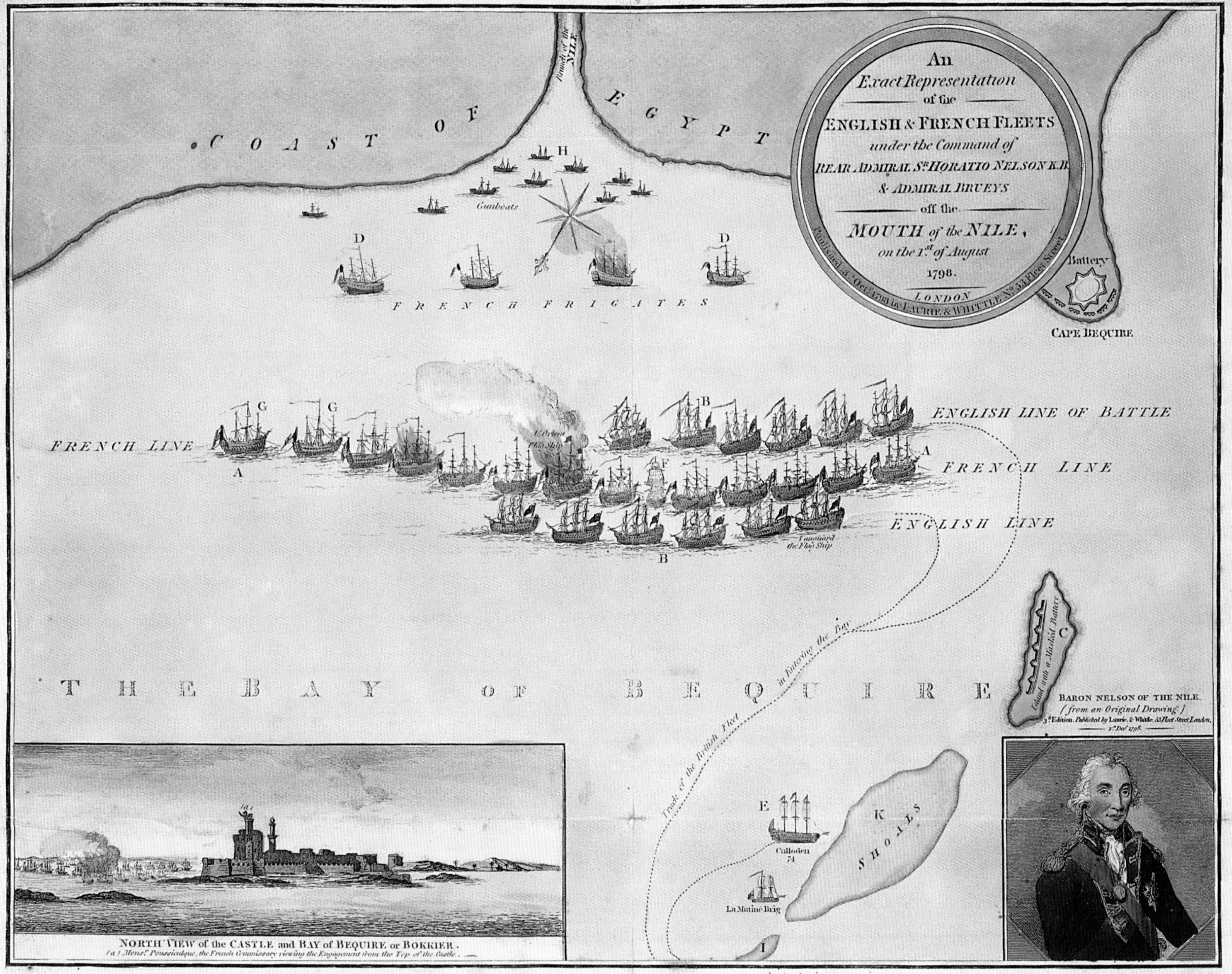

An Exact Representation of the ENGLISH & FRENCH FLEETS under the Command of REAR ADMIRAL Sr. HORATIO NELSON K.B. & ADMIRAL BRUEYS off the MOUTH of the NILE, on the 1st of August 1798.
LONDON
Published 8 Octr. 1798 by LAURIE & WHITTLE No. 53 Fleet Street.
Mouth of the NILE
COAST OF EGYPT
Gunboats
H
D
D
FRENCH FRIGATES
Battery
CAPE BEQUIRE
ENGLISH LINE OF BATTLE
FRENCH LINE
FRENCH LINE
ENGLISH LINE
L'Orient Flag Ship
Vanguard the Flag Ship
A
A
B
B
F
G
G
Island with a Masked Battery
C
THE BAY OF BEQUIRE
Track of the British Fleet in Entering the Bay
E
Culloden 74
La Mutiné Brig
K
SHOALS
I
BARON NELSON OF THE NILE.
(from an Original Drawing.)
3d Edition. Published by Laurie & Whittle, 53 Fleet Street London, 1st Decr 1798.

NORTH VIEW of the CASTLE and BAY of BEQUIRE or BOKKIER.
(a) Monsr. Poussielque, the French Commissary viewing the Engagement from the Top of the Castle.

REFERENCES TO THE PLATE.

AA.—THE French Ships drawn up in a line, and moored on spring cables, to receive our Fleet.
BB. The two Divisions of the British Fleet, after the breaking of the French Line. The dots from each represent the different Courses they took to commence the attack.
C.—Island, with a masqued battery.
D.D.—The French Frigates LA DIANE, LA JUSTICE, L'ARTEMISE, LA SERIEUSE; the two former of which escaped, the third was burnt, and the last dismasted and sunk.
E—The English ship CULLODEN, which got ashore before the action.
F.—The LEANDER, which broke the Enemy's Line, and dropped anchor between the head and stern of two French Ships, both of which she raked with her broadsides for a considerable time, and did them much injury.
GG.—The two French Line-of-battle Ships, LE GUILLAUME TELL, and LE GENEREUX, which escaped.
H.—The Enemy's Gun-boats.
IK.—Shoals.

*** This sketch is meant to give a perfect idea of the commencement of the action. In a short time all the enemies ships became in a great measure unmanageable, and fell into the greatest confusion. The BELLEROPHON, soon after the breaking of the line, engaged L'ORIENT to windward, while the VANGUARD attacked her to the leeward, and both these ships afterwards engaged the French Admiral, both starboard and larboard. Towards the middle of the action their stations were taken by the MAJESTIC and ALEXANDER. The fate of L'ORIENT is already known. She took fire about eleven o'clock at night. LA GUILLAUME TELL and GENEREUX withdrew from the action about one o'clock in the morning, and were pursued for some time by the ZEALOUS. The engagement commenced at five o'clock in the afternoon of the 1st of August, and continued with unabated fury till between one and two the next morning; from this time till five the fire on both sides slackened very considerably, when the conflict was renewed; and soon after the scene terminated in the glory and triumph of the British Fleet, the destruction of two French ships of the line and two frigates, and the capture of nine sail of the line, viz.

LE GUERRIER,	74	LE FRANKLIN	80
LE CONQUERANT	74	LE TONNANT	80
LE SPARTIATE,	74	L'HEUREUX	74
L'AQUILON	74	LE MERCURE	74
LE SOUVERAIN PEUPLE	74		

From the London Gazette Extraordinary, October 2, 1798.

ADMIRALTY-OFFICE, OCT. 2.

The Hon. Capt. Capel, of his Majesty's sloop Mutine, arrived this morning with dispatches from Rear-Admiral Sir Horatio Nelson, K. B. to Evan Nepean, Esq. Secretary of the Admiralty, of which the following are copies:

SIR, *Vanguard, Mouth of the Nile, Aug. 7, 1798.*

HEREWITH I have the Honor to transmit you a Copy of my Letter to the Earl of St. Vincent, together with a Line of Battle of the English and French Squadrons; also a List of killed and wounded. I have the Pleasure to inform you, that Eight of our Ships have already Top-Gallant Yards across, and ready for any Service; the others, with the Prizes, will soon be ready for Sea.

Signed, HORATIO NELSON.

P.S. The Island I have taken Possession of, and brought off the Two 13-Inch Mortars, all the Brass Guns, and destroyed the Iron Ones.

Evan Nepean, Esq.

MY LORD, *Vanguard, off the Mouth of the Nile, Aug. 3, 1798.*

ALMIGHTY GOD has blessed his Majesty's Arms in the late Battle, by a great Victory over the Fleet of the Enemy, whom I attacked at Sun-set on the 1st of August, off the Mouth of the Nile. The Enemy were moored in a strong Line of Battle for defending the Entrance of the Bay (of Shoals), flanked by numerous Gun-Boats, Four Frigates, and a Battery of Guns and Mortars on an Island in their Van; but nothing could withstand the Squadron your Lordship did me the Honor to place under my Command. Their high State of Discipline is well known to you; and, with the Judgment of the Captains, together with their Valour and that of their Officers and Men of every Description, it was absolutely irresistable.—Could any thing from my pen add to the characters of the Captains, I would write it with pleasure, but that is impossible.—I have to regret the Loss of Captain Westcott, of the Majestic, who was killed early in the Action; but the Ship was continued to be so well fought by her First Lieutenant, Mr. Cuthbert, that I have given him an order to command her till your Lordship's pleasure is known. The Ships of the Enemy, all but their two Rear Ships, are nearly dismasted; and those two, with two Frigates, I am sorry to say, made their Escape; nor was it, I assure you, in my power to prevent them. Captain Hood most handsomely endeavoured to do it, but I had no Ship in a Condition to support the Zealous, and I was obliged to call her in.—The Support and Assistance I have received from Captain Berry cannot be sufficiently expressed. I was wounded in the Head, and obliged to be carried off the Deck, but the Service suffered no Loss by that Event. Captain Berry was fully equal to the important Service then going on, and to him I must beg Leave to refer you for every Information relative to this Victory. He will present you with the Flag of the Second in Command, that of the Commander-in-Chief being burnt in the L'Orient.

Signed, HORATIO NELSON.

To Admiral the Earl of St. Vincent, Commander-in-Chief, &c. &c. &c. off Cadiz.

ENGLISH LINE OF BATTLE.

		GUNS.	MEN.
1	Culloden, T. Troubridge, Captain	74	590
2	Theseus, R. W. Miller, Captain	74	590
3	Alexander, Alex. J. Ball, Captain	74	590
4	Vanguard, Rear-Admiral Sir Horatio Nelson, K. B. Edward Berry, Captain	74	595
5	Minotaur, Thomas Louis, Captain	74	640
6	Leander, T. B. Thompson, Captain	50	343
7	Swiftsure, B. Hallowell, Captain	74	590
8	Audacious, Davidge Gould, Captain	74	590
9	Defence, John Peyton, Captain	74	590
10	Zealous, Samuel Hood, Captain	74	590
11	Orion, Sir James Saumarez, Captain	74	590
12	Goliath, Thomas Foley, Captain	74	590
13	Majestic, G. B. Westcott, Captain	74	590
14	Bellerophon, Henry D. E. Darby, Captain	74	590
	La Mutine, Brig		
	Total,	1012	8068

FRENCH LINE OF BATTLE.

		GUNS.	MEN.	
1	Le Guerrier	74	600	— *Taken*
2	Le Conquérant	74	700	— *Taken*
3	Le Spartiate	74	700	— *Taken*
4	L'Aquilon	74	700	— *Taken*
5	Le Souverain Peuple	74	700	— *Taken*
6	Le Franklin, Blanquet, First Rear Admiral	80	800	— *Taken*
7	L'Orient, Brueys, Admiral and Commander-in-Chief	120	1010	— *Burnt*
8	Le Tonnant	80	800	— *Taken*
9	L'Heureux	74	700	— *Taken*
10	Le Timoléon	74	700	— *Burnt*
11	Le Mercure	74	700	— *Taken*
12	Le Guillaume Tell, Villeneuve, Second Rear Admiral	80	800	— *Escaped*
13	Le Généreux	74	700	— *Escaped*
	FRIGATES.			
14	La Diane	48	300	— *Escaped*
15	La Justice	44	300	— *Escaped*
16	L'Artemise	36	250	— *Burnt*
17	La Sérieuse	36	250	— *Sunk*
	Total,	1190	10710	

List of killed and wounded in his Majesty's Ships, under the Command of Admiral Nelson, 1st of August, 1798.

Theseus. 5 Seamen killed; 1 officer, 24 Seamen, 5 Marines, wounded - Total,	35
Alexander. 1 officer, 13 seamen, killed; 5 officers, 48 Seamen, 5 Marines, wounded	72
Vanguard. 3 Officers, 20 Seamen, 7 Marines, killed; 7 Officers, 60 Seamen, 8 Marines, wounded	105
Minotaur. 2 Officers, 18 Seamen, 3 Marines killed; 4 Officers, 54 Seamen, 6 Marines, wounded	87
Leander. 14 Seamen wounded	14
Swiftsure. 7 Seamen killed; 1 Officer, 19 Seamen, 2 Marines, wounded	29
Audacious. 1 Seaman killed; 2 Officers, 31 Seamen, 2 Marines wounded	36
Defence. 3 Seamen, 1 Marine, killed; 9 Seamen, 2 Marines, wounded	15
Zealous. 1 Seaman killed; 7 Seamen wounded	8
Orion. 1 Officer, 11 Seamen, 1 Marine, killed; 5 Officers, 18 Seamen, 6 Marines, wounded	42
Goliath. 2 Officers, 12 Seamen, 7 Marines, killed; 4 Officers, 28 Seamen, 9 Marines wounded	62
Majestic. 3 Officers, 33 Seamen, 14 Marines killed; 3 Officers, 124 Seamen, 16 Marines, wounded	193
Bellerophon. 4 Officers, 32 Seamen, 13 Marines, killed; 5 Officers, 126 Seamen, 17 Marines, wounded	197
16 Officers, 156 Seamen, 46 Marines, killed; 37 Officers, 562 Seamen, 78 Marines, wounded. - Total,	895

Vanguard, off the Mouth of the Nile, August 11, 1798.

MY LORD,

THE Swiftsure brought in this Morning, La Fortune, a French Corvette of 18 Guns and 70 Men.

Earl St. Vincent. Signed, HORATIO NELSON.

*** Since the above glorious victory, the gallant Admiral has been created a British Peer, under the title of Baron Nelson of the Nile, and Burnham Thorpe, in the County of Norfolk; with the following honourable augmentations to his armorial Ensigns, viz. *A Chief undulated Argent, thereon waves of the sea, from which a palm tree issuant, between a disabled ship, on the dexter, and a ruinous battery, on the sinister, all proper;* and for his Crest, *on a Naval Crown Or, the Chelengk, or Plume of Triumph;* presented him by the Grand Signior, as a mark of his high esteem, and of his sense of the gallant conduct of the said Horatio Baron Nelson in the said glorious and decisive victory; with the motto, "PALMAM QUI MERUIT FERAT;" and to his Supporters, being a Sailor on the dexter, and a Lion on the sinister, the honourable augmentations following, viz. *in the hand of the Sailor a Palm Branch, and another in the paw of the Lion, both proper, with the addition of a tri-coloured Flag and Staff in the mouth of the latter;* which augmentations to the Supporters to be borne by the said Horatio Baron Nelson, and by those to whom the said dignity shall descend, in virtue of his Majesty's Letters Patent of Creation; and that the same may be first duly exemplified according to the Laws of Arms, and recorded in the Herald's Office.

ADDITIONAL INFORMATION;

CONTAINING VERY INTERESTING PARTICULARS RESPECTING THE FATE OF THE LEANDER.

THE LEANDER, of fifty guns, commanded by Capt. T. B. Thompson, with Capt. Berry on board, first Captain to Admiral Nelson, having his Dispatches for Lord St. Vincent, who was cruizing off Cadiz, was captured by Le Genereux, of seventy-four guns, one of the French Ships which had escaped in the above Engagement.—The Leander fought her within Pistol-shot for six hours and thirty-five minutes (notwithstanding the part she took in the Engagement of the Nile, when she broke the French Line). In this action with the Genereux, she had thirty-five killed, and fifty-seven wounded, every mast, yard, shroud, and stay, cut away, and only twelve barrels of powder remaining in her: Le Genereux had 900 men on board, of which 100 were killed, and 188 wounded, according to her Surgeon's report.—Capt. Thompson received two wounds from shot, and two from splinters, and also a shot just above the right knee, and another that took off part of his ear; but we add, as an unparalleled instance, of the Leander killing between eighty and ninety more of the enemy than she had actually men on board her at the commencement of the action, as upwards of one hundred of Capt. Thompson's crew, two Lieutenants, and officers in proportion, had been put on board the French Prizes.—The official accounts extracted from the French Papers, contain the following interesting information concerning the fate of their Navy during the above Engagement with Admiral Nelson:—Killed, drowned, burnt, and lost, 5225.—Total number of the Crews on board the French Vessels burnt, taken, or sunk, according to Certificates of the Commissioners and Officers of the different Vessels, amount to 8930.—Letters from Sir Morton Eden, his Majesty's Envoy at Vienna, are arrived, which state, that Commodore Trowbridge, having been joined by a reinforcement of Fire Ships and Bomb Ketches from Constantinople, had on the 1st of September, attacked the French Fleet of Transports in the Port of Alexandria, and burnt near 400 Sail of Vessels, which Admiral Nelson was obliged to leave unaccomplished after the above memorable Battle of the Nile, not having either Bomb-Vessels or Fire Ships with him.—We have also the Satisfaction to state, that the Inhabitants of Malta, tired of the Treachery of the French, had attacked and driven the whole of them into the Forts of Valetta and St. Elmo; and having cut off all Supplies of Water from the Garrison, the French had twice offered to capitulate, which was rejected, the Inhabitants insisting they should surrender at Discretion.

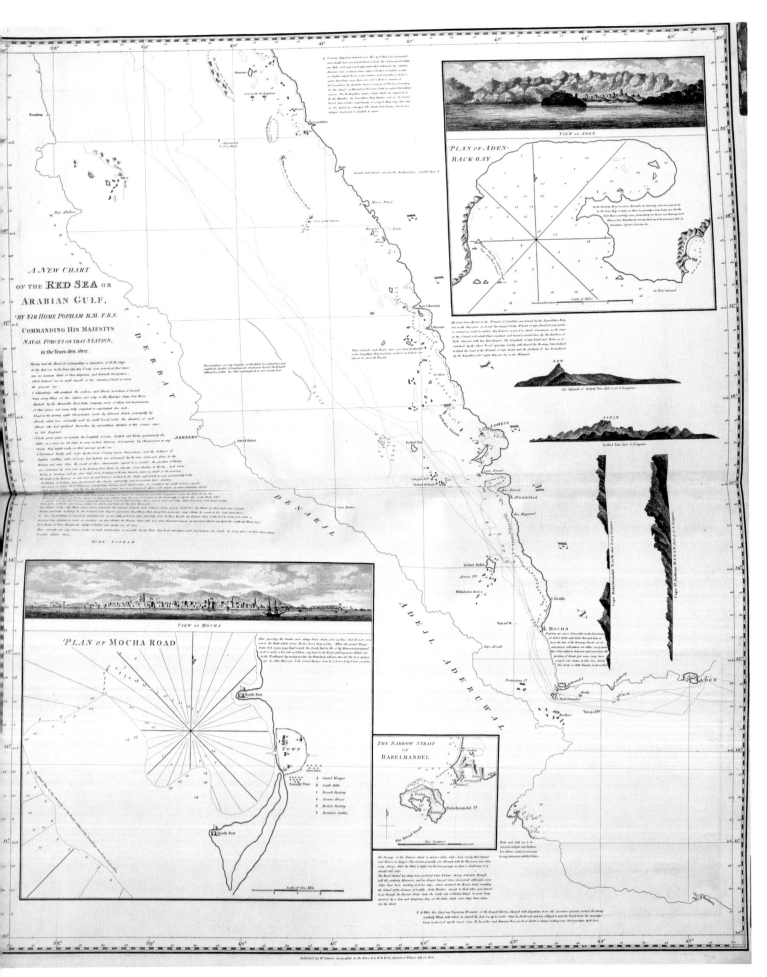

| THE RED SEA BY SIR HOME RIGGS POPHAM, 1801–2 |

Admiral Popham led a highly successful, if controversial, naval career. Between 1787 and 1793 it seems he was personally trading in India and the Far East, of which the East India Company took a dim view, but he learned surveying techniques and carried out many surveys of these waters. He was attached to the Duke of York in Flanders ashore as 'superintendent of inland navigation' and then, whilst 'commanding His Majesty's Naval Forces' in the Red Sea in 1801 and 1802, he supervised surveys, mindful of Bonaparte's ambitions to bring his army to India and of their Lordships' orders to send surveys back for the fledgling British Hydrographic Office.

This survey shows ships' tracks and has incorporated excellent navigational views and details of harbours. It was engraved and published by William Faden in 1804. Popham's surveying talents were recognized when he was appointed to the Chart Committee of the Admiralty and by his election as a Fellow of the Royal Society. They extended to writing a new system of signalling which was adopted by the Royal Navy and used by Nelson at Trafalgar to send his famous signal. (Reproduced by courtesy of the Royal Geographical Society with IBG, 14.C.78 No. 43)

| RIGHT | **PASSAGE THROUGH ORE SUND BETWEEN DENMARK AND SWEDEN, WITH SOUNDINGS, 1801** | The British needed to break up the League of Armed Neutrality formed by Czar Paul of Russia in 1801 with the Danes, Prussians and Swedes – equivalent to a threat of war – to ensure vital supplies of mast timber and hemp for ships and to prevent an imbalance of numbers of ships of the line in Bonaparte's favour. Henry Addington's government decided to send a squadron into the Baltic to either attack the Russians at Rival or to 'neutralize' the Danish fleet at Copenhagen; other countries would then secede from the alliance. Nelson, as Admiral Hyde Parker's second-in-command, and despite Parker's caution, planned the attack, which took place on 2 April 1801. While Faden's chart of the Strait of Ore Sund past Copenhagen, published just after the battle on 12 April, was not available to Nelson's sailing master, Thomas Atkinson, it was based on surveys that would have been. These were compiled by Professor Christian Carl Lous, who worked with Admirals Andreas Lous and Johan Nordenankar, Swedish naval cartographers in the latter part of the eighteenth century. They had completed surveys of the Kattegat and Baltic between 1769 and 1773 and gave enough detail around Copenhagen, including transits to approach the harbour, for Nelson to know that there was a good chance of getting the smaller ships of the line close enough to fight the anchored Danish fleet. However, without up-to-date charts with accurate details on gradient, depth and profile of the seabed between the Middle Ground shoal and the Trekoner fort, he was unable to confirm that there was enough water for at least 74-gun ships of the line to anchor. (The National Archives {PRO} WO 78/2501)

| BELOW | **SKETCH OF THE BATTLE OF COPENHAGEN BY CAPTAIN WILLIAM BLIGH, 1801** | By the time of Copenhagen Captain Bligh, in command of the *Glatton* (54 guns), was a highly experienced navigator and hydrographer, having sailed as Captain Cook's sailing master, aged 23, on his third and final voyage. On 1 April, the night before the battle, Bligh worked with Captain Hardy supervising the hazardous job of surveying the shallow waters around the Danish fleet. This allowed Nelson to surprise the Danes by bringing his ships to attack in front of their anchored line, between them and the Middle Ground shoal.

During the battle there was very little room to manoeuvre and although the Danish fleet was destroyed, it was at an enormous cost in terms of lives to both sides. Furthermore, the Czar, unbeknownst to Nelson, had been assassinated on 23 March and so the alliance would have collapsed anyway: such are the exigencies of war.

The next day Bligh drew this fascinating elevation which shows the positions of the British and Danish fleets, with Copenhagen behind, a rare on-the-spot record of the actual scene. Bligh had laid his ship alongside the Danish flagship, *Danebrog*, and, with the exceptional loss of only 17 of his crew, forced her to strike her colours. For this Nelson gave Bligh the rare honour of inviting him on board the quarterdeck of his flagship, *Elephant*, for public congratulation. (UKHO © British Crown Copyright)

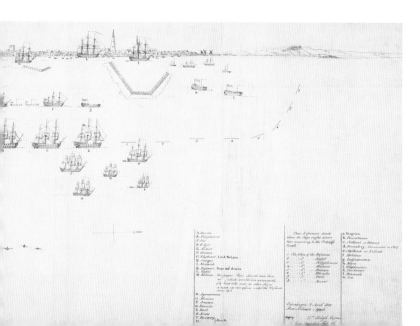

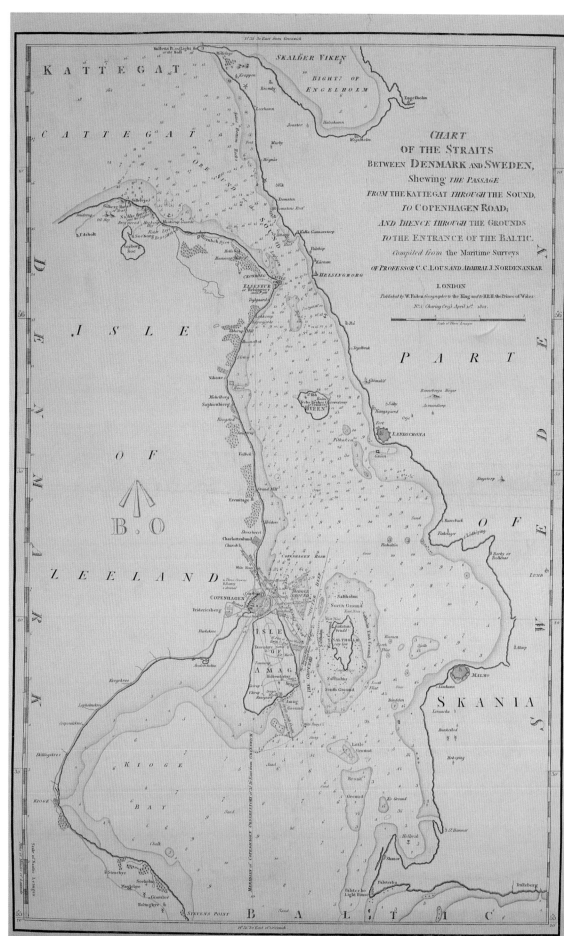

| **TRACK CHART OF THE *GOLIATH* ON THE JAMAICA STATION, 1802** | After distinguishing herself at the Battle of the Nile, the *Goliath* (74 guns) was sent out to the Jamaica station to monitor the fragmenting situation in nearby Haiti, France's most profitable West Indies' colony. Spain had ceded the western part, San Domingo or Saint Dominique, to France in 1697, and prosperous sugar and coffee plantations had been developed. The Black slaves rebelled under their leader Toussaint L'Ouverture and Bonaparte sent out a large punitive army in 1802, but yellow fever and elusive guerrilla bands defeated his brother-in-law, General Charles Leclerc. In an attempt to ensure that the situation in Haiti did not influence a similar slave revolt in their nearby colony of Jamaica, the British had invaded Haiti on 20 September 1793 and did not withdraw troops until 1798. The US President, Thomas Jefferson, anxious to forestall the use of Haiti as a French base to invade Louisiana, provided assistance to the Haitians and by 1804 Haiti was the second European colony after America to achieve independence.

The intensity of the patrol can be appreciated by *Goliath*'s track shown on the working chart, drawn by her sailing master, I Engledue, which is particularly heavy in the Jamaica Channel, between Jamaica and the westward peninsula of Haiti. *Goliath* had joined the squadron from Halifax in Canada, and finished, as the ship's track shows on the chart by approaching the coast of south-eastern Cuba and then sailing north between Cuba and Haiti along the Windward Passage past Great Inagua Island. Leaving the station along Crooked Island Passage between Long Island and Acklins Island, adjacent to 'Watlins' Island, now called San Salvador, she made a rendezvous with a West Indies convoy to escort it to Portsmouth. The chart has latitude and longitude scales and the track would mostly have been fixed with noon sun sights – known as a sun-run-sun – hence the diagonally sharp noted changes of course. (© National Maritime Museum, London, F0027)

| APPROACHES TO THE SCHELDT BY CAPTAIN WILLIAM BLIGH, 1803 |

The possibility of landing a large army on the European continent to support Austria and the Netherlands was a significant part of British strategy against Napoleon. Of immediate importance was a good chart for the blockading fleet off Flushing. Captain Bligh was appointed in October 1803 to make an accurate survey of the approaches to the Scheldt. Sending out the ship's cutters, and anchoring them and the ship during strong tidal flows, he took soundings and bearings to lay down the outline of the coast on a grid anchored to latitude, starting at 51° 03', sub-divided with nine 1-league squares (27 miles) up to 51° 48'. It gives depths in fathoms (6 feet), with those in brown gained from Dutch maps, and clearing bearings to enable an approach clear of shoals and sandbanks. It allows navigation to the mouth of the River Scheldt, the river that drains part of northern France, as the River Escaut, through Cambrai and Valenciennes to Antwerp. Bligh also drew coastal elevations of the Flanders' coast. (UKHO © British Crown Copyright)

| THE ACTION BETWEEN COMMODORE NATHANIEL DANCE AND REAR-ADMIRAL LINOIS OFF MALACCA, 1804 |

Napoleon had little understanding of naval strategy or tactics, but nonetheless decided that, besides attempting an invasion of Britain across the English Channel, he would set up some raiding squadrons overseas to harry the British. One area in which he might succeed with this strategy was in the Indian Ocean where Mauritius was available as a base. Rear-Admiral Linois, with a squadron of four frigates led by his flagship *Marengo*, had raided the East India Company's factory at Bencoolen, Sumatra, and on 14 February 1804 he waited about 50 miles off the Malayan coast in the South China Sea on the same latitude as Mersing, knowing that the homeward bound East India convoy was due and would almost certainly take this route to go into the eastern entrance of the Malacca Strait from the Singapore Strait, to make for India.

Commodore Dance had a convoy of 16 East Indiamen, 11 merchantmen and a brig when he first saw Linois. He detached four East Indiamen that could be mistaken at a distance for small men-of-war, the *Alfred*, *Royal George*, *Bombay Castle* and *Hope*, to investigate. As night approached, both fleets anchored, the convoy displaying similar lights to British men-of-war, but with Linois holding the weather gage to the south west. The next morning Linois tried to cut off the stern-most ships. Dance, with no escort, knew he had to rely on bluff, and the four East Indiamen boldly formed a line of battle with Royal Navy ensigns flying, tacked straight to the French who, after some long-range exchange of shot, fled.

Dance drew this chart when he got back to London, where it was published by William Daniell. Dance was able to plot the actual events as five stages in relation to the adjacent Malayan coast and nearby islands of Palau Aur and Palau Tinggi. For his victory he was knighted, given £5000 and a £500 per year pension plus £50,000 to distribute among the ships' companies. Napoleon said of Linois however: 'He has made the French flag the laughing stock of the Universe'. (© National Maritime Museum, London, F0316)

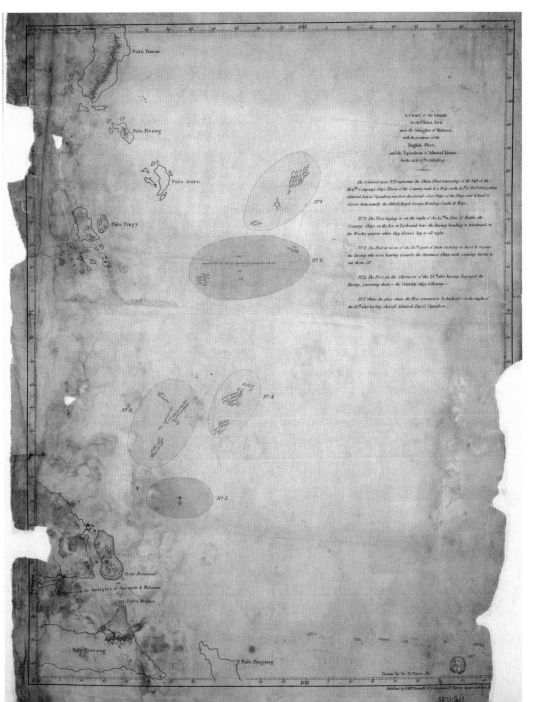

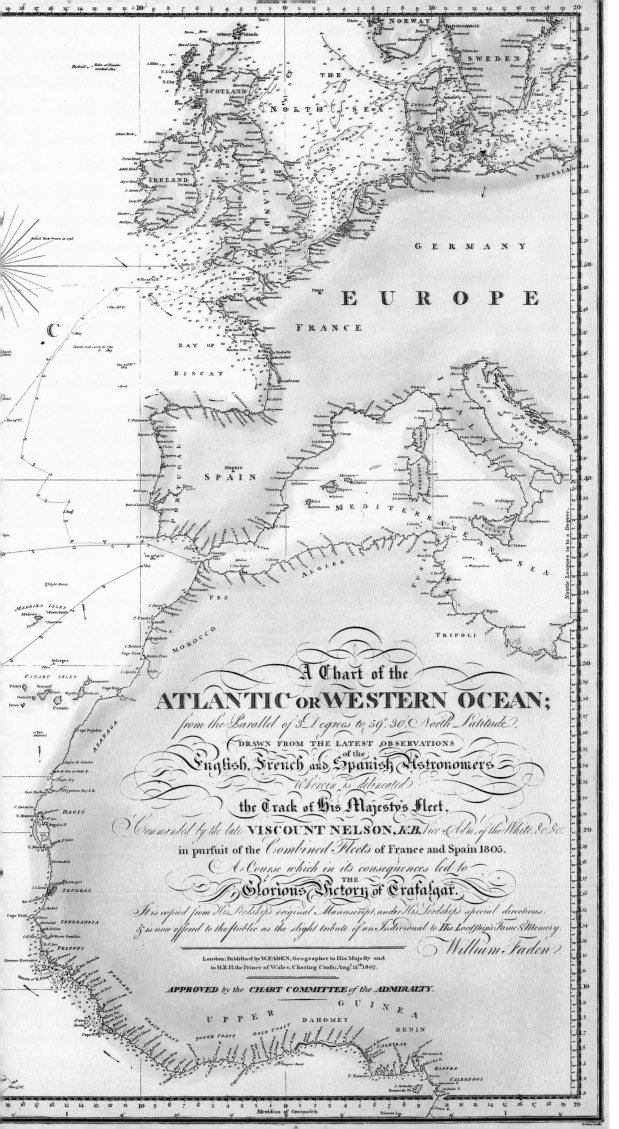

A Chart of the
ATLANTIC OR WESTERN OCEAN;
from the Parallel of 3 Degrees to 59°. 30' North Latitude
DRAWN FROM THE LATEST OBSERVATIONS
of the
English, French and Spanish Astronomers
Wherein is delineated
the Track of His Majesty's Fleet,
Commanded by the late VISCOUNT NELSON, *K.B. Vice Adm. of the White &c &c.*
in pursuit of the *Combined Fleets* of France and Spain 1805.
A Course which in its consequences led to
THE
Glorious Victory of Trafalgar.
It is copied from His Lordship's original Manuscript, under His Lordship's special directions.
& is now offered to the public as the slight tribute of an Individual to His Lordship's Fame & Memory.
William Faden.

London: Published by W. FADEN, Geographer to His Majesty and
to H.R.H. the Prince of Wales, Charing Cross, Aug'st 12th 1807.

APPROVED by the **CHART COMMITTEE** of the **ADMIRALTY.**

| CHART OF THE ATLANTIC SHOWING ADMIRAL
NELSON'S PURSUIT OF ADMIRAL VILLENEUVE, 1807 |
The chart is dated 1807 and is one of the first Atlantic charts to
be approved by the Chart Committee of the Admiralty, formed
to accelerate the distribution of charts into the fleet, which had
hitherto been delayed by the Hydrographer, Alexander Dalrymple,
who was reluctant to release charts until he was satisfied as to
their perfection.

Published by William Faden, it dramatically shows almost
every day-by-day noon-sight position, with the track of Nelson
chasing Villeneuve out to the West Indies and back, between 12
May and 18 July 1805, along with Admiral Calder's track to
intercept Villeneuve on his return.

As part of his invasion plan of Britain Napoleon had intended
to distract the Mediterranean Fleet by encouraging it on a chase of
the Toulon Fleet, commanded by Villeneuve, across the Atlantic
to be lost in a fruitless search among the Caribbean islands, while
Villeneuve made his way back to form a larger force with other
squadrons that could overwhelm the Channel Fleet and allow the
invasion ships carrying the troops to leave Boulogne. (UKHO
© British Crown Copyright)

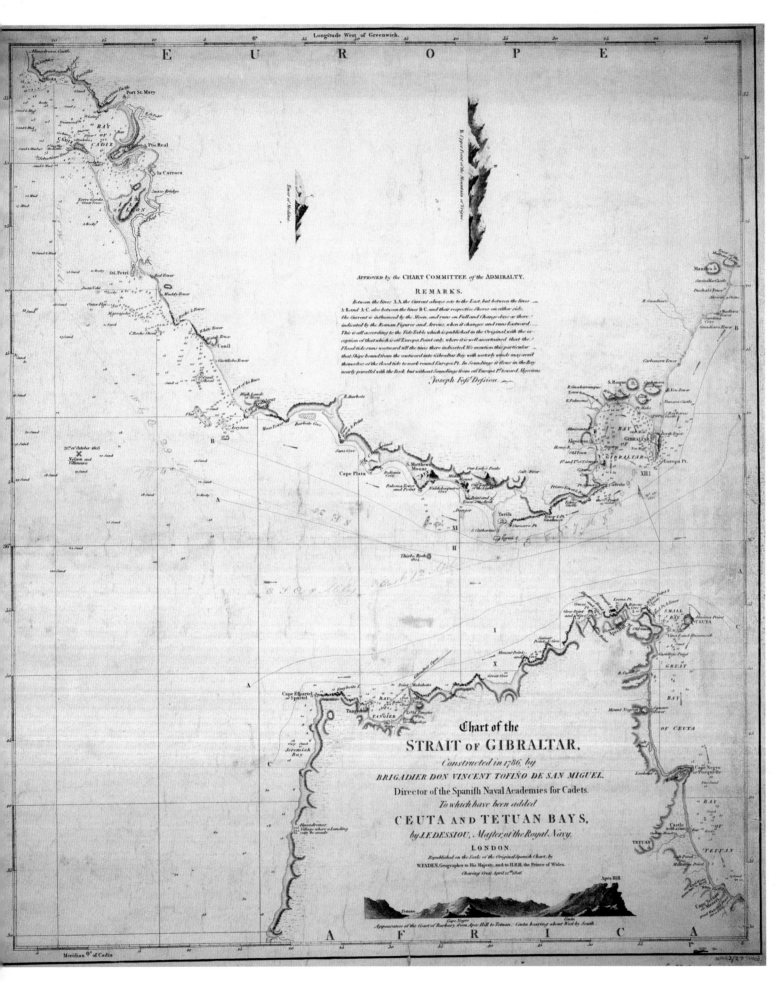

Chart of the STRAIT of GIBRALTAR,

Constructed in 1786, by

BRIGADIER DON VINCENT TOFIÑO DE SAN MIGUEL,

Director of the Spanish Naval Academies for Cadets.

To which have been added

CEUTA AND TETUAN BAYS,

by J.F. DESSIOU, Master of the Royal Navy.

LONDON.

Republished on the Scale of the Original Spanish Chart, by
W. FADEN, Geographer to His Majesty, and to H.R.H. the Prince of Wales.

Charing Cross, April 12th 1806.

| **CHART OF THE STRAIT OF GIBRALTAR, SHOWING THE BATTLE OF TRAFALGAR, 1807** |

The Battle of Trafalgar needs little introduction as the tactics and results have been debated in countless books. However, its significance for the future shape of Europe was immense. It ended forever Napoleon's muddled maritime aspirations to invade Britain and gave her command of the sea, ensuring the continuing supply of food and materiel from her growing colonies with which to ultimately win the fight on land. It boosted, too, the rest of Europe's determination to stop Napoleon's ambitions and fuelled the uprising in Spain against French over-lordship and ultimately to her alliance with Britain.

It is unsurprising that this chart, brought out six months after the Battle of Trafalgar on 12 April 1806, should patriotically mark the spot of the battle by crossed guns. J F Dessiou, a highly respected master in the Royal Navy has added his own surveys of Ceuta and Tetuan Bays and knowledge of currents to this essentially Spanish chart, created by Brigadier Don Vincent Tofino de San Miguel, Director of the Spanish Naval Academies. It was one of 200 charts approved by the Chart Committee of the Admiralty. It is useful for an interested public in that it shows the site of the battle in relation to the Spanish coast, including Cadiz, to the safety of which the Franco-Spanish fleet was heading when it was attacked by the British, and also Gibraltar to where a squadron of Nelson's fleet had departed for re-victualling and repairs, leaving him with less ships than Villeneuve. (© National Maritime Museum, London, F1968)

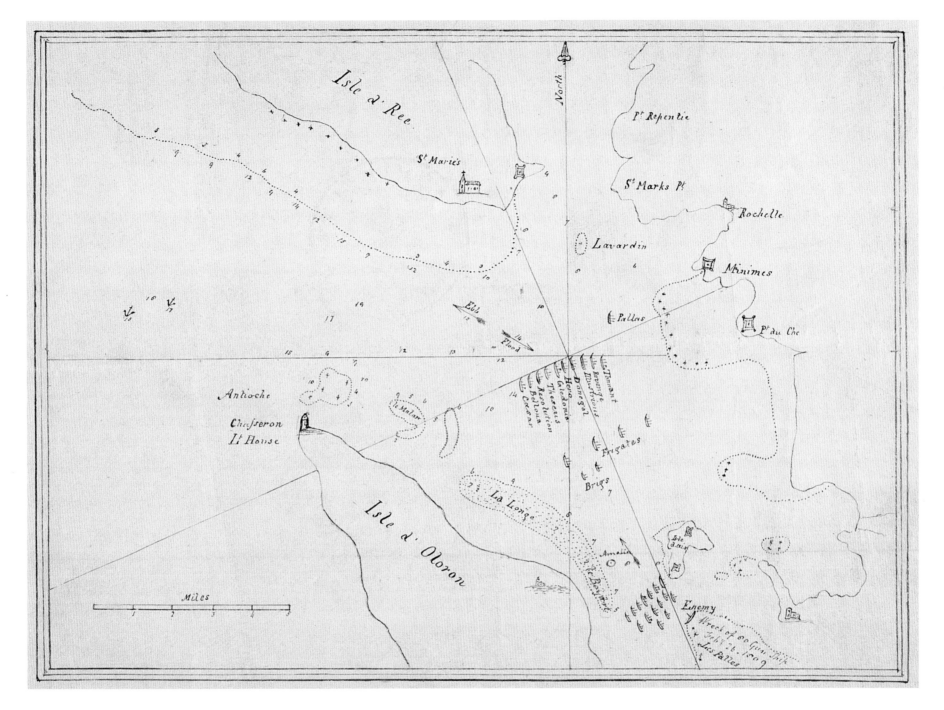

| THE BATTLE OF AIX AND BASQUE ROADS BY LORD THOMAS COCHRANE,
1809 | In February 1809 a French squadron under Admiral Willaumez escaped from Brest and, missing its intended port of L'Orient, hastily sought shelter, and joined up with the Rochefort squadron under Admiral Zacharie-Jacques-Théodore Allemand, making 11 ships of the line at the anchorage of Aix Roads in the estuary of the River Charente, which leads into the great arsenal of Rochefort and the harbour of La Rochelle.

The Admiralty realized an opportunity and sent Admiral Gambier's squadron to watch and wait. The tides and sandbanks made the normal method of assault difficult and the Admiralty sent a young but brilliant naval captain, Lord Cochrane, to plan and execute a fireship attack. Cochrane drew up this chart with which to brief his force.

Admiral Allemand, in anticipation of any British attack, had arranged his squadron in two lines across the 2-mile wide entrance channel between the fort on the island of D'Aix and the Boyart shoal, with a strong floating wooden boom in front, three frigates to starboard of the formation, and 73 small boats packed with men to board and tow away any fireships.

On 11 April Cochrane launched his attack with 20 fireships packed with explosives and Colonel William Congreve's rockets. Cochrane, in the leading fireship, bore down on the French fleet, propelled by a south westerly gale and a strong flood tide at 9 p.m., breaking through the boom. The French, in confusion, cut their mooring cables and drifted on to the Pallas mud flats, easy targets the next morning as the tide ebbed leaving them high and dry. However, Gambier neglected to follow up the advantage until the early afternoon of the next day, by which time many of the French had re-floated. Four French ships were taken or burnt, but Cochrane, his repeated signals for Gambier to engage disregarded, denounced his Admiral's leadership, and a court martial was held at which Gambier was exonerated. (Admiralty Library Manuscript Collection: F/21)

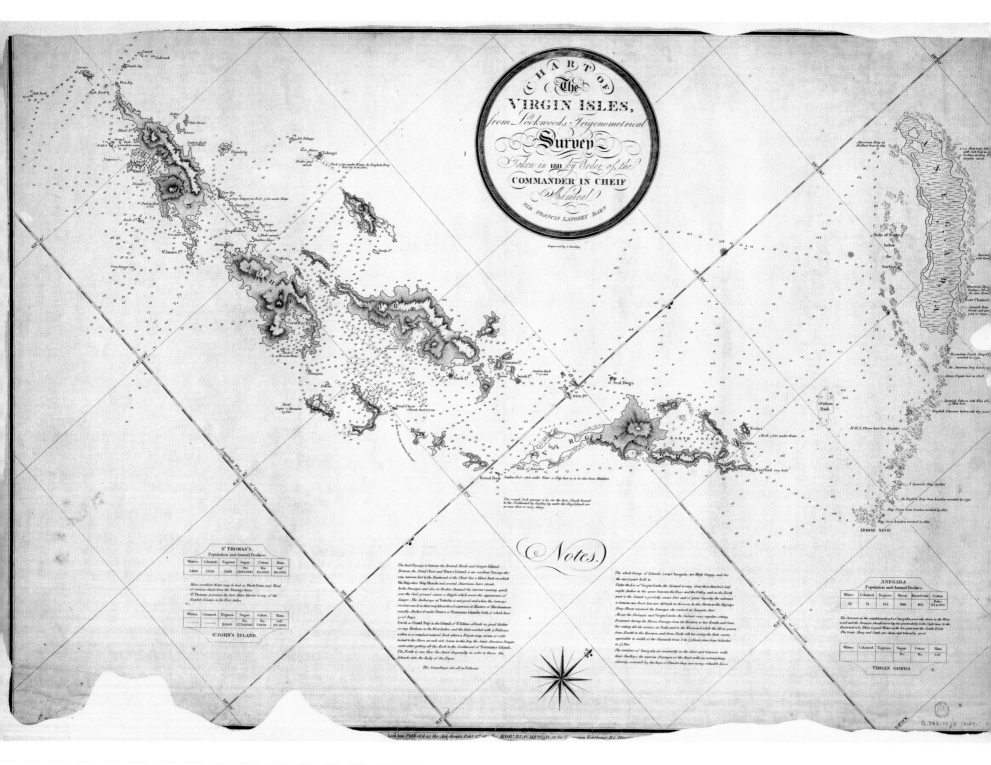

| TRIGONOMETRICAL CHART OF THE VIRGIN ISLANDS, 1812 | By 1807 the Admiralty had appointed the Chart Committee of the Admiralty to sort through some 1000 British commercial charts, known as Bluebacks from the blue lining that distinguished them from the Admiralty chart, and purchase sufficient to provide a portfolio for the fleet. The Committee came to the unfortunate conclusion that all charts, including Admiralty charts, were not of a safe standard of accuracy. They bought some 200 of the least worse, of which half were from Faden, but none from the publisher, Robert Blachford. Perhaps this example, published by Blachford in 1812, was not considered by the Committee, although it was based on an 1811 survey carried out on the order of the Commander-in-Chief West Indies, Admiral Sir Francis Laforey, which used the trigonometrical survey technique developed by Murdoch Mackenzie.

Discovered by Columbus, the Virgin Islands were occupied by the Danish in 1666, who were keen, as were so many European countries , to supplement their small tropical colonies along the Coromandel Coast and at Accra on the Gold Coast in West Africa. The Danish West Indies, as they were called, prospered until the war with Britain in 1801, from which time the British occupied them until 1815. Admiral Laforey, had captained the *Spartiate* at the Battle of Trafalgar and was appointed Commander-in-Chief West Indies based at Barbados in 1811, where he realized the need for better charts for both his men-of-war and for the burgeoning commercial shipping using the Virgin Islands port of Charlotte Amalie, and he ordered his surveyors to chart them. The 14 wrecks marked off the north coast of Anegada bear testimony to the need. (© National Maritime Museum, London, F0120)

| RIGHT | **SUGGESTED PLAN OF ATTACK OF WEST SCHELDT, BY CAPTAIN NICHOLAS TOMLINSON, 1811** | Returned to power, the port of Antwerp and the dockyard of Flushing on the Dutch island of Walcheren at the mouth of the River Scheldt were still key to Napoleon's plans to invade England where he had ships building. After the abortive invasion attempt by the British in 1809 that resulted in 4000 dead from Walcheren fever, the French were still blockaded in 1811 when Captain Tomlinson drew this proposal to attack with fireships. We would call it a feasibility study today, and it shows the fortifications, depths and channels, along with suggested formation of the attacking force to cripple the French squadron. Although his plan was not put into action by the Admiralty it shows the aggressive thinking of those officers at the scene encouraged by their Lordships, and is an example of how such attacks were then planned. (© National Maritime Museum, London, F0464)

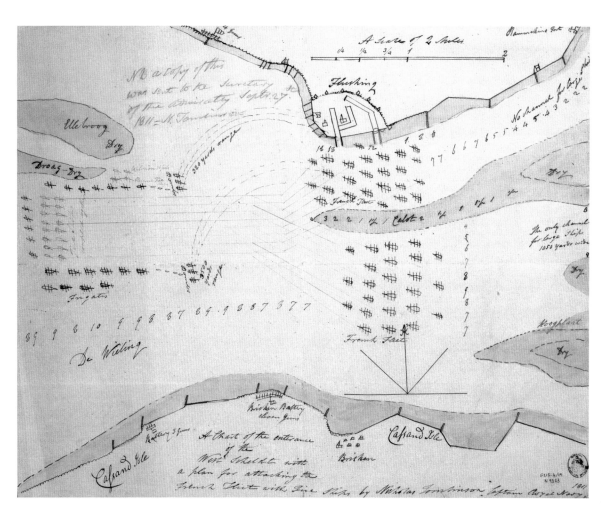

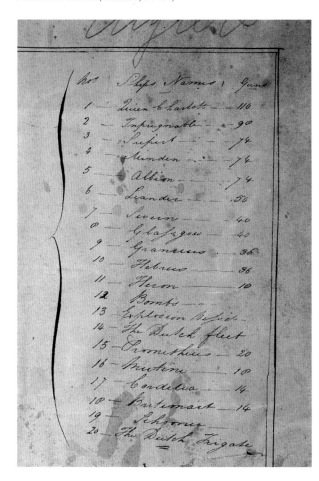

|RIGHT | **BOMBARDMENT OF ALGIERS BY J B SANDSBURY, 1816** | The elimination of piracy in the Mediterranean became possible during the peace after the Napoleonic Wars and was achieved when a combined Dutch and British fleet of 11 British men-of-war and four Dutch, led by the *Queen Charlotte* of 110 guns, with bomb and explosion vessels, bombarded Algiers on 27 August 1816, as featured on this chart. The key (detail above) lists the ships, with the guns they mounted. The chart shows the attack formation against the town and harbour. It is by J B Sandsbury, who is thought to have been one of the ship's masters, and provided a visual report to the Admiralty. They paved the way for France to attack Algiers in 1831 and annexe the country. (© National Maritime Museum, London, F0011)

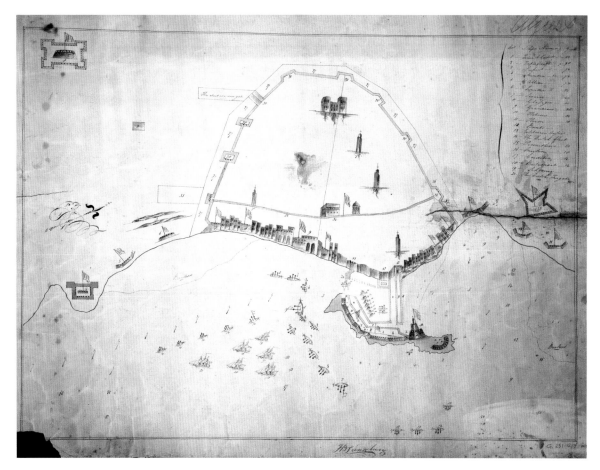

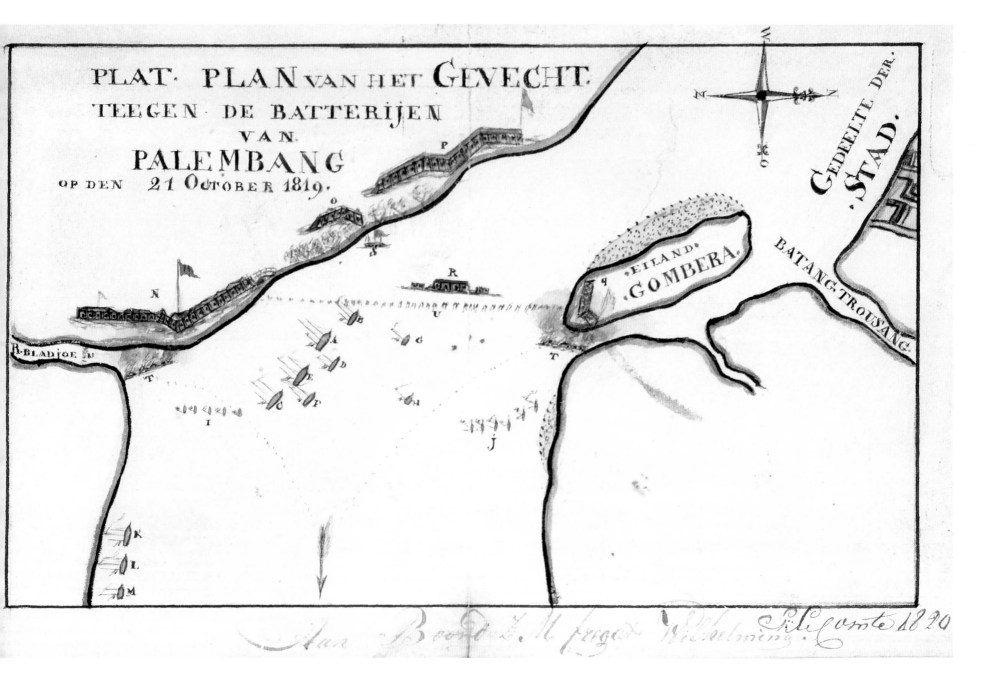

| ABOVE | **THE DUTCH RE-CAPTURE OF PALEMBANG (SUMATRA) BY PIETER LE COMTE, 1819** | After Napoleon's final defeat in 1815 the Dutch wanted to re-establish their influence and rule over their colonies in the Far East. The island of Sumatra, rich with spices and raw commodities, had been governed by Sir Thomas Raffles from 1811 while the Netherlands was occupied by Napoleon's forces. Returned to the Dutch in 1815 by the British, who sought to maintain a balance of colonies in the Far East between the maritime powers of Europe and the United States, a Dutch naval flotilla sailed up the Palembang river to force the Sultan to accept their rule. This chart, drawn by a naval officer present, who made a number of drawings in situ on board the frigate *Wilhelmina*, shows how the assault was planned with an attacking force of frigates, brigs and troop-carrying transports that would land troops to capture the Sultan's palace, the fort and the town. (Scheepvart Museum, Netherlands)

| RIGHT | **THE BATTLE OF NAVARINO BY LIEUTENANT A B BECHER, 1827** | The nationalistic uprising by the Greeks against the Ottoman Empire in 1821 sparked a wave of sympathy in Britain and France, who valued Hellenic cultural traditions. The poet Lord Byron was among a group of sympathizers who went out to fight for their cause. Lord Cochrane, who had lead the navies of Chile and Brazil in their fights for independence, was asked by the Greeks to put together a fleet to fight the Turks. When the Turkish sultan sought Egyptian help, other nations' interests were compromised and Russia, France and Britain sent a combined fleet under Vice-Admiral Sir Edward Codrington to enforce a truce and persuade the Turks to negotiate an acceptable treaty.

The chart was drawn by Lieutenant Becher, the first Naval Assistant at the Hydrographic Office appointed in 1823, from an original chart by Lieutenant S Smyth in HMS *Dartmouth*, part of the British fleet in the action in Navarino Bay on the western side of the Peloponnese peninsula on 27 October 1827. It depicts the last battle to be fought under sail. The combined French, British and Russian squadrons (each nationality is shown by colour coding), totalling 12 ships of the line and 14 frigates, with smaller ships, anchored in an arc around the bay enclosing a Turkish and Egyptian fleet of 7 ships of the line, 15 frigates and 26 corvettes. As tension mounted, a small ship taking a message from Codrington was shot at and within minutes British and French gunners were firing heavily. In an action lasting two and a half hours all but one of the Turkish and Egyptian ships were either sunk or set on fire. (© National Maritime Museum, London, F0159)

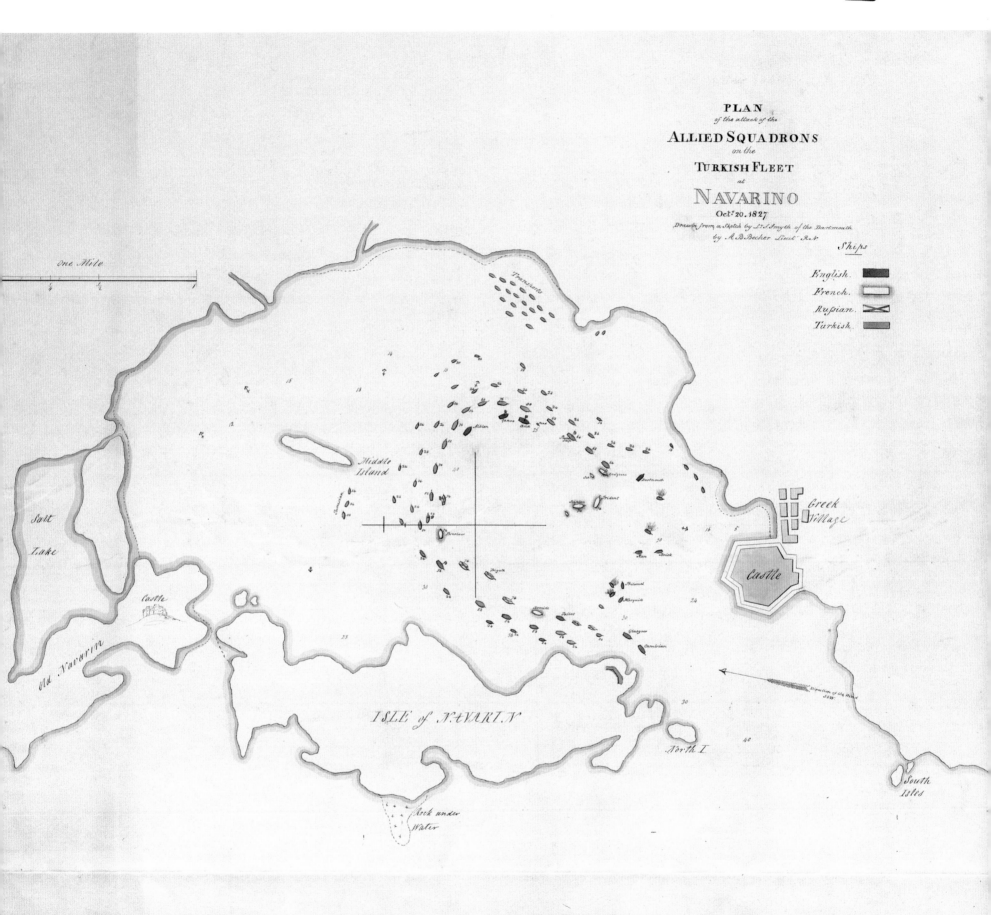

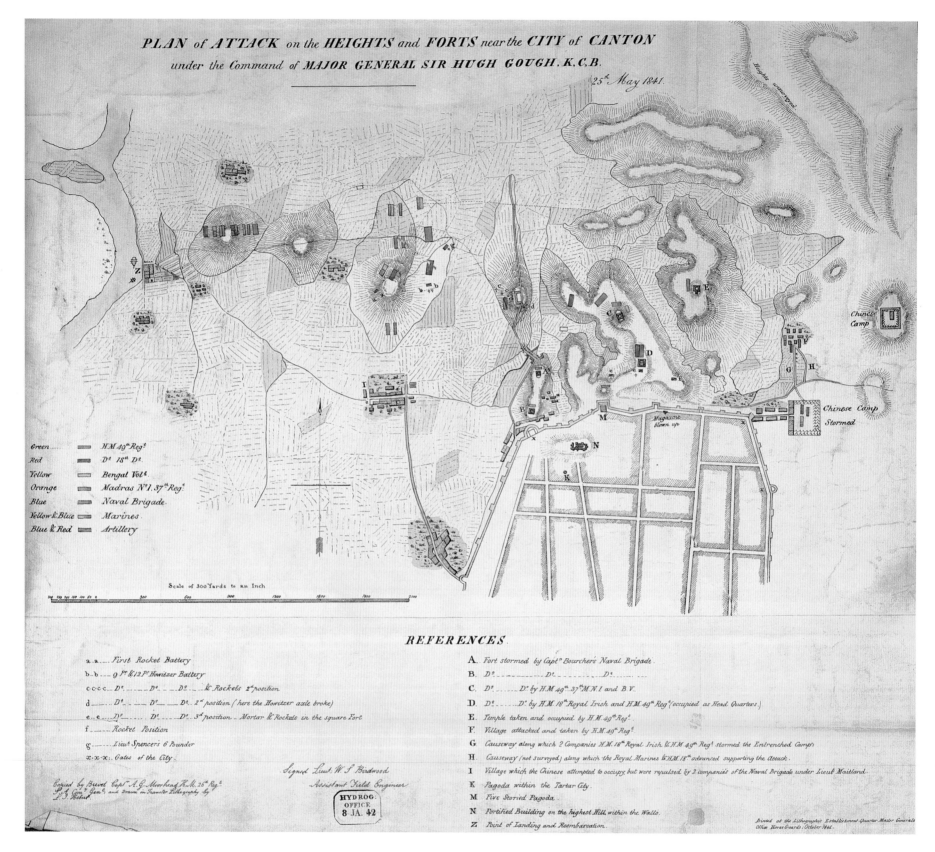

PLAN of ATTACK on the HEIGHTS and FORTS near the CITY of CANTON
under the Command of MAJOR GENERAL SIR HUGH GOUGH, K.C.B.
25th May 1841.

Green ——— H.M 49th Regt.
Red ——— Do 18th Do.
Yellow ——— Bengal Volrs.
Orange ——— Madras No 1. 37th Regt.
Blue ——— Naval Brigade.
Yellow & Blue ——— Marines.
Blue & Red ——— Artillery.

Scale of 300 Yards to an Inch

REFERENCES

a.a.— First Rocket Battery
b.b.— 9 Pr & 12 Pr Howitzer Battery
c.c.c.— Do — Do — Do & Rockets 2d position
d.— Do — Do — Do. 2d position (here the Howitzer axle broke)
e.e.— Do.— Do.— Do.— 3d position - Mortar & Rockets in the square Fort
f.— Rocket Position
g.— Lieut Spencers 6 Pounder
x.x.x.— Gates of the City.

Copied by Brevet Capt. A.G. Moorhead H.M. 26th Regt.
J.G. Cor. Gen's and Drawn in Transfer Lithography by

Signed Lieut. W.S. Birdwood
Assistant Field Engineer
HYDROG:
OFFICE
8 JA. 42

A.— Fort stormed by Capt Bourchers Naval Brigade.
B.— Do.— Do.— Do.
C.— Do.— Do. by H.M. 49th 37th M.N.1 and B.V.
D.— Do.— Do. by H.M. 18th Royal Irish and H.M. 49th Regt (occupied as Head Quarters.)
E.— Temple taken and occupied by H.M. 49th Regt.
F.— Village attacked and taken by H.M. 49th Regt.
G.— Causeway along which 2 Companies H.M. 18th Royal Irish & H.M. 49th Regt stormed the Entrenched Camps.
H.— Causeway (not surveyed) along which the Royal Marines & H.M. 18th advanced supporting the Attack.
I.— Village which the Chinese attempted to occupy, but were repulsed by 2 companies of the Naval Brigade under Lieut Maitland.
K.— Pagoda within the Tartar City.
M.— Five Storied Pagoda.
N.— Fortified Building on the highest Hill, within the Walls.
Z.— Point of Landing and Reembarcation.

Printed at the Lithographic Establishment Quarter Master Generals
Office Horse Guards : October 1841.

| **PLAN OF ATTACK ON FORTS AND THE CITY OF CANTON BY LIEUTENANT S J BIRDWOOD, 1841** | The naval brigades of the Royal Navy came about from the need and opportunity to supplement the army's cannon usually during a naval landing or amphibious operation. The navy frequently landed guns during the Napoleonic Wars and later during the Crimean War, and the concept of a naval brigade, who went ashore to fight alongside the army, arises from then.

The Chinese Government's resistance to British traders importing opium from India, which had appalling consequences for the Chinese population, led to the first Opium War of 1839–42.

This carefully drawn map of the final battle of the war records the fall of Canton (Guangzhou today) on 25 May 1841. It is by an army engineer, Lieutenant Birdwood, and shows the role of two naval brigades in the assault on key positions, and the point of landing and embarkation of the troops by the navy. Printed by the Army Lithographic Establishment in Horseguards, London, a copy was sent to the Hydrographic Office to be kept with other plans and surveys of the Canton area, and be available for future planning or for reference in drawing up a detailed chart of the Canton Estuary and approaches. (Admiralty Library Manuscript Collection: A/63)

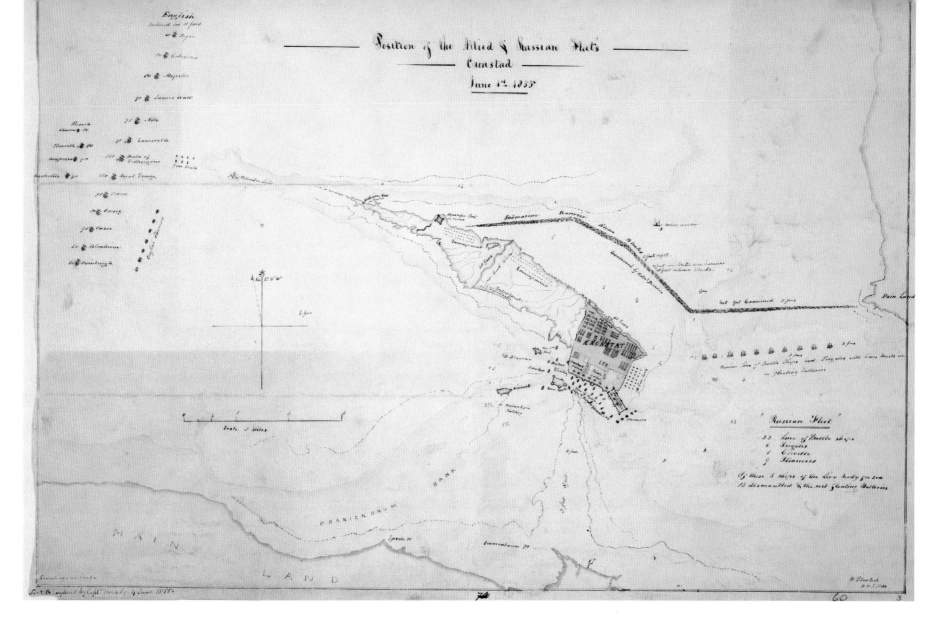

| ABOVE | CHART WITH POSITIONS OF THE ALLIED AND RUSSIAN FLEETS AT KRONSTADT BY W SILVERLOCK, 1855 | The war with Russia to prevent her domination of Turkey, known as the Crimean War, was also fought out in the Baltic, mainly by the British. To prevent the Russian fleet at Kronstadt from prosecuting the Russian war around the Black Sea, the British decided to attack. This chart by Captain George Rodney Mundy's master. W Silverlock, with soundings taken from his ship the *Nile*, one of the first wooden sailing ships to be converted to propeller-driven, was forwarded to the War Office in June 1855. It showed the strength of the fort and how the Russians had supplemented it with a fleet of 22 ships of the line, of which five were ready for sea, but the remainder had been set up as floating gun batteries. Once the strength of Kronstadt was appreciated by the War Office from the information on this chart, an attack was planned on the seemingly easier fort at Sveaborg, near Helsinki, and a bombardment took the fort on 11 August. Realizing that Kronstadt, which protected the approaches to St Petersburg, would be next, put pressure on the Tsar to discuss peace terms, and the allies' preparations for a massive attack in the summer of 1856 became unnecessary. (The National Archives {PRO} WO 78/1130)

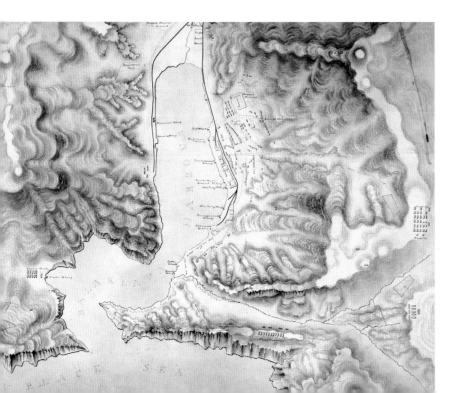

| LEFT | MAP OF BALAKLAVA HARBOUR, 1855 | In situations where their presence would be required for some time, it was always useful for naval ships to have a detailed map of an area to show more of the layout and disposition of the harbours and wharves, along with principal buildings, than would be shown on a maritime chart, although later Admiralty and other nations' charts put details of dockyards and naval bases onto their harbour charts. This survey showing the terrain of Balaklava harbour in the Crimean penin-sula, is attractively but accurately drawn to a scale of 24 inches to the mile. Produced under the direction of Major-General Richard Airey, the Quarter-Master General under Lord Raglan, it was copied and made available by the Director of Topographical and Statistical Depot in the War Department, and used by both Services. The small harbour of Balaklava was the British Headquarters but could barely take all the transports trying to offload stores and equipment needed during the Crimean War.

The aim of the allies in helping Turkey was to prevent Russian domination of the Black Sea by crushing the Russian Black Sea Fleet and return the Danube territories taken by the Russians to Turkey. The biggest problem was in sustaining the supply lines to the army of clothing, to combat the extreme cold, food and equipment, which the British could not achieve adequatelyfrom Balaklava 30 miles to the front line. The well-known Balaclava woollen hood was created out of necessity during this campaign. The incompetence and hardship caused Lord Aberdeen's government to fall in consequence. It was also the last time that the old wooden three-decker ships of the line were used in war, ignominiously towed by steam-driven ironclads to carry out bombardment. The Turkish wooden fleet had been annihilated by the Russians at the outset of the war at the Battle of Sinope. (The National Archives {PRO} WO 78/1030)

MAP
SHEWING THE SEVERAL ROUTES
Proposed for the
PASSAGE OF GUN-BOATS
TO THE LAKES
VIA
Erie and Oswego — Canal
Champlain
Illinois River and Chicago
Wisconsin „ Green Bay

PREPARED BY
S. H. SWEET
DEP. STATE ENGR AND SURVEYOR
1862

Brother Against Brother

The American Civil War, 1861-5

| **MAP TO SHOW POSSIBLE ROUTES FOR THE GUNBOATS INTO THE LAKES BY S N SWEET, 1862** | Although the threat of Southern action against the Federal forces in and around the Great Lakes was small, guerrilla action 'behind the lines' was possible, and besides the release and escape of Southern prisoners from island prisons had to be guarded against. One such attempt at the Johnson Island prison in Lake Erie in August 1864 was foiled in part by attendant gunboat *Michigan*. This route map, held in the archives of the Library of Congress, was drawn by the Department of State Engineer and Surveyor S N Sweet to work out the most propitious routes for gunboats to the Great Lakes via the Erie and Oswego canal, the Champlain canal, the Illinois river and so on. Comparative distances using the lakes and canals are given in the notes and remarks. (Library of Congress)

THE bloody confrontation of the American Civil War bore the most severe war losses of the nineteenth century. Nevertheless, this war also witnessed a significant period of naval technological innovation by both sides: the ironclad ship with steam propulsion, the gun turret, the submersible and the torpedo, and the mine.

From the infancy of colonization, the North and South had developed along different and sometimes conflicting political, economical and cultural lines, which were finally brought to a head over the issue of slavery. In 1861, following Abraham Lincoln's election as President on a strong anti-slavery ticket, seven Southern states – South Carolina, Mississippi, Florida, Alabama, Georgia, Louisiana and Texas – seceded from the Union and formed the Confederate States of America with Jefferson Davis as President. Many naval officers had to make the soul-searching decision of resigning from the US Navy to join the new Confederacy. A good example is Matthew Fontaine Maury, who was born in Virginia and became a US Navy midshipman in 1825. He devoted himself to the study of navigation, and, to be known as the 'Pathfinder of the Seas', became world-recognized for his work in oceanography. As a distinguished hydrographer he represented the US at the International Oceanography Conference at Brussels in 1853 and his uniform system of recording oceanographic data was adopted worldwide. His background illustrates the dichotomy of conscience that faced many serving officers when the Civil War broke out. As a Virginian, he opposed secession of his State, but felt obliged to lend support when it did, resigning his commission in the US Navy and accepting a Confederate commission. He went to Europe to use his reputation to obtain delivery of navy ships for the south. At the end of the war he was specifically excluded from the amnesty and settled in Mexico, then England, before finally returning as Professor at the Virginia Military Institute.

Following secession, Jefferson announced that any federal forts within a seceded State became the property of the Confederacy. This view was tested on 12 April 1861 when General Pierre Beauregard demanded that Major Robert Anderson surrender and leave Fort Sumter in Charleston. When Anderson asked for two days to consume his supplies, Beauregard refused and opened fire. These were the first shots of the war.

Lincoln responded by asking the Union States for 75,000 men and a navy to blockade the south. This would embrace a seaboard of around 3000 miles and clearly this was not going to be possible with a navy of just 40 ships. But the North had the economic advantage with the shipyards, more money and a greater population. The Confederacy lacked the industrial might of the Union: for every Southern factory there were six in the North. The South wanted to keep their sea ports open and bring supplies over from Europe and the Caribbean, in practice via blockade runners. They hoped to break the Union blockade with ironclads which would ram, fire on and sink their wooden ships. In reality, however, ironclads were inherently unseaworthy and the South's ironclad tactics became more of a threat to the Union in defensive operations out of Confederate ports or up river: the ships never wholly fulfilled their promise as blockade busters. Confederate hopes, too, were that commerce raiders built by Laird in Britain would inflict sufficient damage on Union trade that Lincoln would sue for peace and the South would be recognized as independent, but these were not completed in time.

The tenacious Confederates had one advantage; the majority of naval officers joined the South on secession. With only enough munitions to start the war from the capture of Federal arsenals and shipyards, they turned to innovation with extraordinary drive and initiative to try to tip the balance. However, time was not on their side. Charleston was the Southern naval base for submarine experiments. It resisted attack from Du Pont's Union ironclads and was the seaport of advantage for Caribbean blockade runners. Work on submarine design lead to the 'Davids' (to attack the 'Goliaths' of the US Navy), a series of small submersibles, which carried a star torpedo over the bow. In 1864 the *Hunley*, which was actually built in Mobile, Alabama, became the first submersible to sink a ship. She fired on the USS *Housatonic*, a sloop of war which was on blockade duty off the Charleston Bar, but she also sank, taking her crew of nine men with her.

The Confederates also developed a range of underwater and floating mines, known as 'infernal machines', which were the forerunners of the sea mines that were so effective during twentieth-century war at sea.

In April 1861 the Southerners were able to raid the navy yards at Gosport and Norfolk, take away 1000 cannon and salvage the steam frigate USS *Merrimac*. Holding the port they converted her with an all-over iron shield, and installed 10 guns that fired armour-piercing shells and added a heavily built solid metal bow, renaming her the CSS *Virginia*. The Union Navy had full intelligence about the project and in response gave a Swedish engineer, John Ericsson, a hundred days to build a new kind of ship of iron, with shallow draft, a rotating gun turret and two guns within, and a steam engine. She was named USS *Monitor*.

The *Virginia* moved down-river from Portsmouth on 8 March 1862 and into Hampton Roads to attack the Union blockade. She rammed the wooden ship USS *Cumberland* and fired on the *Congress*. Four other Union ships ran aground. The *Monitor*, by now launched in New York, laboured south to Norfolk, nearly sinking twice, to arrive a few hours after the *Virginia* had wrought havoc there, and attacked the next morning. The ensuing three-and-a-half hour fight at Hampton Roads was inconclusive but goes down in history as the first engagement between ironclads. The *Virginia* was later destroyed by her own crew when the Confederates evacuated Norfolk, and the *Monitor* foundered in December that year. But both naval secretaries, Gideon Welles for the North and Stephen R Mallory for the South, ordered more, so spawning a completely new style of ship that was the direct antecedent of the Dreadnought battleships of the early twentieth century.

A selection of eight charts shown in this chapter, all from the collection at the US Library of Congress in Washington, gives an illuminating view of the naval war, particularly the imbalance in resources of the two sides. The first map depicts the battle between the ironclads CSS *Manassa* and the USS *Monitor*, published in the *New York Herald*. Maps and charts had from time to time appeared in US journals. But during the Civil War, using recently developed printing technology that was largely denied to the South, they were printed by the North in profusion, and were highly popular with their readership. Roger Butterfield writing in 'Pictures in Papers' in *American Heritage* (June 1962) notes that '*Harper's*, *Leslie's* and their lesser rival, the *New York Illustrated News*, employed twenty-seven "special" or combat artists during the war, and also used the work of more than 300 identified amateurs as well as a great many photographers. All together these three northern weeklies printed

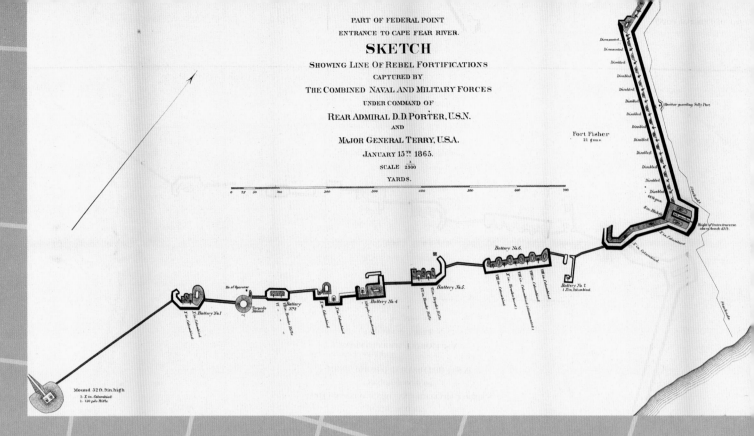

PART OF FEDERAL POINT
ENTRANCE TO CAPE FEAR RIVER.

SKETCH
SHOWING LINE OF REBEL FORTIFICATIONS
CAPTURED BY
THE COMBINED NAVAL AND MILITARY FORCES
UNDER COMMAND OF
REAR ADMIRAL D.D. PORTER, U.S.N.
AND
MAJOR GENERAL TERRY, U.S.A.
JANUARY 15TH 1865.
SCALE 2500
YARDS.

|RIGHT| LINE OF CONFEDERATE FORTIFICATIONS ALONG CAPE FEAR RIVER, 1865 | Rear-Admiral Porter's aide-de-camp, J S Bradford, submitted a full report at the first session of the 39th Congress of the combined attack on Fort Fisher by military and naval forces under Rear-Admiral Porter and Major General Terry in January 1865. It included this sketch of the Confederate fortifications along Cape Fear River and two others that are illustrated on page 137. (Library of Congress)

nearly 6000 war pictures'. This is indicative of the number of maps and charts printed. They were printed with images cut on wood blocks, and place names in metal cemented in place, as can be noticed on the map. A metal electrotype copy was made for the printing. The chart depicting the attack on Charleston is typical of the genre that appeared. Competition spawned great efforts and *The New York Daily Tribune* published *The Tribune War Maps*. The Confederates by comparison suffered from material shortages of all sorts during the war, including printing presses, paper, as well as lithographers and wood engravers, and their output was far less then the North.

Another source of charts and maps is the reports by the Secretary of the Navy made to Congress (see the charts on pages 136 and 137). The chart of Beaufort Harbour and Port Royal (page 133) is a good example of a propaganda chart, produced in great numbers during the two World Wars, although fewer during the American Civil War.

In the end the policy of strangling the South with a blockade and then the capture of their main ports and harbours won the war for the North. Lack of charts in the South through inadequate printing facilities with control of existing charts held by the North, was a handicap, too. Although defeat was acknowledged by generals on the battlefield, it was the lack of guns and ammunition, which they tried to get from Europe (and Britain's decision not to support the Confederacy was crucial), that ground the Confederate army to a halt.

With the Unites States a complete country at the conclusion of the Civil War, she started to think imperially, and the great naval historian Alfred Mahan's writings on war became a compelling influence on Congress and the country's psyche. He advocated building capital ships and bases to protect trade, then any conflicts arising from US expansion could be met with power. Capital ships were built in the 1890s and a squadron was based in San Francisco to cover the Pacific, and by the mid-1890s America had established naval bases and coaling stations from Puget Sound to San Diego: now America was truly a two-ocean navy. US charting of the western seaboard, already started by Charles Wilkes in 1841 during the circumnavigation by the USS *Vincennes* surveying the Strait of Juan de Fuca, Puget Sound, the

Columbia River, San Francisco Bay and the Sacramento River, was continued by George Davidson, the pioneer west coast surveyor. Born in England, his family emigrated to America in 1832 and Davidson was taught surveying by Alexander Dallas Bache when he joined the US Coast and Geodetic Survey (as it was then called) in 1845. He charted the US Pacific coast from 1850 for 10 years and his surveys were published in the Pacific Coast Pilot. After his Alaskan survey in 1867 he continued surveys along the west coast for the next 20 years, using what are now called Davidson quadrilaterals, the basis for its primary triangulation.

Visions of empire began to come true for the US when circumstances led to the Spanish-American war of 1898. Strategically, Cuba became important if America was to build a canal through Panama, which she had tried to buy three times. An uprising in Cuba in 1880 was brutally suppressed by the Spanish over 18 years, but in 1898 the USS *Maine* sailed into Havana to protect American lives and property. She blew up that evening. Although now thought to have been triggered by a fire that caused a magazine to explode, the newspaper magnate William Randolph Hearst headlined sabotage, and with the cry, 'Remember the Maine, to hell with Spain', America went to war. The conflict marked the end of Spanish colonial power and in the ensuing peace treaty the US gained the Philippines, Guam, and Cuba with the establishment of a permanent naval base at Guantánamo Bay.

The expanded United States needed charts worldwide, too, and over the next century Congress gave the funds to enlarge the US Office of Coast Survey (OSC), which now produces charts for US waters including its possessions and territories. The OSC is the United States' oldest scientific organization established in 1807 by Congress to make a survey of the coastline, concentrating on coast-hugging surveys with observations of the tides, currents and sea bed. Ferdinand Hassler was its first superintendent. He was succeeded in 1843 by Alexander Dallas Bache, a great-grandson of Benjamin Franklin, who had first promulgated the Gulf Stream. Today the OCS is administered under the National Oceanic and Atmospheric Administration (NOAA). Depending on activity the OCS reviews and re-issues charts of the US coast from between six months and 12 years.

| RIGHT | **WAR MAP FROM THE**
NEW YORK HERALD, **1861** | From the
spark that ignited the American Civil
War – the bombardment of Fort Sumter
guarding the entrance to Charleston on
12 April 1861 – the Federal Union of the
Northern States' Navy, the US Navy, was
given a near-impossible task by President
Abraham Lincoln: to blockade some
3000 miles of Confederate coastline.

The *New York Herald* reported the
war to an eager population in the North
with explanatory maps and charts to
illustrate major conflicts, and this map,
engraved by Waters & Son of New York,
is typical. It marks the 11 October
engagement in 1861, when the
Confederate ship *Manassas* attacked the
wooden-hulled blockading ships at the
Head of Passes, where the Mississippi
river splits into some half a dozen tribu-
taries as it flows into the Gulf of Mexico.
The *Manassas*, converted into an ironclad
along the lines of the first ironclad CSS
Merrimack with 10 guns and the USS
Monitor with a revolving turret, transformed warship design. She was fitted
with a metal ram and given a gun that
fired forward, and her design was good
enough for inshore and river waters. The
attack was countered by Captain David
Farragut's incursion up the Mississippi in
April 1862, capturing the river forts,
sinking the *Manassas* and forcing the surrender of New Orleans. The blockade
that eventually strangled Confederates
supplies had now successfully started.
(Library of Congress)

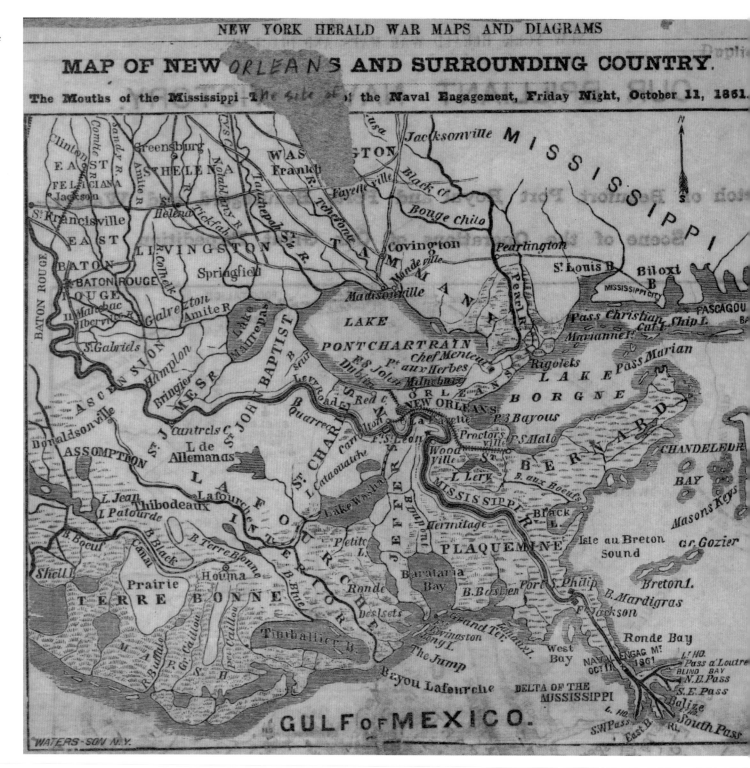

| RIGHT | **THE UNION ATTACK ON PORT ROYAL AND BEAUFORT HARBOR,**
1861 | Maps and charts are used to help unite and strengthen the sense of purpose and identity
of a nation, particularly a young one, and during the American Civil War the Unionist public of
the North were, for example, encouraged to have a copy of this and other similar patriotic charts,
which, as stipulated on the chart, 'should be in every loyal household', where the symbolism of
the image of the Union Eagle attacking the Confederate Snake would not be lost.

Under Lincoln's energetic Navy Secretary, Gideon Welles, the first amphibious operation of the
US Navy was to procure a deep-water harbour from which to operate, refuel and replenish blockading ships. An attack was planned under Flag Officer Samuel F Dupont with 74 wooden ships, the
largest US fleet amassed to date, and transports carrying 12,000 men under General Thomas

Sherman. As can be seen on the plan, after severe weather delays and the Southerners alerted to the
secret operation, Dupont took the fleet inside the 3-mile broad entrance guarded by Forts Walker
and Beauregard. He cleverly attacked from behind, i.e. the north, around Skull and Mackeys
Creeks to bombard Fort Walker, and St Helena and Phillips Islands to bombard Fort Beauregard,
while the forts' guns were designed to withstand an attack from seaward. The Union forces captured the forts with great skill (skills learned from whaling and privateering), as the waters inside
the headland are confined, and went on to capture Port Royal and Beaufort harbour some 10 miles
along Broad river, but just 50 miles from Charleston, the birthplace of the Southern States secession, giving them their southern defendable, deep-water harbour for re-supplying the blockade, and
a launching point for land operations deep into the Southern States. (Library of Congress)

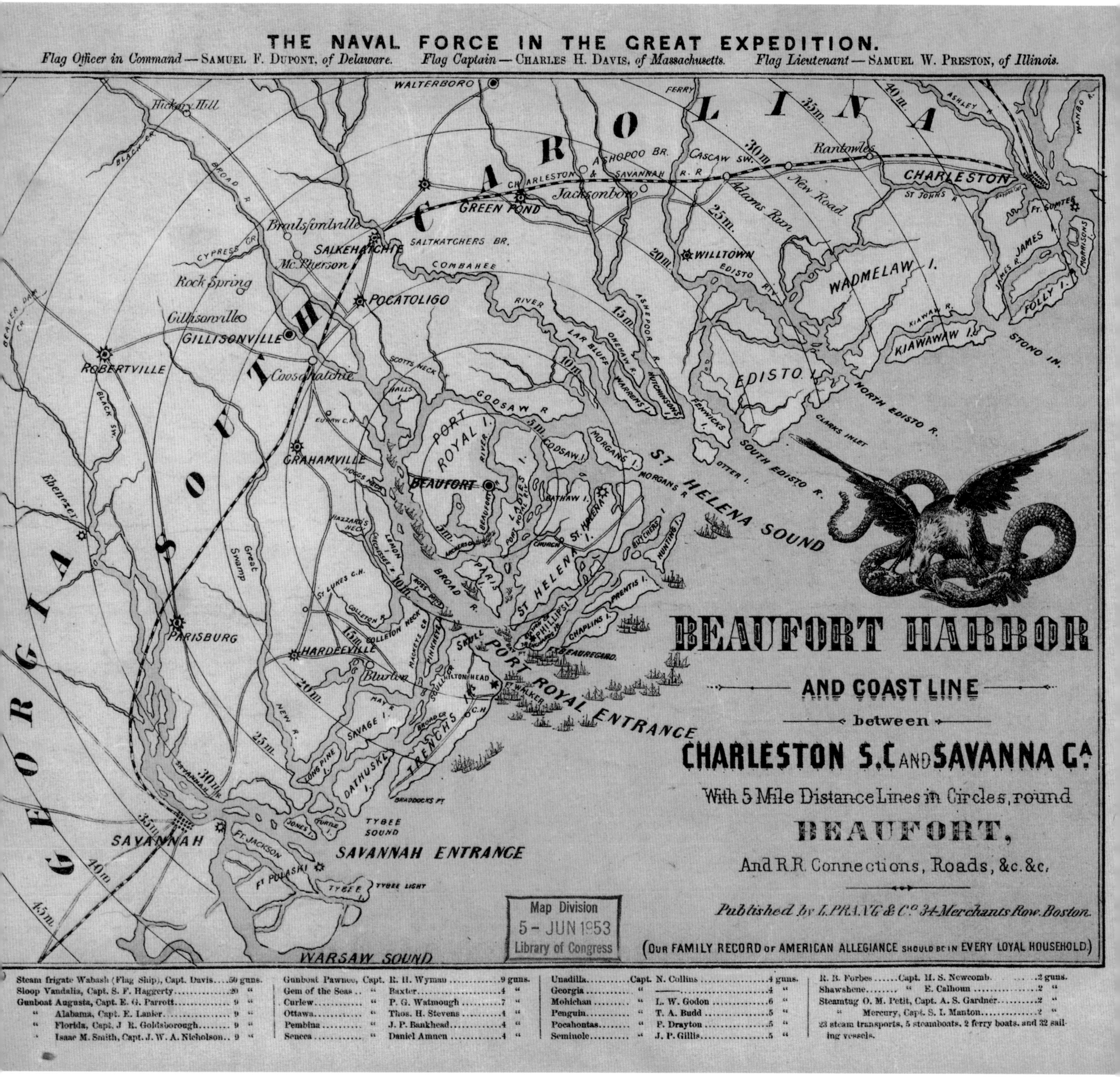

THE NAVAL FORCE IN THE GREAT EXPEDITION.

Flag Officer in Command — SAMUEL F. DUPONT, *of Delaware.*   *Flag Captain* — CHARLES H. DAVIS, *of Massachusetts.*   *Flag Lieutenant* — SAMUEL W. PRESTON, *of Illinois.*

BEAUFORT HARBOR

AND COAST LINE

between

CHARLESTON S.C. AND SAVANNA G.ª

With 5 Mile Distance Lines in Circles, round

BEAUFORT,

And R.R. Connections, Roads, &c. &c.

Published by L. PRANG & C.º 34 Merchants Row, Boston.

(Our FAMILY RECORD of AMERICAN ALLEGIANCE should be in EVERY LOYAL HOUSEHOLD.)

Steam frigate Wabash (Flag Ship), Capt. Davis....50 guns.	Gunboat Pawnee, Capt. R. H. Wyman ....9 guns.	Unadilla............Capt. N. Collins ....4 guns.	R. B. Forbes ......Capt. H. S. Newcomb.......2 guns.
Sloop Vandalia, Capt. S. F. Haggerty.............20 "	Gem of the Seas ... Baxter.....................4 "	Georgia .... " ....4 "	Shawshene...... " E. Calhoun ....2 "
Gunboat Augusta, Capt. E. G. Parrott............9 "	Curlew............ P. G. Watmough ....7 "	Mohican .... " L. W. Godon ....6 "	Steamtug O. M. Petit, Capt. A. S. Gardner......2 "
" Alabama, Capt. E. Lanier................9 "	Ottawa............ Thos. H. Stevens ....4 "	Penguin............ " T. A. Budd ....5 "	" Mercury, Capt. S. L. Manton......2 "
" Florida, Capt. J. R. Goldsborough.......9 "	Pembina............ J. P. Bankhead ....4 "	Pocahontas.......... " P. Drayton ....5 "	23 steam transports, 5 steamboats, 2 ferry boats, and 32 sailing vessels.
" Isaac M. Smith, Capt. J. W. A. Nicholson.. 9 "	Seneca............ Daniel Ammen ....4 "	Seminole............ " J. P. Gillis ....5 "	

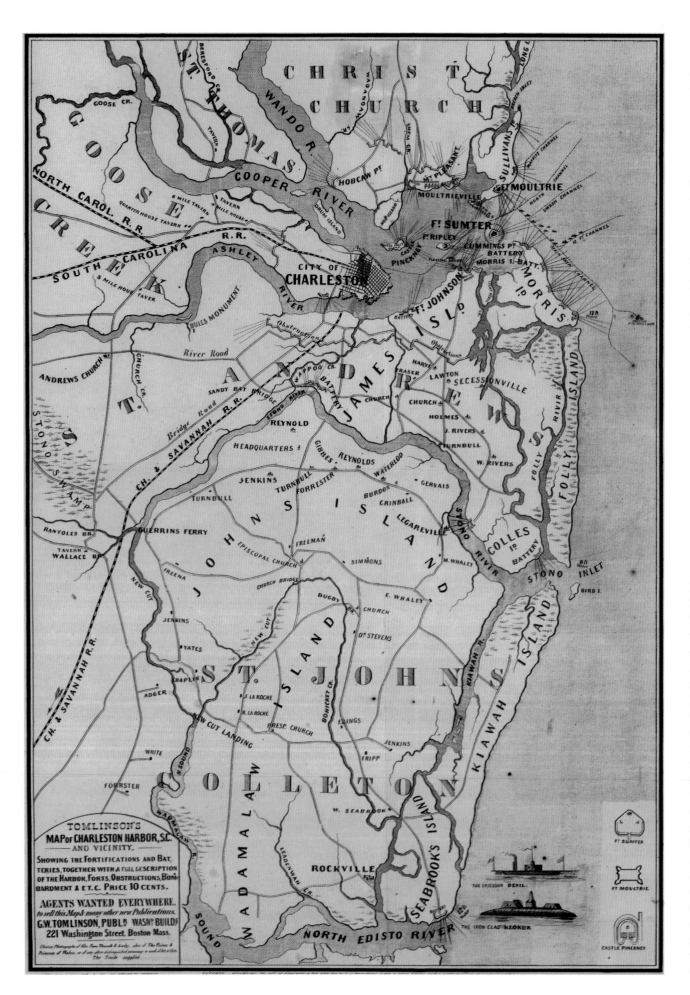

TOMLINSON'S
MAP OF CHARLESTON HARBOR, S.C.
AND VICINITY.

SHOWING THE FORTIFICATIONS AND BATTERIES, TOGETHER WITH A FULL DESCRIPTION OF THE HARBOR, FORTS, OBSTRUCTIONS, BOMBARDMENT & E.T.C. PRICE 10 CENTS.

AGENTS WANTED EVERYWHERE.
to sell this Map & many other new Publications.
G.W. TOMLINSON, PUBLʳ. WASHⁿ. BUILDᵍ.
221 Washington Street, Boston, Mass.

| LEFT | **MAP OF CHARLESTON HARBOR, SOUTH CAROLINA, 1863** | This 1863 lithograph broadsheet by J Mayer & Co. of Boston, Massachusetts, sold to the general public for 10¢, shows the scene of the bombardment of Fort Sumter in April 1863 by US ironclad monitors in support of Major General Hunter's attempted troop landing to take Charleston. It describes the Confederate defences, forts, number of guns, obstructions, and shows the Confederates' withering lines of fire from the various forts that repulsed the fleet of nine ironclad warships, including the 677-ton USS *Keokuk* featured on the bottom of the map, which sank the next day with 90 projectiles holing her. Another attempt to take Charleston in August failed, as part of the stranglehold the US Navy was implementing on all American Atlantic ports to prevent blockade runners bringing supplies in and exporting cotton. (Library of Congress)

| RIGHT | **CHART OF REAR-ADMIRAL DAVID FARRAGUT'S ENTRANCE INTO MOBILE BAY BY ROBERT WEIR, 1863** | The port of Mobile was the second to last to fall to the Federal forces. The attractive lithograph chart, drawn and compiled after the action for Rear-Admiral Farragut by Robert Weir, and then printed as part of the report, shows the action in five stages. Farragut took a fleet of four ironclads and 14 wooden ships into Mobile Bay on 5 August 1863, audaciously past the guns of Fort Morgan and through underwater obstructions and a line of moored mines or 'torpedoes' as they were then (confusingly) called, which blew up the leading 15-inch gun ironclad *Tecumseh*. Farragut issued his famous order, 'Damn the torpedoes, full speed ahead', and his ships surrounded the Confederate ironclad *Tennessee* forcing her to surrender. Although Mobile itself did not capitulate until April 1865, the destruction of the seaward defences denied blockade runners another major port. The narrow entrance in shoaling waters required fine seamanship to avoid running aground and contemporary charts, of sufficient accuracy to allow for this, were also used by Weir in compiling this chart. (Library of Congress)

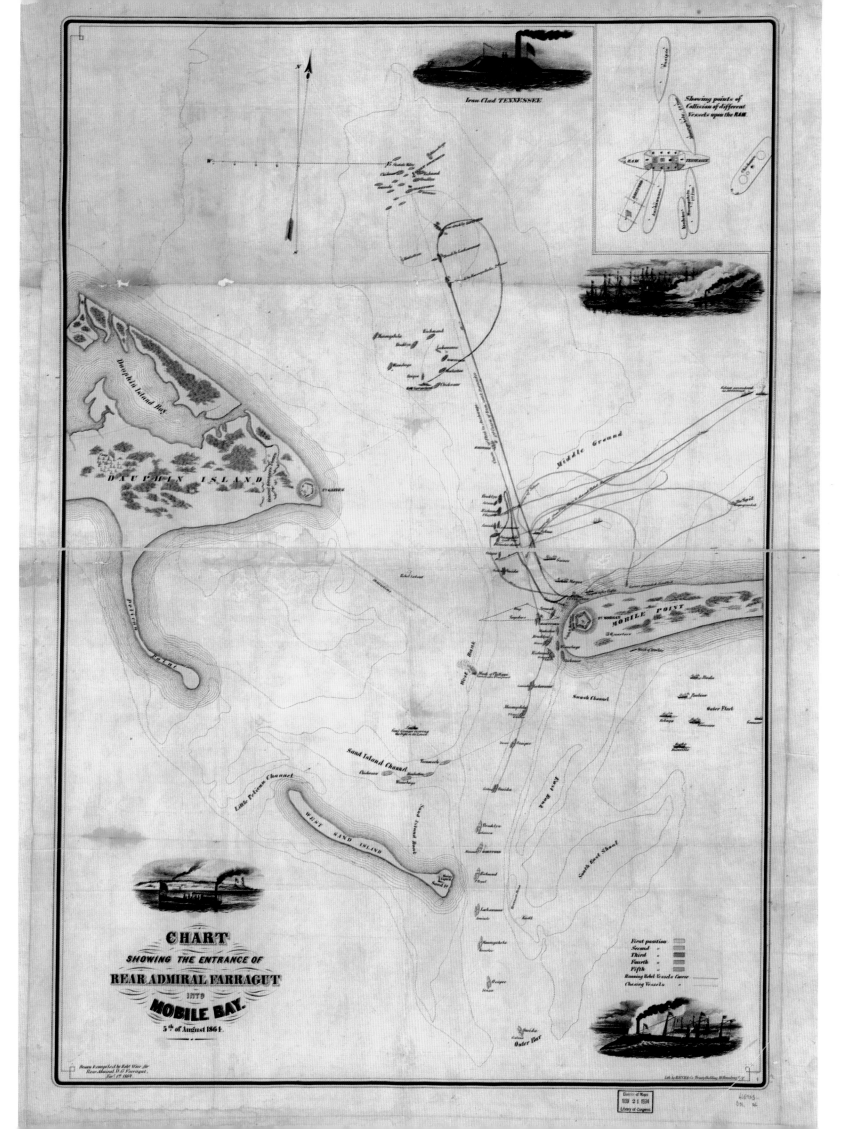

Iron-Clad TENNESSEE

Showing points of
Collision of different
Vessels upon the RAM.

CHART
SHOWING THE ENTRANCE OF
REAR ADMIRAL FARRAGUT
INTO
MOBILE BAY.
5ᵗʰ of August 1864.

First position
Second
Third
Fourth
Fifth
Running Rebel Vessels Course
Chasing Vessels

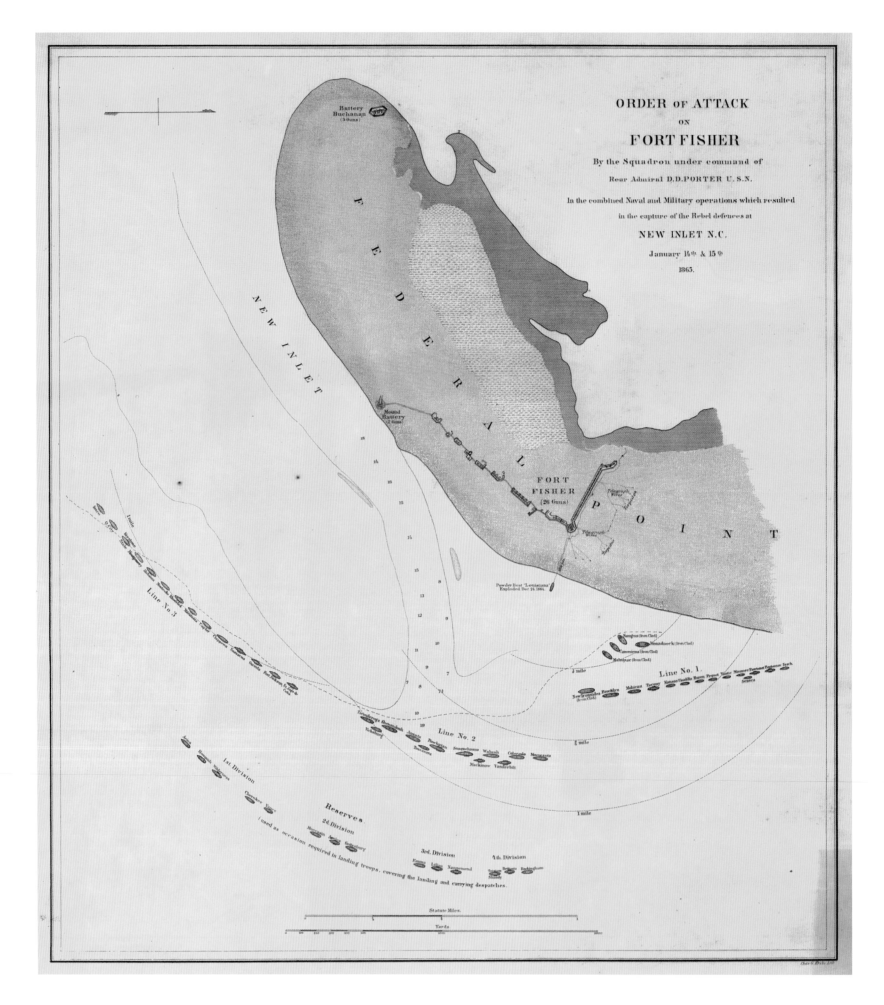

ORDER of ATTACK
ON
FORT FISHER
By the Squadron under command of
Rear Admiral D.D. PORTER U.S.N.

In the combined Naval and Military operations which resulted
in the capture of the Rebel defences at

NEW INLET N.C.

January 14th & 15th
1865.

|LEFT | **REAR-ADMIRAL DAVID PORTER'S ATTACK ON FORT FISHER, 1865** |
Wilmington was the last Confederate port to fall to the Federal forces. Fast, shallow-draft steamers from the British West Indies, often skippered by the British or French, consistently ran the blockade, taking shelter under the Confederate gun batteries, from where local pilots guided the runners with their military cargoes 28 miles upriver to Wilmington. Immense quantities were brought in: for example, in the last four months of 1864 alone a total of 750 tons of lead, 100 tons of powder, 69,000 muskets and thousands of tons of food and clothing was reached. They were transferred to trains that raced north to Richmond and General Lee's Virginian army. The key to capturing Wilmington was to take Fort Fisher, strategically placed at Cape Fear, the entrance to

Cape Fear river. Rear-Admiral Porter was Farragut's foster brother, and naturally they knew each other well and had developed many of the tactics for the new ironclad ships. The chart was based on the US Coast Survey of 1857, part of a set of navigational charts used by both navies during the Civil War, and prepared for the first report to Congress after cessation of hostilities. It shows the second attempted assault on 14 and 15 January with four ironclads pulverizing Fort Fisher with 11- and 15-inch shells and the remainder of the massive North Atlantic Blockading Squadron drawn up in three lines. Troops were then landed and the final amphibious operation of the Civil War concluded with the fall of Wilmington a month later. (Library of Congress)

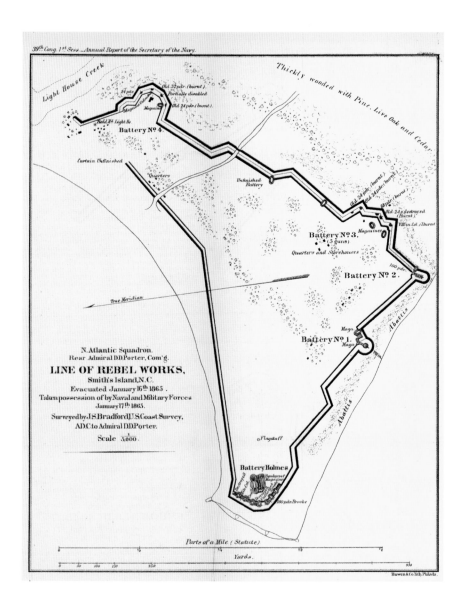

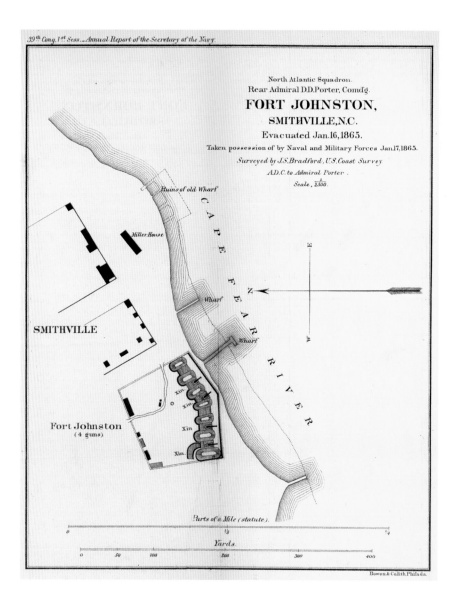

| **LINE OF CONFEDERATE WORKS AT SMITH'S ISLAND, CAPE FEAR RIVER, BY J S BRADFORD, 1865** | The day after Fort Fisher was captured Admiral Porter laid down naval gunfire support on the Confederate fortifications on Smith Island, identifiable with its lighthouse erected in 1794, and army forces then took possession. This survey, with notes on the damage and destruction, was made by Porter's aide-de-camp, J S Bradford, to become part of the US Coast Survey, as part of the official annual report to a Congress that represented the whole of the United States, and presented at the first session of the 39th Congress. (Library of Congress)

| **FORT JOHNSTON, SMITHVILLE, BY J S BRADFORD, 1865** | The pilots who guided ships through the difficult shoals of Cape Fear and the river settled at Fort Johnston, naming the port Smithville, to be changed to Southport in 1887. The fort was occupied by Admiral Porter after it was evacuated by the Confederates on 16 January, and this survey, also by J S Bradford, similarly formed part of the report to Congress. (Library of Congress)

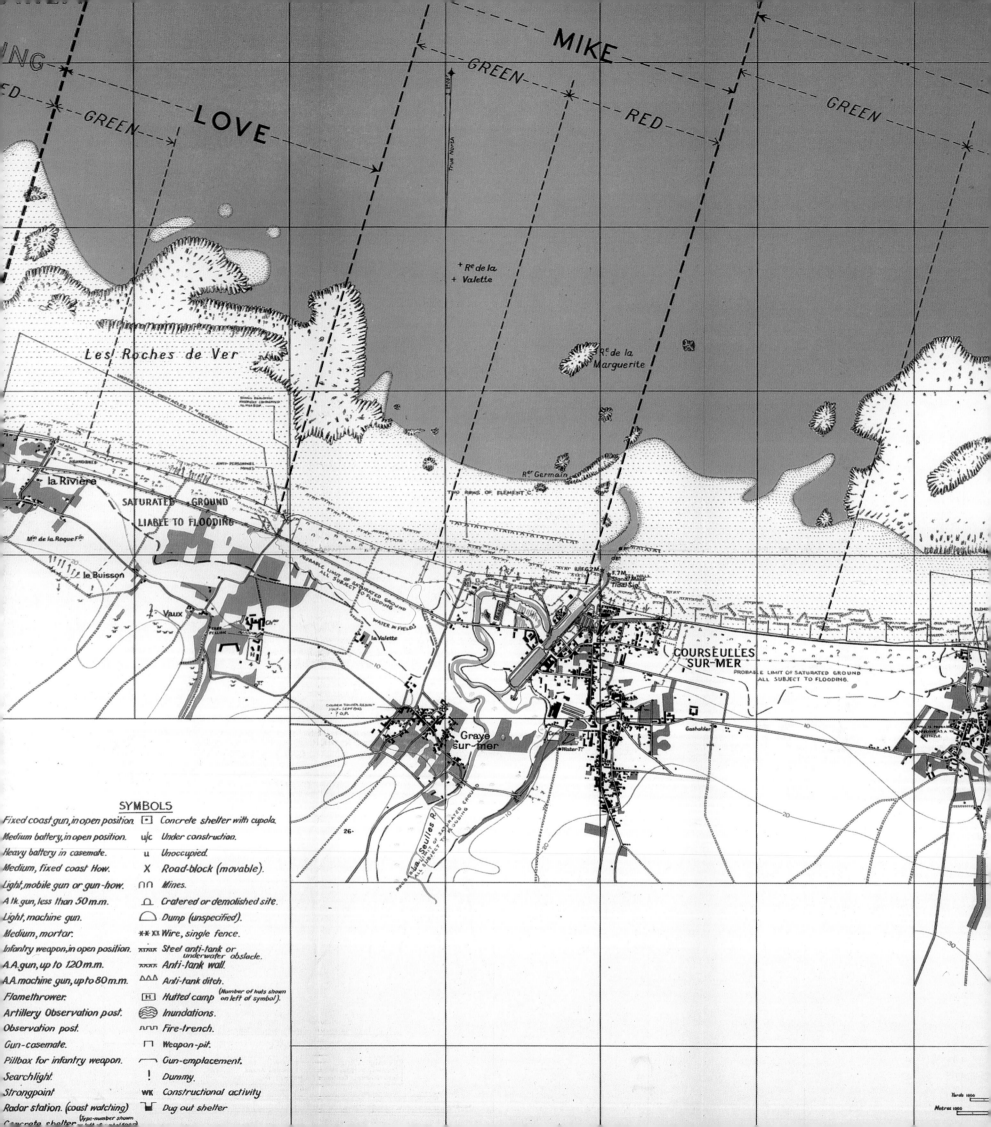

MIKE

LOVE

GREEN

RED

GREEN

GREEN

+ R⁺ᵉ de la
+ Valette

Les Roches de Ver

R⁺ᵉ de la
Marguerite

la Rivière

R⁺ᵉ Germain

SATURATED GROUND
LIABLE TO FLOODING

Mⁿ de la Roque Fᵐᵉ

le Buisson

COURSEULLES
SUR-MER

Vaux

la Valette

PROBABLE LIMIT OF SATURATED GROUND
ALL SUBJECT TO FLOODING.

Graye
sur-mer

Gasholder

SYMBOLS

Fixed coast gun, in open position.	⊡	Concrete shelter with cupola.	
Medium battery, in open position.	u/c	Under construction.	
Heavy battery in casemate.	u	Unoccupied.	
Medium, fixed coast How.	X	Road-block (movable).	
Light, mobile gun or gun-how.	∩∩	Mines.	
A tk.gun, less than 50 m.m.	⌂	Cratered or demolished site.	
Light, machine gun.	⌒	Dump (unspecified).	
Medium, mortar.	✶✶ ××	Wire, single fence.	
Infantry weapon, in open position.	×⊼⊼×	Steel anti-tank or underwater obstacle.	
A.A.gun, up to 120 m.m.	×××	Anti-tank wall.	
A.A. machine gun, up to 80 m.m.	△△△	Anti-tank ditch.	
Flamethrower.	H	Hutted camp (Number of huts shown on left of symbol).	
Artillery Observation post.	≋	Inundations.	
Observation post.	∩∩∩	Fire-trench.	
Gun-casemate.	⊓	Weapon-pit.	
Pillbox for infantry weapon.	⌐	Gun-emplacement.	
Searchlight.	!	Dummy.	
Strongpoint.	wk	Constructional activity	
Radar station. (coast watching)		Dug out shelter	
Concrete shelter			

Yards 1000

Metres 1000

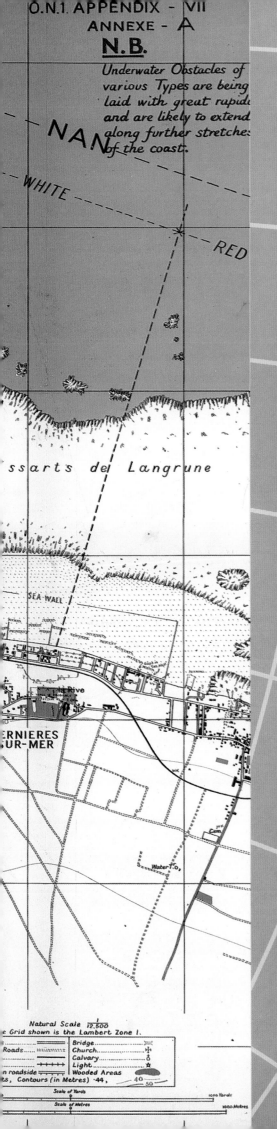

CHAPTER 8

The Modern Chart of War

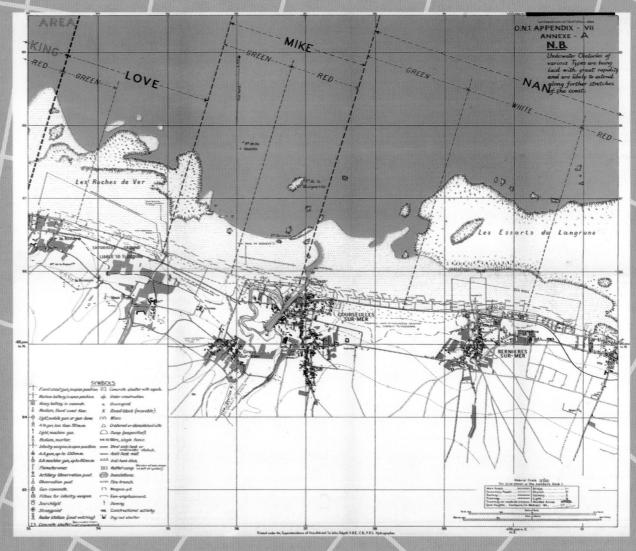

| **ASSAULT MAP FOR JUNO BEACH, 1944** | An essential element in the preparations for D-Day was a set of specially drawn maps, one for each of the five landing sites, code-named Juno, Sword, Gold, Utah and Omaha. This one concentrates on Juno for the use of Force J, the 3rd Canadian Division. It includes all the main topographical features and contours inland for about 2 miles, the drying line or low water mark, with exposed rocks but no soundings. The facility of these maps lay in covering the landing areas for each assault force on one plan, whereas the use of military maps would have involved two or more joined together. (UKHO © British Crown Copyright)

As they entered the twentieth century, nearly every maritime nation had established a hydrographic office that dealt only with the collation, issue and publication of charts, and coordination and execution of marine surveys. While the world's coastlines have been surveyed to a high degree of accuracy, a comparatively small part of the ocean and ocean floor are well charted. The paradox is that in a century of three-dimensional warfare, above, on and below the sea, hydrographical data still relies to a large extent on work that was surveyed by men in small boats from vessels under sail using fairly basic instruments many years ago.

The opening years of the twentieth century saw the disruption of the British policy that had, to a significant extent during the nineteenth century, kept the world in relative peace. By allowing the older established European countries a sort of balance of colonies, competitive wars that had marked previous centuries were avoided. But a significant exception was the 'Scramble for Africa'. In the 1870s only the coastal belts of this great continent were known, the rest was a *terra nullius*, a no-man's land, and most Europeans saw the continent as vacant; not to rent, but to occupy. Within half a generation almost the entire continent was claimed with 30 new colonies shared between Britain and France (testing each other's claims), Portugal, Italy and Germany, with Belgium a portion in the middle. The Franco-Prussian war revealed an emerging young Germany whose pride was at stake. She wanted an Empire like Britain's and felt excluded in the final colonial stampede across Africa. She would fight for one. The German drive to naval armament, combined with imperial and mercantile ambitions created a power imbalance between maritime nations and propelled the revolution in ship design towards the end of the century. Years ahead of its rivals, the Royal Navy designed and built a battleship with the attributes of high speed, elaborate protections and all big-gun armament that rendered obsolete all other battleships. Launched in 1906 she was named HMS *Dreadnought* and her design became a generic. She combined ten 12-inch guns with 11-inch armour plate and a maximum speed of 21 knots. Other maritime nations felt compelled to compete and in the subsequent 'Dreadnought race' Britain managed to keep ahead: by 1918 she had 48 to Germany's 26. The competition continued between the USA and Japan, until a treaty limitation was signed in 1921.

In the Far East at the turn of the century, Russia was trying to maintain her influence, while Japan, in an echo of German nationalism, was building Dreadnoughts with British know-how, and starting to expand by attacks on China and Pacific Russia. The elimination of Russia's Far East Fleet at the Battle of Tsushima, initiated by the attack in 1904 on Port Arthur that is highlighted by the British Naval Attaché's chart on page 144, was the first naval action of an emergent nationalistic Japan, which would ultimately lead to Pearl Harbor. In Europe the Franco-Russian alliance of 1893, and the Anglo-French 'entente cordiale' of 1904 isolated Germany. France moved in to Morocco in 1905, which irritated Germany, but Anglo-Russian differences in Persia were resolved. Austria-Hungary annexed Bosnia-Herzegovina in 1908 and threatened Serbia. It is surprising that the First World War didn't break out earlier, but the scene was set, and the assassination of the Arch-Duke Ferdinand of Austria in 1914 ignited the volatile situation. In preparation for war, hydrographic offices issued charts that would cover the areas where conflict was envisaged. The British Hydrographic Office issued special charts to cover the areas where the fleets were based – in Portsmouth, the Nore, Gibraltar and Malta – in more detail. Equally, old charts for potential wartime anchorages

strategically placed to cover the new German threat, such as Scapa Flow in the Orkneys and Kinsale in Ireland, were dusted off and up-dated. Charts to a large scale were needed by the Director of Naval Intelligence, and 10 sets of German charts of the German coastline were prepared for operational rather than navigational use. Surveys were ordered for contingency harbours as naval bases, particularly in the North Sea such as at Harwich for destroyers and the firths and lochs of Scotland.

Once war was declared British principal naval policy was to contain the German High Seas Fleet with the British Grand Fleet, which it largely did until the fateful encounter off Jutland in 1916. The outcome of this battle is mostly assessed with historical hindsight as a tactical victory for the Germans who lost fewer ships, and as a strategic victory for Britain as the German fleet never left Wilhelmshaven again. The charts on pages 145 and 146, one British, one German, give a detailed appraisal of this juggernaut encounter. A landsman might think that the Royal Navy, with professionally trained navigators and with, by the time of the battle, relatively sophisticated equipment and charts, would have a consistently accurate position. Great advances had been made in the understanding and design of the magnetic compass to compensate for deviation caused by a ship's magnetism and variation caused by the earth's changing magnetic poles. But navigation is not that straightforward. One of the most surveyed and best-charted seas in the world is the North Sea and the site of the Battle of Jutland was well covered. The two major squadrons of the British fleet were to rendezvous at the entrance to the Skagerrak. Admiral Lord Jellicoe, Commander-in-Chief of the Grand Fleet, had sailed from Scapa Flow in the Orkneys to meet up with Vice-Admiral Sir David Beatty's battle cruisers from Rosyth off Jutland Bank. A hundred miles separated Scapa Flow from Rosyth and the rendezvous was 200 miles steaming for both fleets. On arrival, position comparisons were signalled visually between the two fleet navigators and it was found that the combined dead reckoning error was 10 miles.

With the German High Seas Fleet confined and inactive following the battle, the crews grew discontented to the point of mutiny in 1918, but while this festered, an unrestricted U-boat campaign went into full throttle to try to deny supplies from the US. The convoy system was the only way to overcome this and charts were designed and issued solely for convoy use. These were adapted from standard Admiralty charts that gave specific and adequate coverage for convoy routes to avoid known U-boat haunts. In this war and the next, Convoy commodores conducted zigzag patterns followed by all the ships in the convoy, whereby turns of successive different courses were made together at various time intervals designed to foil an enemy submarine's torpedo-firing capability based on steady course and speed assumptions.

An attempt to overcome the trench stalemate in Europe by a concentrated attack to the east on the Turks firstly by a naval bombardment in the Dardenelles, then an amphibious landing at Gallipoli, failed, and is highlighted with the chart illustrated on page 144 from the journal of a young officer at the battle. Photography, as shown on this particular chart, was still a young technology, but was being used by chart compilers along with traditional drawings to provide coastal views on charts.

Sea power had greater significance in the Second World War than in any other war since 1815. Napoleon and Hitler fought land wars successfully on a blitzkrieg basis, but over-extended their lines of communications by trying to attack Russia. Combined operations won wars by taking the soldier to the

| RIGHT | **A TYPICAL GOOSEBERRY, 1944** | Operation Overlord required minute and detailed planning. If it was to succeed, every stage of the process of securing the beachheads and then following this with a massive infrastructure to keep the newly landed armies supplied, had to be carefully thought through. The Gooseberry was an essential element of this. Fifty-five ageing merchant ships and four obsolete battleships and cruisers were brought across the English Channel, filled with concrete and sunk in a semi-circle, as the diagrammatic chart shows, to provide a breakwater as part of the artificial harbours, knows as Mulberries. (The National Archives {PRO} DEFE 2/499)

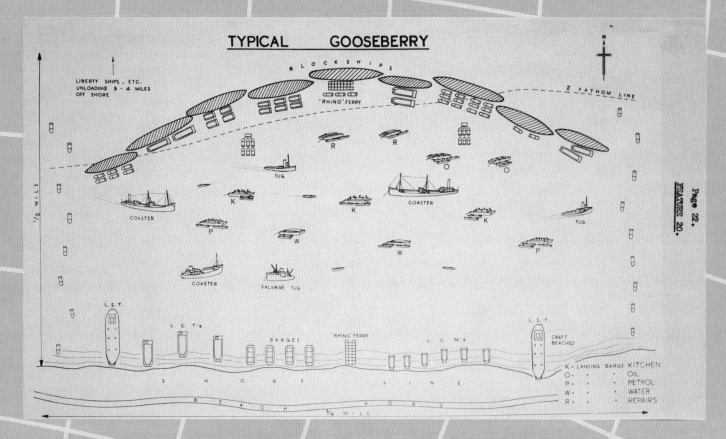

aggressor country, and never have amphibious operations played so important a role as in this war. The island-hopping operations in the Pacific against the Japanese must have seemed never ending, but in the European theatre Operation Torch, the Allied invasion of French North Africa and the first large-scale amphibious operation of the war, landed American troops at Casablanca who had steamed directly from the US. Allied troops in North Africa drove out the Germans and Italians, followed by Operation Husky where they were landed in Sicily and then crossed the Strait of Messina into Italy. All relied on the chart which was key to each operation and as the D-Day charts featured on pages 152–157 indicate, the Allied amphibious operations were meticulously planned, using charts of multi-layered information for all the different units involved, based on good intelligence. Deception also played a role. The Germans were fooled as to the landings in northern France in part by the planting of a 'secret' chart. It purported to show the Allied invasion at the northern part of the Cherbourg peninsula. Codenamed Operation Mincemeat, it was later featured as a major film *The Man Who Never Was*. An unknown body was given the identity of a Royal Marines major called Martin, from Admiral Mountbatten's Combined Operations staff, and was 'washed up' on the Spanish shore near Huelva, purportedly from a ditched aircraft, but actually released from a submarine at night, with the deceptive charts and information in an attached briefcase.

The chart on page 151 sums up the US strategy to win the war against Japan, by taking control of supplies and materiel. In fighting the Pacific War, Japan expanded outwards like a blown-up balloon until its logistics could no longer maintain its forces, while the Americans established an entirely new system of logistical supply of materiel, whereby replenishment of fuel, ammunition and equipment was perfected by a system of supply ships and tankers passing these essentials to warships while underway, rendering a return to

land bases to replenish unnecessary. This enabled them to wear down the Japanese. The Japanese transport fleet, for example, was shattered by the US and Royal Australian Air Forces in the Battle of the Bismarck Sea, and Japan lost any chance of re-supplying its position in New Guinea. Pre-emptive strikes on Japanese forward air bases destroyed most of their aircraft. New Guinea and the Marshall Islands fell and American forces moved quickly to re-take the Philippines.

Another technological breakthrough, code-breaking, consistently revealed German and Japanese intentions, particularly in the Pacific War when an early appreciation allowed the Americans to concentrate what were meagre forces, outnumbered in the overall theatre, entirely on to a division of the Japanese carrier strength – first the ambush at Coral Sea in May 1942 with equal losses; secondly at the Battle of Midway in June 1942 with the loss of four Japanese carriers to one US, which tipped the balance of carriers in America's favour; the third enabled the Americans to take Guadalcanal in August 1942. This lead to an 18-month campaign, which finally broke the Japanese. The island-hopping fight was won because intelligence showed where the enemy was weakest and as such where to strike next. But ultimately, in a war where losses were high, victory was won by the side that could replace them the quickest.

The twentieth century produced a number of significant developments that totally changed the concept of the war at sea: the mine, the submarine, amphibious operations on a grand scale, and the aircraft carrier which facilitated air reconnaissance and attack at sea. Charts and navigation had to develop rapidly in concert to match them. Charts were now being designed to meet many supplementary requirements, for example the D-Day chart on page 152 indicates the planned safe channels, which would be cleared of mines to be used by the amphibious attack force.

| LEFT | **ADMIRALTY CHART OF THE FALKLANDS ISLANDS, 1982**| This Admiralty chart was one of those used on the bridge of the frigate *Antelope*, which was part of the British Task Force and is in the modern style with depths in metres and inshore waters less than 20 metres coloured in blue. It shows the track *Antelope* took escorting two support vessels via the Ascension Islands into San Carlos Water via Falkland Sound between the two main islands. (By kind permission of Captain N J Tobin DSC RN)

In 1911 naval experiments with aircraft resulted in the American aviator Eugene Ely getting airborne and landing on a platform erected over the guns of a cruiser, and a few months later Commander Sampson flew a Short biplane on and off a similar arrangement on the battleship HMS *Africa*. In 1923 HMS *Hermes*, the first ship to be built as an aircraft carrier from the keel up, was launched and by the Second World War naval carriers had become a potent force. The operational chart on page 148 shows the cat-and-mouse hunt for the *Bismarck* in 1941 during which Swordfish aircraft from the *Ark Royal* played a vital role, and the chart of the dash up the English Channel by the German battle cruisers *Scharnhorst* and *Gneisenau* illustrates the use of British air attack.

Similar to surface ships and submarines, charts for air navigators were rapidly developed. In Britain today these are compiled and distributed by the RAF for RAF and Fleet Air Arm aircraft, while Ordnance Survey land maps (with particular attention to electric pylons) and sea charts with local information overlays have been adapted for helicopters. Global Position System (GPS) gives real time position, while Tacan (Tactical Air Navigation) electronic transmission and response systems set up in aircraft carriers and military airfields give aircraft a range and bearing position, and air radar, designed to intercept an enemy fighter, can be used to find prominent headlands or islands to fix position.

Submarines by their nature are designed to stay submerged for long periods of time, but this has created its own challenge for navigation in a new environment. Techniques have progressed rapidly since the Second World War when submarines would either rely on a quick periscope fix if near land or surface at night to re-charge batteries and take a star sight with a sextant. British and US submarines today use bottom contour charts specially prepared from Admiralty charts with manifold sea-bed contour lines and depths, now in metres, and Royal Navy survey ships regularly re-survey areas frequented by submarines, for example, the approaches to the submarine base at Faslane along the Firth of Clyde. Positions on these charts can be found from a running fix obtained by measuring depths with a specialized echo sounder, which can give a position accurate to within 30 metres.

By the time of the Second World War a whole range of systems had been devised to facilitate the deployment of the submarine in warfare and, by extension, to be included on board a warship. The principle of beaming out a sound wave, and listening for a returning echo, then measuring the time taken to give range and the bearing gave us Asdic (Anti-*S*ubmarine Detection Investigation Committee), now called Sonar (Sound Navigation and Ranging), which hunted the submarine and helped to win the war against the U-boat, and the two charts on page 150 demonstrate the use of the chart firstly on a wartime operations room plotting table searching for survivors of a U-boat attack, and secondly in hunting a U-boat following a reported sighting by an aircraft. The echo sounder, now accurate to less than a metre, is the direct derivative, and the submarine also uses this tool to navigate. Techniques such as 'down slope enhancement' allow a submarine to receive a tracing of the sea bed profile ahead of her and compare this with a bottom profile chart to assess position. Forward pointing sonar should pick up uncharted pinnacles on her course. Nuclear submarines can stay submerged for weeks, but can still pick up a position fix by coming to periscope depth and receiving a Satellite Navigation (SatNav) position through the radio aerial. Another means is through a trailing wire aerial. A thin wire inconspicuously reaches to the surface and picks up a satellite navigation position.

A second use of beamed radio waves, which would have a profound effect on the outcome of the Second World War, and for navigation, was Radar (Radio Direction And Range). It worked on a similar principle to Sonar but with a different wavelength under 10 centimetres and presenting the range and bearing electronically on a screen. The war against Japanese and German surface fleets and German U-boats was transformed once the Allies had this piece of kit which could detect enemy surface movement at night, including a submarine periscope in calm water, and at ever-increasing range beyond visibility. If Jellicoe at Jutland had had this he would have annihilated the enemy. It is now very useful as a collision warning device in fog and a secondary aid to navigating by giving a range and bearing of land, but this fix should never be relied on in isolation, but rather used to confirm other positional indications.

SINS (Ship's Inertial Navigation System) was developed after the war for nuclear submarines, but is now fitted to many warships and larger merchant ships. It is a highly sophisticated dead reckoning system that uses accelerometers, which respond to every movement of the ship forward, but eliminates any interference from rolling or pitching. Its accuracy is such that after a circumnavigation a submarine's margin of error is expected to be no more than 100 to 200 yards.

Another development using radio waves was the radio direction finder where a radio beacon on shore sends out a signal, which is picked up by the receiving ship. Two or more stations on different bearings give crossing position lines and a fix on the chart. Various systems were developed during and after the Second World War, and used for accurate navigation on D-Day, including Loran and QM, and charts were issued that had the hyperbolic lines (which is how radio waves travel, as a great circle) on to assist in taking a fix. Similar systems called Consol and Omega all together give worldwide coverage, although today the wide spread availability of SatNav systems has overtaken these methods.

With the advent of Satellite Navigation (colloquially named SatNav) it has become possible to fix the land with absolute accuracy. More important is the accurate positioning of the coast relative to latitude and longitude on charts. Even as recently as 1982 the Navigating Officer of HMS *Glamorgan* was using the most modern chart available to bombard Port Stanley in the closing stages of the Falklands War during the night of the 11 June to 'soften up' the incumbents with naval gunfire support. This was done by patrolling up and down a line drawn on the chart at just outside the surface-to-surface missile range. Unfortunately the chart in use at the time was based on the survey made at the end of the nineteenth century and was slightly inaccurate. *Glamorgan* was actually just inside missile range. The quick-thinking navigating officer was able to turn the ship's stern to the incoming missile which was at the end of its trajectory and damage was minimized.

All these improvements to charts and aids to navigation make the average bridge look more like an amusement arcade when compared to the open bridges of Second World War warships. GPS relies on satellites to triangulate through radio. No longer is the three-compass bearing needed (although two might do; with caution) to make a fix on the chart during coastal navigation, or heavenly bodies out of sight of land. But visual navigation and dead reckoning in the twenty-first century should not be a dying art. Every navigator or pilot would be prudent to practice visual navigation – for the science depends on complex systems running seamlessly without electrical or mechanical faults.

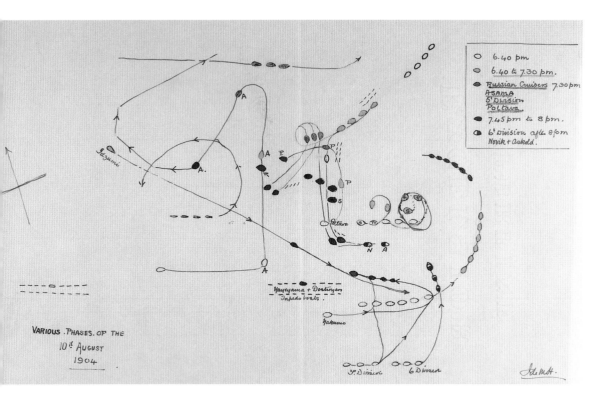

Various Phases of the 10ᵗʰ August 1904

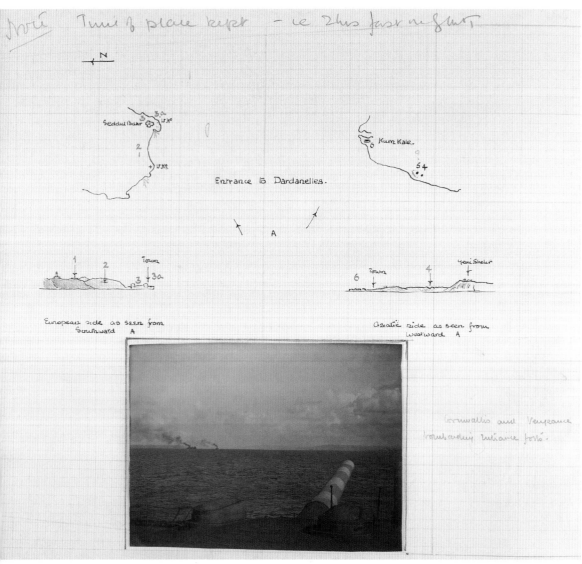

Entrance to Dardanelles.

European side as seen from Southward A

Asiatic side as seen from Westward A

Cornwallis and Vengeance bombarding entrance forts.

| LEFT | JAPANESE ATTACK ON THE RUSSIAN FLEET AT PORT ARTHUR BY CAPTAIN JOHN DE MESTRE HUTCHINSON, 1904 | Captain Hutchinson was appointed as extra naval attaché to the Imperial Navy and joined one of four battleships built by the British, the *Asaki*, on 20 July 1904. He forwarded his journal, marked Strictly Confidential, to the Admiralty, as well he might, for he had just witnessed the first engagement between the Russians and Japanese that would lead to the destruction of the Russian Pacific fleet in the following year. His journal included the chart he drew during the action.

After the Japanese successfully won the war with China in 1894, the European powers and the US allowed the Russians to pay China's war indemnity to Japan in exchange for the right to build the Trans-Siberian Railway through Manchuria to Vladivostok, giving her the facility to bring military and commercial power into the disputed area. Four years later Russia leased Port Arthur, on the southern tip of the Liaodong Peninsula on the Manchurian coast, from China. It had been captured and destroyed by the Japanese in 1894 but now Russia made it her main Asiatic naval base and fortified it accordingly. Britain wanted to see Japan as a counter-balance to Russia's imperialism and gave Japan assistance and know-how to build a formidable new fleet so that by 1903 Japan had six modern battleships and the Russians, although they received similar assistance from France, were falling behind. Japan launched a pre-emptive strike against the Russians at Port Arthur in February 1904. When the Russians under Admiral Vitgeft tried to break out in August they were met by the Japanese fleet under Admiral Togo. The chart shows the second action of 10 August when the Japanese scored a direct hit on the Russian flagship *Tsarevitch*, damaging her steering. The rest of the fleet broke up in confusion. In consequence, the western Russian fleet left the Baltic in October 1904 to sail halfway round the world intent on resolving the Japanese situation. The fleet eventually reached the Tsushima Strait (Korean Strait) where Togo was waiting for them and the Russian fleet was annihilated. (Admiralty Library Manuscript Collection: RNM 2005.14/3)

| LEFT | DARDANELLES LOG, 19 FEBRUARY 1915 | Midshipman Rowland Langmaid on board the battleship *Agamemnon* kept a journal, as required by the Admiralty. Signed monthly by the captain, and sometimes by the flag officer, the keeping of journals not only ensured that junior officers kept abreast of events and were well informed, but they often served to assist hydrographers in the compilation of charts and sailing directions. During the First World War *Agamemnon* was part of the Franco-British fleet of nine British and four French battleships sent to take the Dardanelles Strait, the narrow entrance to the Black Sea some 38 miles long but a mile across at its narrowest. If they could silence the Turkish forts, then a large army of British, French, Australian, New Zealand and Indian troops could be landed. Attacking Turkey, Germany's weakest ally in the war, would also open the supply route to the Russians through the Black Sea. The abstract from Langmaid's journal gives a profile of the approach to the Dardanelles and the photograph taken over the after gun of one of *Agamemnon*'s two pairs of 12-inch gun barrels shows HMS *Cornwallis* and HMS *Vengeance* bombarding the entrance forts, which could not be put out of action as a minefield had been sown across the strait. To break the stalemate in which minesweepers could not clear the mines until the guns were inoperative but the guns could not be silenced while the minefields were un-swept, an amphibious landing was ordered. The Turks stuck to their guns and in spite of appalling soldier losses by the Allies, after eight months a successful naval evacuation of 83,000 men and equipment, with no more than half a dozen casualties, was achieved. Paradoxically the Turkish armistice was signed on board *Agamemnon* in October 1918. Many lessons were learned from this operation and put into practice in the amphibious operations of the Second World War. (Admiralty Library Manuscript Collection: MSS 198)

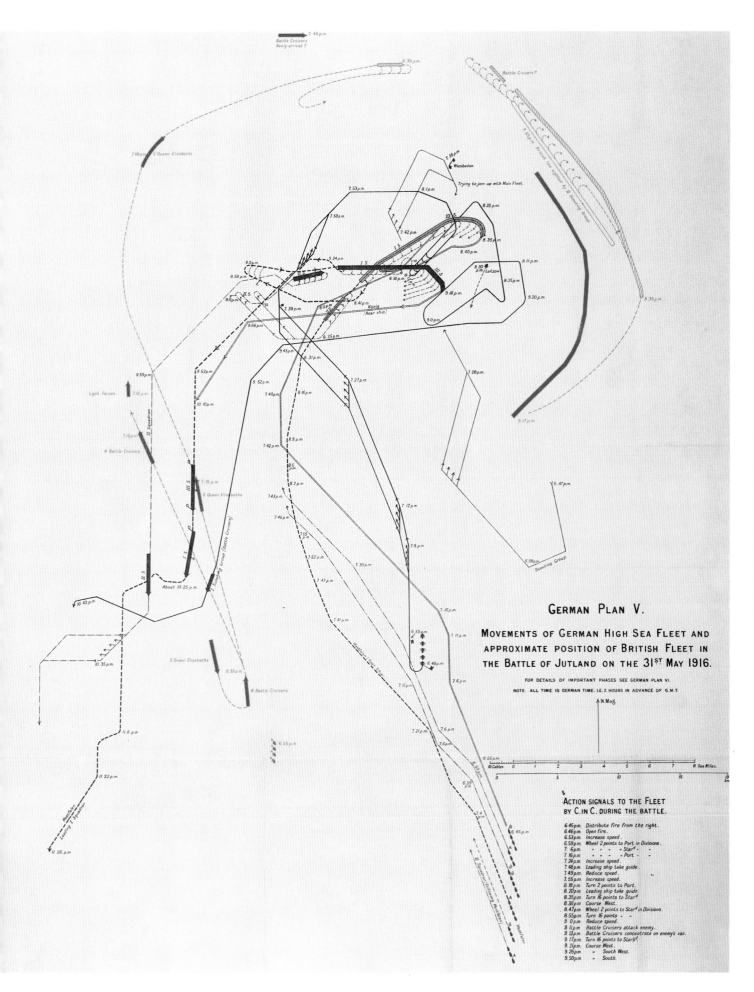

GERMAN PLAN V.

MOVEMENTS OF GERMAN HIGH SEA FLEET AND
APPROXIMATE POSITION OF BRITISH FLEET IN
THE BATTLE OF JUTLAND ON THE 31ST MAY 1916.

FOR DETAILS OF IMPORTANT PHASES SEE GERMAN PLAN VI.

NOTE. ALL TIME IS GERMAN TIME. I.E. 2 HOURS IN ADVANCE OF G.M.T.

N.Mag.

ACTION SIGNALS TO THE FLEET
BY C.IN C. DURING THE BATTLE.

6.45 p.m. Distribute fire from the right.
6.46 p.m. Open fire.
6.53 p.m. Increase speed.
6.59 p.m. Wheel 2 points to Port in Divisions.
7. 6 p.m.   "   "   "   "   Star.
7. 16 p.m.   "   "   "   "   Port.
7.24 p.m. Increase speed.
7.46 p.m. Leading ship take guide.
7.49 p.m. Reduce speed.
7.55 p.m. Increase speed.
8. 12 p.m. Turn 2 points to Port.
8. 20 p.m. Leading ship take guide.
8.35 p.m. Turn 16 points to Star.
8.38 p.m. Course West.
8.47 p.m. Wheel 2 points to Star in Divisions.
8.55 p.m. Turn 16 points .
9. 0 p.m. Reduce speed.
9. 11 p.m. Battle Cruisers attack enemy.
9. 13 p.m. Battle Cruisers concentrate on enemy's van.
9.17 p.m. Turn 16 points to Starb.
9. 21 p.m. Course West.
9.26 p.m.   "   South West.
9.50 p.m.   "   South.

MOVEMENTS OF THE
BRITISH AND GERMAN FLEETS
AT THE BATTLE OF JUTLAND,
1916 | The Battle of Jutland, fought on
31 May 1916, was the main naval
engagement of the First World War.
The official dispatches, now held at the
Admiralty library, Portsmouth, and the
National Archives, from the British
Commander-in-Chief Home Fleet,
Admiral Sir John Jellicoe, to Sir
Charles Walker, Deputy Secretary of
the Admiralty, contain plans, narrative,
and an account of the damage sus-
tained. The chart reproduced here is
from those dispatches and shows the
movements of the British battle and
cruiser fleets and the German battle-
fleet, under Admiral Reinhardt Scheer
during the afternoon and early evening
of 31 May. The Germans, by sailing
their High Seas Fleet, intended to draw
the British fleet out of their bases at
Rosyth and Scapa Flow in the Orkneys
over recently laid mines and into the
path of waiting U-boats. Bad weather
spoiled the U-boat plan and that afternoon the two fleets engaged inconclu-
sively. During the night Admiral
Scheer managed to slip back to base at
Wilhelmshaven, while Jellicoe, lacking
important intelligence that was known
at the Admiralty, covered the wrong
one of three routes through shoals and
minefields while the German fleet took
another. (The National Archives
{PRO} MPI 1/671)

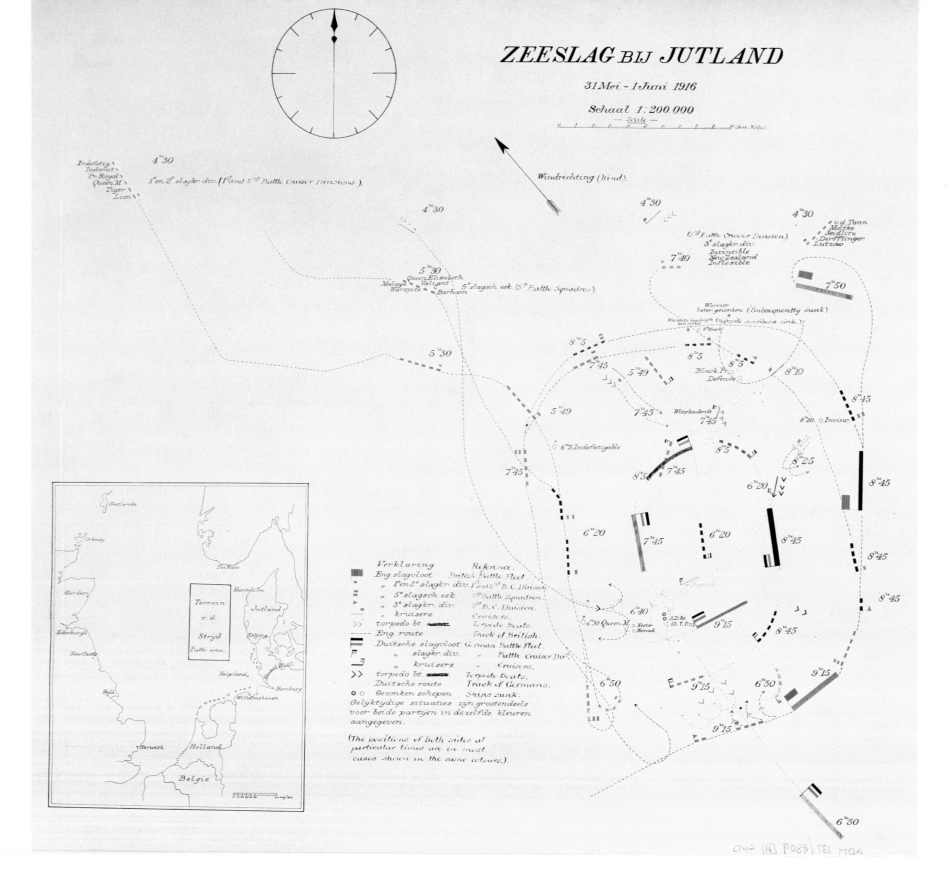

| **GERMAN PLAN OF JUTLAND, 1916** | This German track chart was included in a dispatch of 12 August 1916 sent by Rear-Admiral R Purefoy, Naval Attaché in the British Embassy at the Hague to the Admiralty. We can surmise that it was secretly obtained from the somewhat ramshackle German Naval High Command (where the Kaiser had said, 'I am the German High Command') and then English translations added in later.

The British ships' tracks are in brown and the German ships' in red and the chart shows the approach of Jellicoe's 5th Battle Squadron and Beatty's 3rd Battle Cruiser Division from the north. None of the contenders had a clear idea of where the others were, and this was not helped by the difficulties of keeping an accurate dead reckoning position with fog and tidal currents. Broadly speaking, Beatty's battle cruiser squadron was lured south with the prospect of action by Vice-Admiral Franz von Hipper's battle cruisers into a trap – the German battleship squadron commanded by Vice-Admiral Reinhardt Scheer. As soon as Beatty realized the trap he sharply altered course to the north to lure Scheer's battleship squadron into Jellicoe's squadron. The inset shows the main area of the battle, and the two main fleets got visual contact just after 6 p.m. about 80 miles west of the Jutland peninsula. Jellicoe's aim now had to be to cut the German fleet off from their retreat to their base to the south at Wilhelmshaven, and in a masterly tactical stroke he turned the fleet from line abreast with a turn to port into line ahead, which placed the British fleet across the German line of retreat and crossed the T of the German line of battle, giving the British superiority of fire. As darkness fell and mists appeared, the fleets lost contact and settled into night steaming south with Jellicoe anticipating rejoining battle at daylight. But Scheer had slipped past the British fleet during the night and into harbour. (The National Archives {PRO} MFQ 1/366)

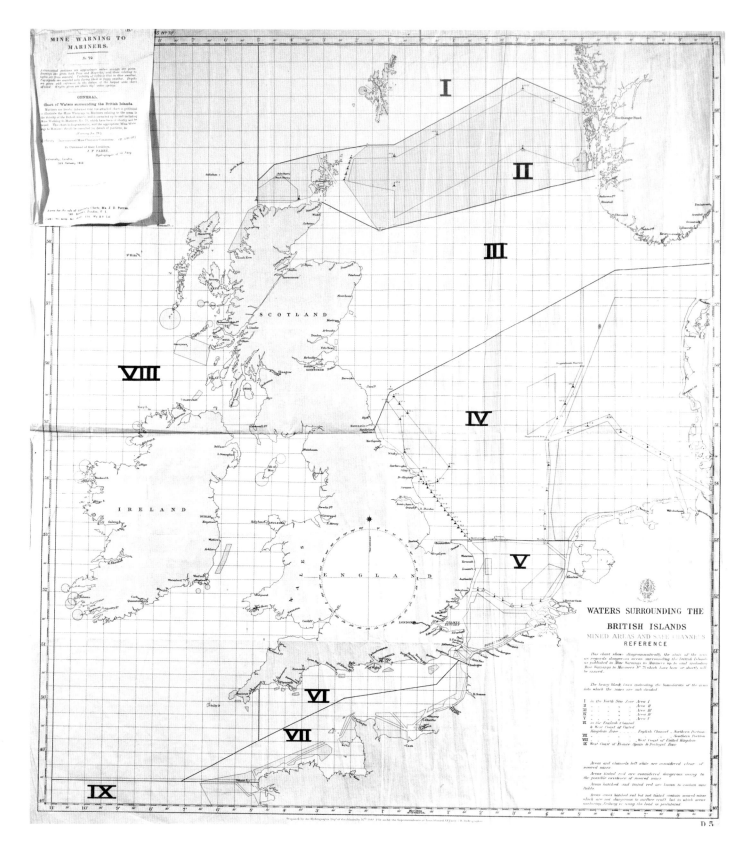

| CHART OF UK WATERS SHOWING MINED AREAS AND SAFE CHANNELS, 1915 |

After the war the UK Hydrographic Office was responsible for compiling and updating charts showing known minefields and issuing them to the Royal Navy as well as making them available to merchant and military navies worldwide. This Admiralty mine warfare chart, first issued in 1915, highlights the possible dangers around the British Isles, information that during the war was of course top secret. Areas tinted red with hatching indicated the known presence of mines; areas just tinted red suggested there was still a problem, while white areas were clear of mines. The note attached to the top left corner is a 'Mine Warning to Mariners'

No. 79, dated 10 February 1919 and issued by the authority of the International Mine Clearance Committee. Although crude mines had first been developed during the American War of Independence, and used as already discussed during the American Civil War, the Russians developed a more sophisticated type to detonate on impact in harbours, and contact mines were first laid in great numbers during the First World War. By the time of the Korean War enemy mines caused 70 per cent of all US Navy casualties and sank the only four US naval vessels lost in that combat. (Reproduced by courtesy of the Royal Geographical Society with IBG, Admiralty Chart no. D.9)

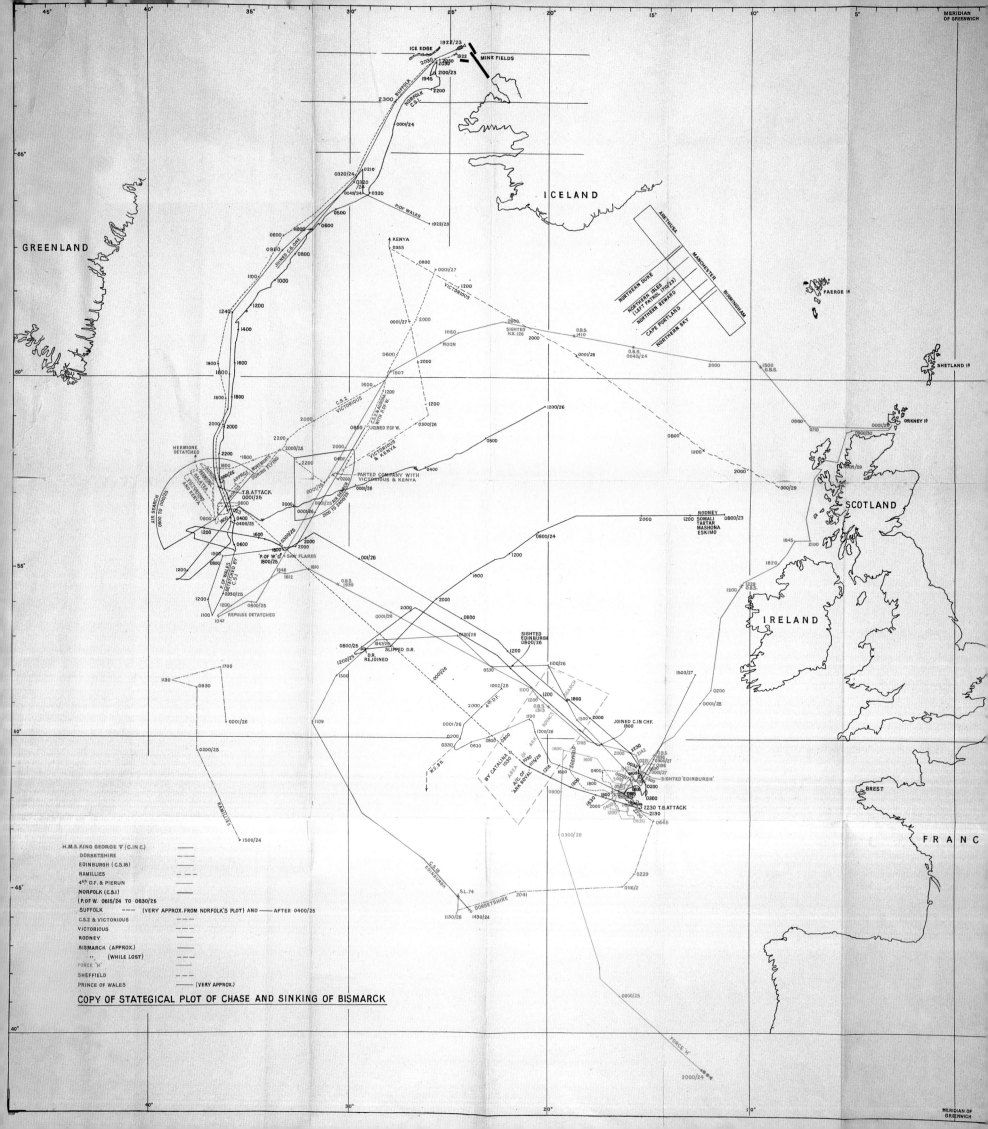

COPY OF STATEGICAL PLOT OF CHASE AND SINKING OF BISMARCK

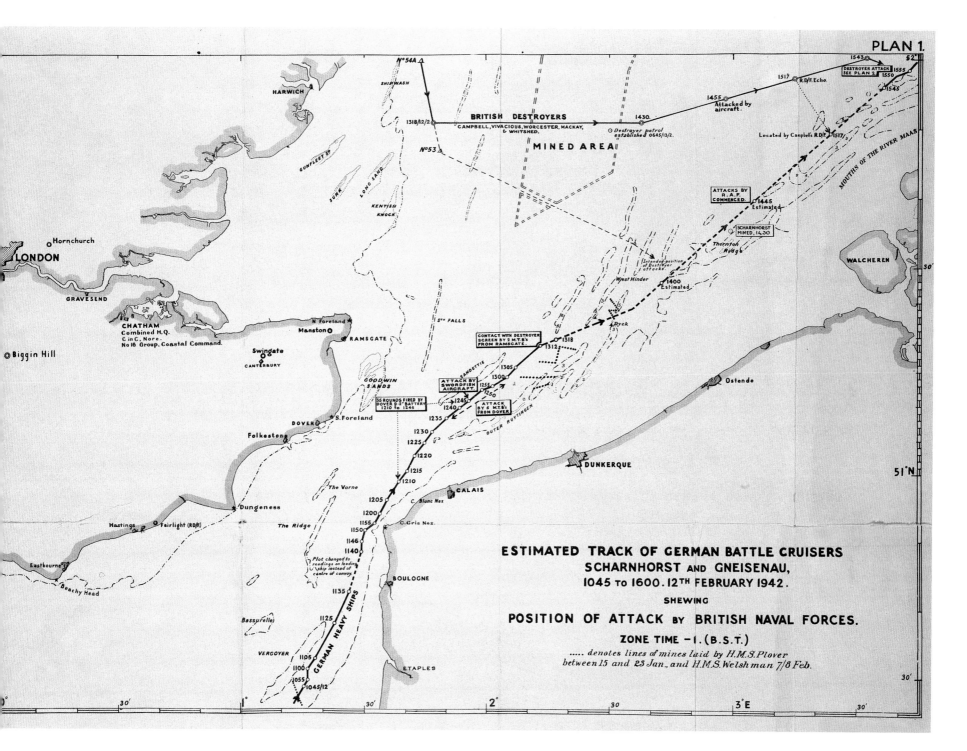

PLAN 1.

ESTIMATED TRACK OF GERMAN BATTLE CRUISERS
SCHARNHORST AND GNEISENAU,
1045 TO 1600. 12TH FEBRUARY 1942.
SHEWING
POSITION OF ATTACK BY BRITISH NAVAL FORCES.
ZONE TIME -1. (B.S.T.)
..... *denotes lines of mines laid by H.M.S. Plover
between 15 and 23 Jan., and H.M.S. Welshman 7/8 Feb.*

| LEFT | **CHASE AND SINKING OF THE *BISMARCK*, 1941** | From the dispatch of the sinking of the German battleship *Bismarck* on 27 May 1941 by Admiral Sir John C Tovey, Commander-in-Chief Home Fleet, the Admiralty compiled this exciting chart as a strategic record directly off the operations room plotting tables of the ships taking part and shows the chase as well as the sinking of the mighty battleship. The *Bismarck*, together with her sister-ship *Tirpitz*, was the largest and heaviest warship ever to be completed by a European nation. On 18 May she set out in company with the heavy cruiser *Prinz Eugen* to carry out Operation Kheinübung against Atlantic convoys. She was responsible on the 24th for the loss of HMS *Hood* after a dramatic encounter. By concentrating all available forces, including the aircraft carriers *Victorious* and *Ark Royal*, whose swordfish aircraft damaged the *Bismarck*'s rudder, her guns were finally silenced by the British battleships *King George V* and *Rodney*, and she was torpedoed and sunk by the *Dorsetshire* 960 kilometres off the west coast of France. (The National Archives {PRO} ADM 234/510)

| ABOVE | **THE CHANNEL DASH, 1942** | The German battlecruisers *Scharnhorst* and *Gneisenau* operated as a team, involved in attacking the British blockade between Iceland and the Faroes, providing cover for the invasion of Norway and hindering the disembarkation of the British Army from Narvik. In February 1942 they broke out of Brest to escape eleven months of constant RAF bombing in a daring and well-planned dash up the English Channel to Germany. The chart, prepared by the Admiralty from reports by the different units involved in the chase, recounts the estimated position and track of the German ships and the positions of the various attacks. Almost home, both ships struck mines and had to make for Kiel, well within range of RAF bombers. *Gneisenau* was so seriously damaged that she never sailed again, while the *Scharnhorst* was sunk on 26 December 1943 by the British battleship *Duke of York* when she attacked a British convoy bound for Russia. (The National Archives {PRO} ADM 186/803)

| **TRACK CHART OF HMS *EXE*, SEARCHING FOR SURVIVORS FROM HMS *VETERAN* IN THE ATLANTIC, 1942** | While rescuing survivors from three American passenger and merchant ships, the *New York*, *Boston* and *Yorktown*, in the Gulf of Cadiz, sunk by *U-404*, one of three U-boat 'wolf packs' comprising 17 German submarines, HMS *Veteran*, a V and W class destroyer, was herself torpedoed. The *Exe*, a River class frigate based at Londonderry and part of the convoy escort screen, was detached with the *Gentian*, one of 229 Flower class corvettes built during the war for crucial convoy escort duties, to search for survivors. Doggedly from 21:15 on the 19 September 1942 until 18:32 on 2 October the two ships carried out the search pattern recorded on this chart from the ARL (Admiralty Research Laboratory) table plot in the operations room below the frigate's bridge, but sadly found no survivors. This chart was included in the captain's report to Admiral Percy Noble, Commander-in-Chief, Western Approaches in Liverpool, who laid the groundwork for the convoy system that his relief, Admiral Sir Max Horton, perfected to overcome the North Atlantic U-Boat threat to Britain. (The National Archives {PRO} MPI 1/689)

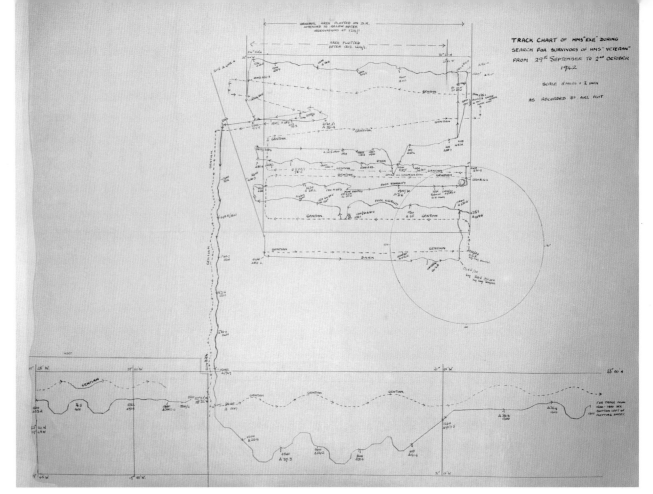

| **TRACK CHART OF ATTACK ON ANTI-SUBMARINE CONTACT, 1942** | During the escort of the US aircraft carrier *Wasp* in April and May 1942 to Malta, where her fighter aircraft helped defend the beleaguered island, HMS *Vidette* and HMS *Ithuriel* were detached with HMS *Salisbury* and HMS *Georgetown* to investigate a reported sighting by a routine Gibraltar reconnaissance aircraft of a submarine in the Gulf of Cadiz. The chart, taking the coastal outline of Spain from the Admiralty navigational chart in use on the bridge chart table, shows the flotilla's sonar (Asdic) search path, centred on the position of the reported siting, taken in formation line abreast 2000 yards (1 nautical mile) apart. The plot chart, coordinated in the operations room by the senior officer in the *Salisbury*, was then forwarded as part of the report of proceedings from 28 April to 15 May to the Admiralty. It gives an idea of the enormous area that had to be covered to find a submarine unless the time of sighting was still very fresh, a tedious but necessary task for the ships. But the U-boat destruction of Allied shipping, known as the Battle of the Atlantic, after catastrophic losses up to 1943, was effectively won from September with consistent use of the convoy system, long-range aircraft, vital assistance from the Canadian and US navies and adequate numbers of anti-submarine escorts. (The National Archives {PRO} MPI 1/689)

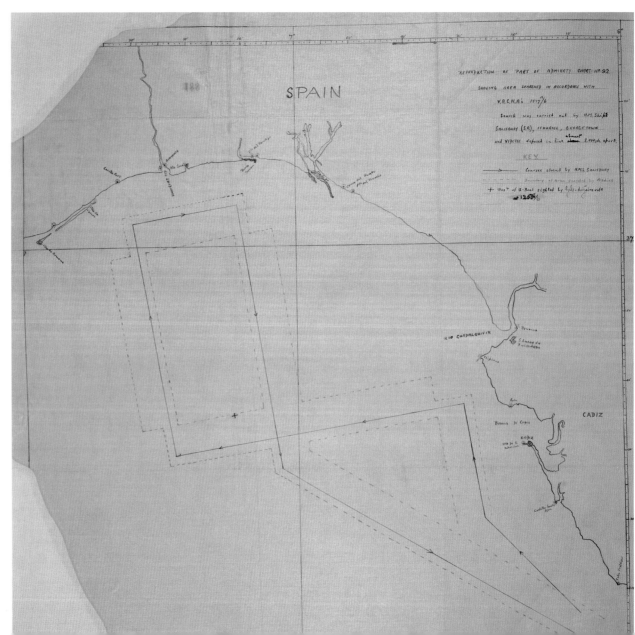

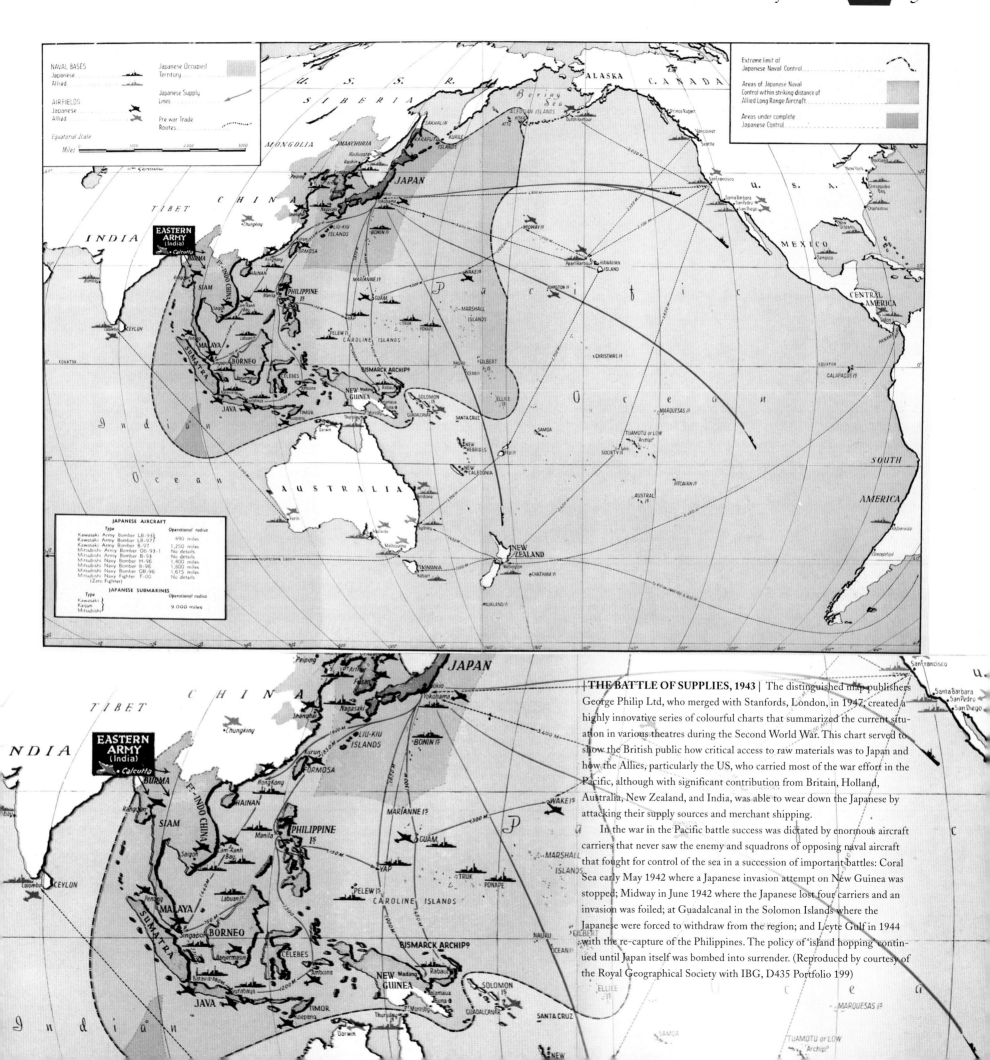

| THE BATTLE OF SUPPLIES, 1943 | The distinguished map publishers George Philip Ltd, who merged with Stanfords, London, in 1947, created a highly innovative series of colourful charts that summarized the current situation in various theatres during the Second World War. This chart served to show the British public how critical access to raw materials was to Japan and how the Allies, particularly the US, who carried most of the war effort in the Pacific, although with significant contribution from Britain, Holland, Australia, New Zealand, and India, was able to wear down the Japanese by attacking their supply sources and merchant shipping.

In the war in the Pacific battle success was dictated by enormous aircraft carriers that never saw the enemy and squadrons of opposing naval aircraft that fought for control of the sea in a succession of important battles: Coral Sea early May 1942 where a Japanese invasion attempt on New Guinea was stopped; Midway in June 1942 where the Japanese lost four carriers and an invasion was foiled; at Guadalcanal in the Solomon Islands where the Japanese were forced to withdraw from the region; and Leyte Gulf in 1944 with the re-capture of the Philippines. The policy of 'island hopping' continued until Japan itself was bombed into surrender. (Reproduced by courtesy of the Royal Geographical Society with IBG, D435 Portfolio 199)

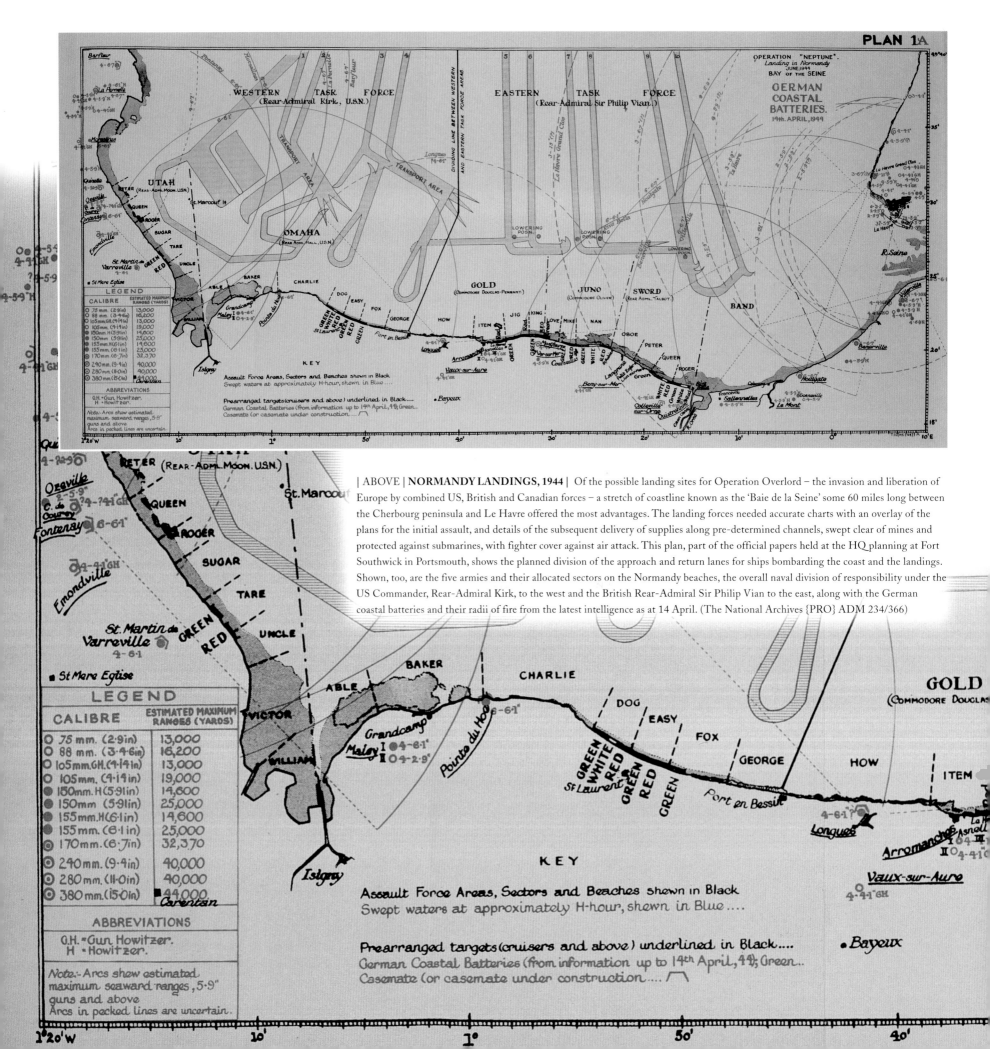

| ABOVE | **NORMANDY LANDINGS, 1944** | Of the possible landing sites for Operation Overlord – the invasion and liberation of Europe by combined US, British and Canadian forces – a stretch of coastline known as the 'Baie de la Seine' some 60 miles long between the Cherbourg peninsula and Le Havre offered the most advantages. The landing forces needed accurate charts with an overlay of the plans for the initial assault, and details of the subsequent delivery of supplies along pre-determined channels, swept clear of mines and protected against submarines, with fighter cover against air attack. This plan, part of the official papers held at the HQ planning at Fort Southwick in Portsmouth, shows the planned division of the approach and return lanes for ships bombarding the coast and the landings. Shown, too, are the five armies and their allocated sectors on the Normandy beaches, the overall naval division of responsibility under the US Commander, Rear-Admiral Kirk, to the west and the British Rear-Admiral Sir Philip Vian to the east, along with the German coastal batteries and their radii of fire from the latest intelligence as at 14 April. (The National Archives {PRO} ADM 234/366)

| RIGHT | **OPERATION BELLPUSH CHARLIE, 1943–4** |

Pivotal to the D-Day landings along the Normandy coast, accurate charts had to be drawn up that would not only show depths but the position of underwater obstacles placed by the Germans to hinder any landing, as well as the gradient and nature of the seabed. This little known, but extraordinary and courageous task, was undertaken by a unit specially set up under the Chief of Combined Operations, Lord Louis Mountbatten, and codenamed 'Operation Bellpush Charlie'. Headed by Lieutenant Commander F M Berncastle, the unit was initially allocated two Landing Craft Personnel, which was later increased to six. They were 32 feet long, camouflaged, with a low profile designed to evade enemy radar, and one engine with an underwater silencer, which pushed them along at 10 knots on passage, but were awkward to handle at the 3 knots needed for sounding. They had to be towed across the Channel by an MGB to within 10 miles of the French coast in order to embark on their task. Over the course of a year they made several operations using a mishmash of surveying techniques ancient and modern to take soundings and samples of the seabed, and make notes on tidal streams, all completed at night under the eyes of the Germans in strong seas. This chart, understandably marked 'Most Secret', shows one such survey which gave the beach approach information along a 2-mile stretch of shoreline in the Baie de la Seine, by Arromanches, in the middle of Juno beach, between Manieux and Asnelles-sur-mer using their church spires for position lines. (UKHO © British Crown Copyright)

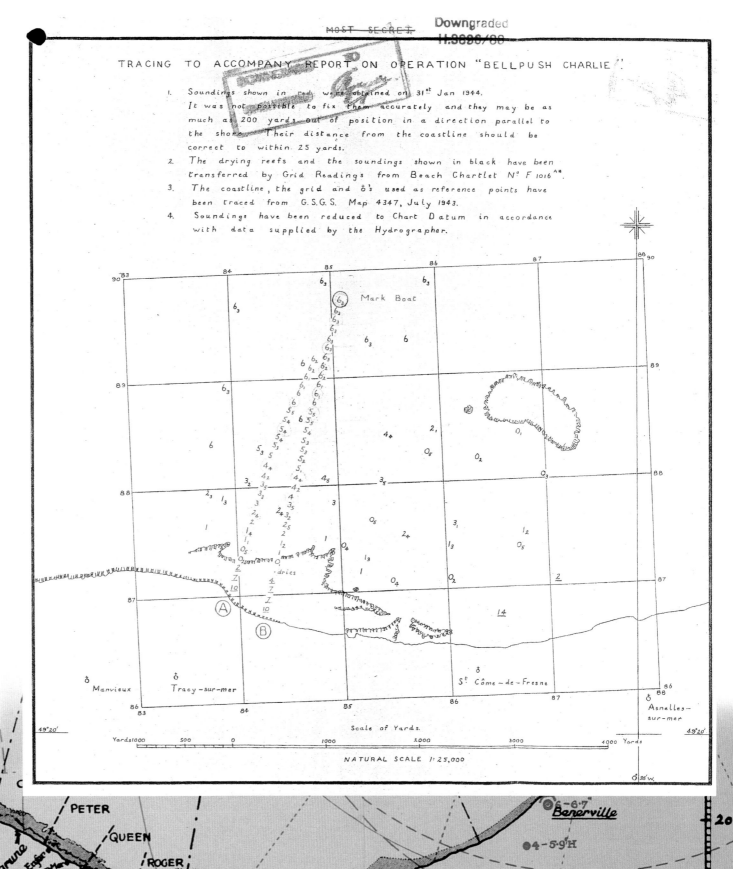

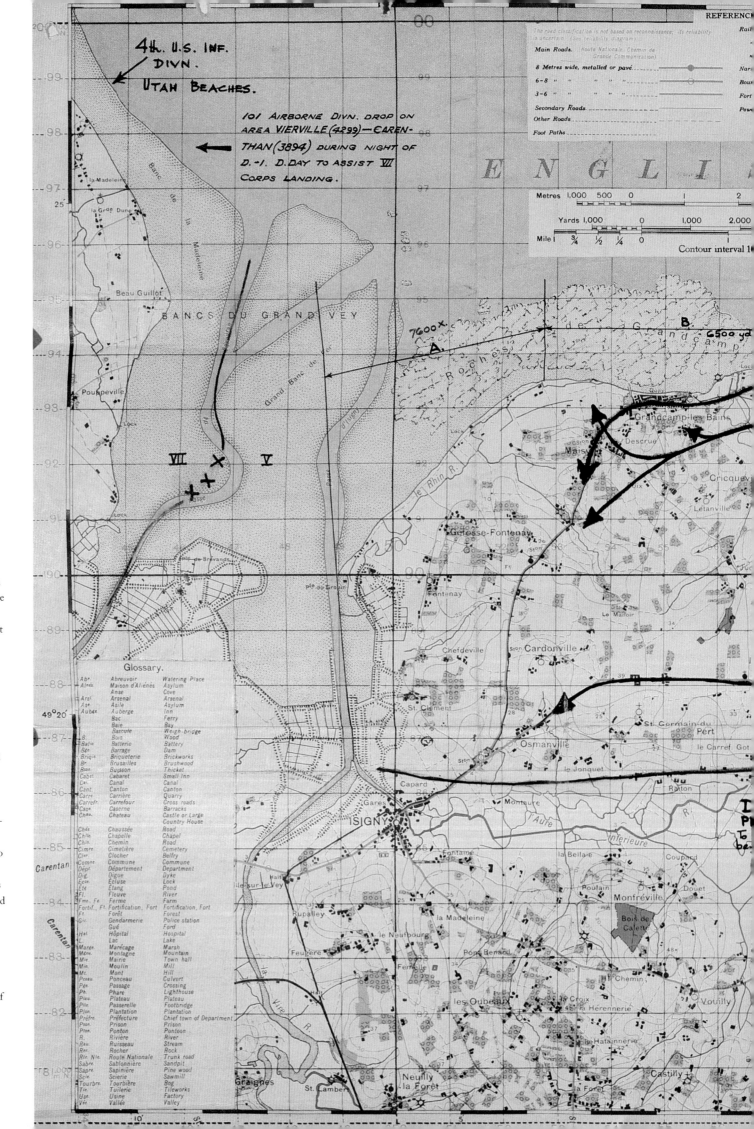

| PLAN OF OMAHA BEACH AND HINTERLAND, 1944 | This is an example of the practical use of a French map of the landing area of Omaha beach with the detailed secret aims of where the various US army units should be landed, including the airborne division, the night before. The ambitious line prepared by Combined Operations Headquarters to show how far inland they should have penetrated at two hours before dark on D-Day is also drawn on with, for the English-speaking forces, a useful translating glossary of features. On D-Day (6 June) the landings at Sword, Juno and Gold (British and Canadian forces) and Utah (American) went well and objectives were consolidated by nightfall, but Omaha (American) ran into severe problems. Unfortunately, the tanks were launched from the tank landing ships too far from the beach, in deeper water then anticipated, and were swamped. The loss of heavy armour coupled with unexpected stiff German resistance meant that by nightfall only land up to the beachhead maintenance line, drawn on the chart, had been secured. Indeed, during the afternoon, it had seemed likely that this sector, suffering the heaviest casualties of around 3000 men, would have to be abandoned. (The National Archives {PRO} DEFE 2/436)

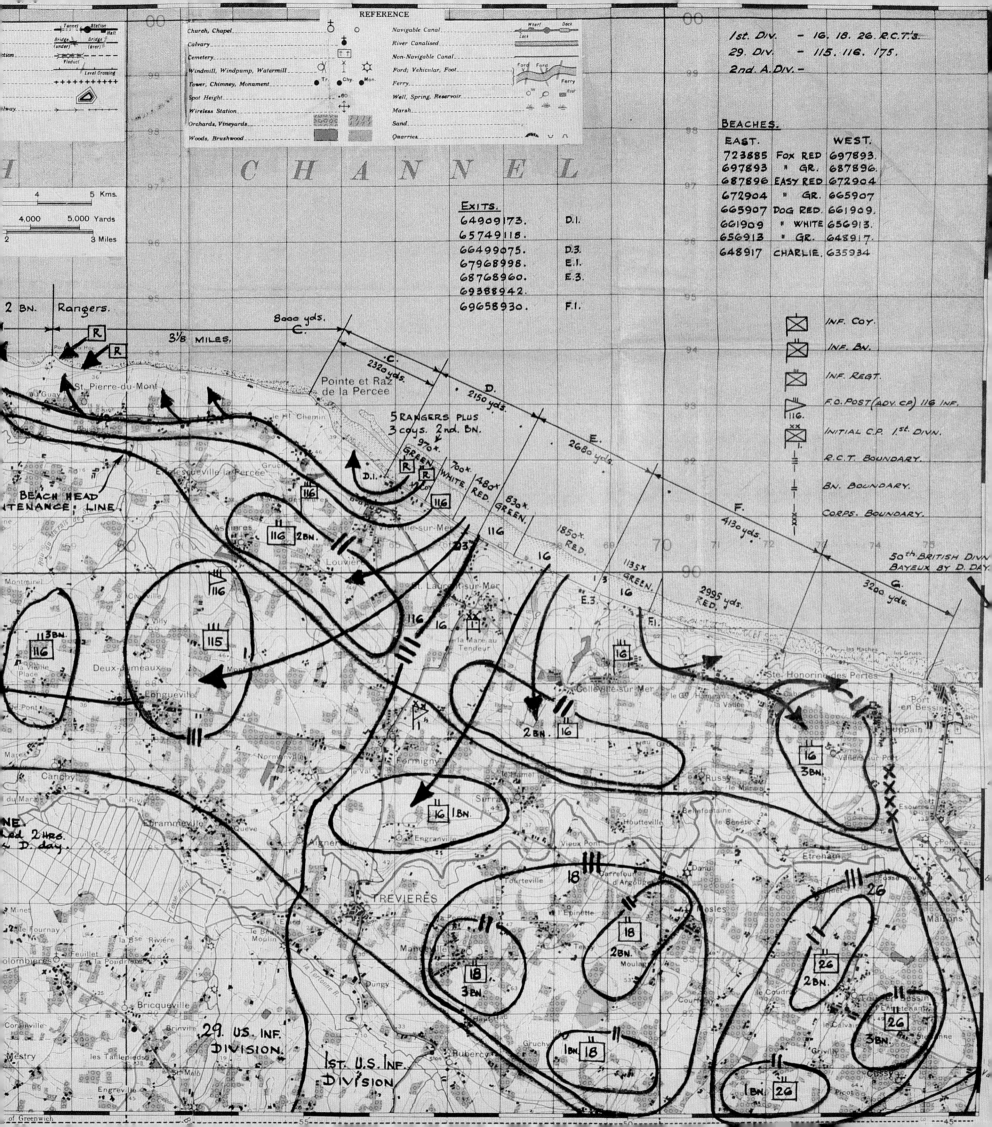

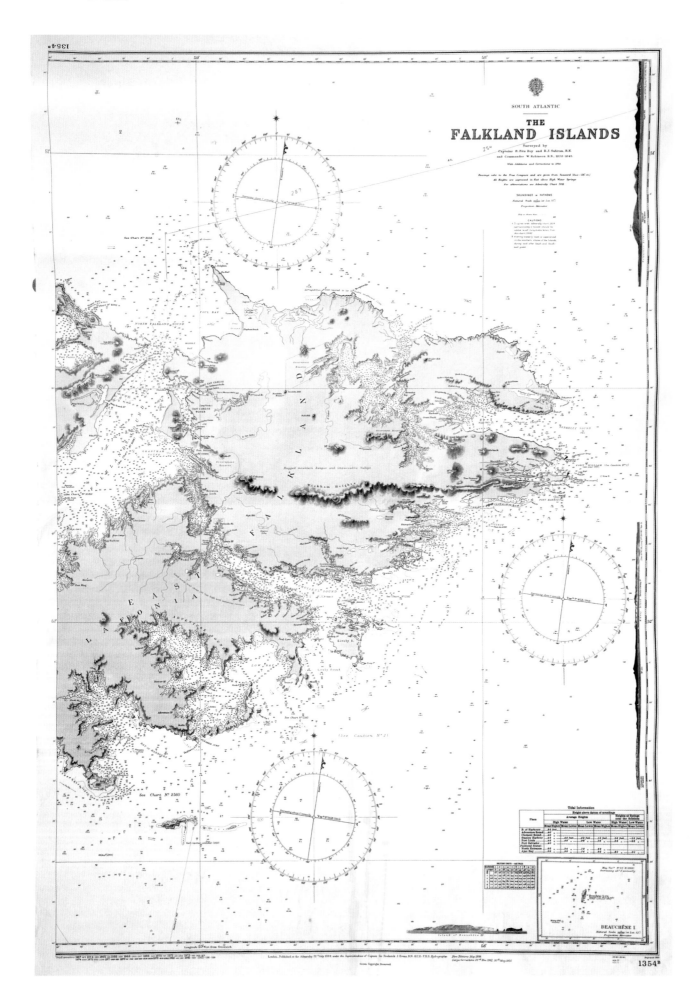

| **THE FALKLANDS ISLANDS, 1982** | The Argentinean decision to take the Falkland Islands by force with a landing on 2 April 1982 was made to divert public attention from the country's economic problems, and thereby prop up the ruling junta, and in response to the defence cuts planned by the British Government, in particular axing the ice patrol ship *Endurance*. Although earlier reports had been received by the British Government of Argentinean intentions, and even that the UK Hydrographic Office had unexpectedly sold out of all charts of the Falkland Islands, political reaction to early warnings was slow.

Royal Navy ships sailed from Gibraltar, Portsmouth and Plymouth in early April and rendezvoused in mid-Atlantic to form the Falklands Task Force. The chart shown here was used on the bridge of the *Antelope*, a Type 21 frigate primarily designed to defend against aircraft and commanded by Captain Nick Tobin, which escorted the slower elements of the amphibious task group and entered the Total Exclusion Zone around the Falklands on 22 May.

The role of frigates such as *Antelope* was to defend support shipping in the Amphibious Operating Area against any Argentinean counterattack and provide air defence against Argentinean Skyhawks and Mirage III's that got past the defending British Harrier fighter aircraft. An attack by four A4 Skyhawks during the early afternoon of 23 May lodged two unexploded 1000-pound bombs into *Antelope*'s hull, one of which detonated while being disarmed during the evening. The subsequent fire spread to the missile magazine and the frigate blew up. (By kind permission of Captain N J Tobin DSC RN)

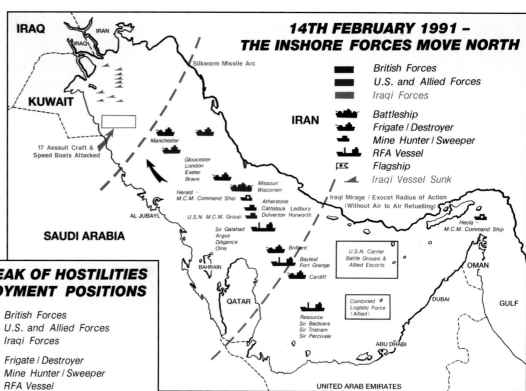

| THE GULF WAR BY COMMODORE CHRIS CRAIG, 1991 | Saddam Hussein's invasion of Kuwait threatened to escalate into a second invasion into Saudi Arabia, destabilizing the region and threatening the world's supplies of oil. Once the UN had sanctioned a US-led coalition to liberate Kuwait, a massive sealift operation was mounted as part of Operation Desert Storm, with the US Navy providing huge naval carrier air strikes, cruise missile and 16-inch gun attacks from veteran battleships *Wisconsin* and *Missouri*. However, the Iraqi navy offered threats from their fleet of small but fast patrol craft, equipped with surface-to-surface missiles, and from extensive minefields they had sown across

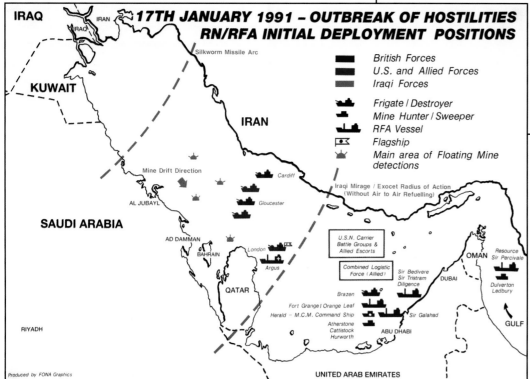

the approaches to Kuwait City and the Iraq naval bases of Umm Qasr and Basra, unfortunately allowed while political clearance to operate north of 29°N was politically denied by the Coalition. Commodore Chris Craig was appointed in command of all British naval forces in the Gulf, working on board his flagship *London*, and directly with the US and coalition HQ in Saudi Arabia. They effectively wiped out the Iraqi patrol craft with Lynx helicopter Sea Skua anti-ship missile attacks, and the multinational mine countermeasure ships led by British Hunt class ships which cleared safe channels for ships giving air defence and shore bombardment support, and tied down three Iraqi divisions with the ruse of landing a force of 16,000 marines.

These three diagrammatic charts were prepared by Commodore Craig to describe the three pivotal phases of the sea operations: the start of hostilities on 17 January; the inshore naval forces moving towards Iraq on 14 February; and the final day of the war on 28 February. He used them to brief the Press and for PR, to debrief the MOD and politicians and to later illustrate his post-war lectures. (By kind permission of Captain C J S Craig CB DSC RN)

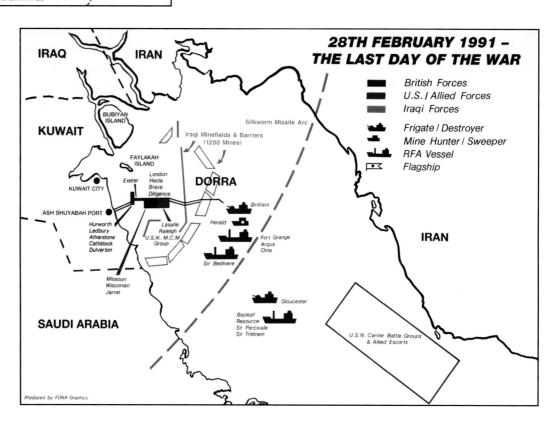

Bibliography

Admiralty Charts and Publications *The Sea Pilot*, various volumes

Admiralty Charts and Publications, *Admiralty Ocean Passages for the World* NP136, 4th edition, 1987

Admiralty Charts and Publications, *The Mariner's Handbook* NP100, 1979

Admiralty Manual of Hydrographic Surveying, 2nd edition, HMSO, 1963

Admiralty Manual of Navigation, Volumes II and III, HMSO, originally printed 1955

Andrewes, William J H (ed.), *The Quest for Longitude*, Collection of Historical Scientific Instruments, 1996

Archer, Christopher and others, *World History of Warfare*, Cassell, 2002

Bathurst, Bella, *The Wreckers*, HarperCollins Publishers, 2005

Binns, Alan, *Viking Voyagers*, William Heinemann Ltd, 1980

Black Jeremy (ed.), *The Seventy Great Battles of All Time*, Thames & Hudson, 2005

Bluett, Mary, *Surveys of the Seas: A Brief History of British Hydrography*, Macgibbon & Kee, 1957

Brown, David, *The Royal Navy and the Falklands War*, Leo Cooper Ltd, 1987

Campbell, Tony, 'Portolan Charts from the Late Thirteenth Century to 1500', in *The History of Cartography Vol. 1 & Vol II, (generally)* , J B Harley and David Woodward (eds), University Chicago Press, 1987

Canney, Donald L, *Lincoln's Navy: The Ships Men and Organization, 1861-65*, Conway Maritime Press, 1998

Conner, Daniel, and Miller, Lorraine, *Master Mariner*, Douglas & Macintyre, 1978

Craig, Captain Chris CBE DSO RN, *Call for Fire*, John Murray, 1995

Crane, Nicholas, *Mercator, The Man who Mapped the Planet*, Weidenfeld & Nicolson, 2002

Crone G R, *Maps and Their Makers*, Hutchinson & Co Ltd, third edition, 1966

Dampier, William, *A Voyage to New Holland*, Alan Sutton Publishing Ltd, 1981

Dawson, Commander L S, *Memoirs of Hydrography*, Henry Keay, 1885

Day, Vice-Admiral Sir Archibald, *The Admiralty Hydrographic Service*, HMSO, 1967

Dyson, John, *Columbus for Gold, God and Glory*, Simon & Schuster/Madison Press, 1991

Encarta 98, 'Encyclopaedia', Microsoft 1997 CD Rom

Evans, Colonel M H H OBE RM, *Amphibious Operations: The Projection of Sea Power Ashore*, Vol IV, Brasseys (UK) Ltd, 1990

Evans, G N D, *Uncommon Obdurate: The Several Public Careers of J F W Des Barres*, Peabody Museum of Salem, Massachusetts, 1969

Featherstone, Neville, and Lambie, Peter, *Reeds OKI Nautical Almanac*, Adlard Coles Nautical, 2005

Feldbæk Ole (translated by Tony Wedgwood), *The Battle of Copenhagen 1801*, Leo Cooper (Pen & Sword Books Ltd), 2002

Firstbrook, Peter, *The Voyage of the Matthew*, BBC Worldwide Publishing Ltd, 1997

Fisher, Susanna, 'Organisation of Hydrographic Information for English Navigators', *Journal of Navigation*, Volume 54, No. 2, Cambridge University Press, May 2001

Fisher, Susanna, *The Makers of the Blueback Charts*, Imray Laurie Norie & Wilson Ltd, 2001

Fraser, Antonia (ed.), *The Lives of the Kings and Queens of England*, Weidenfeld & Nicholson, 1975

Freiesleben, H C, 'The Origin of the Portolan Charts', *Journal of Navigation*, Volume 37, No. 2, Cambridge University Press, May, 1984

Freycinet, L, *Voyage au Tour du Monde Paris*, (Freycinet) 1825

Gardiner, Robert (ed.), *Nelson Against Napoleon*, Caxton Editions, Chatham Publishing, 1997

Hapgood, Charles, *Maps of the Ancient Sea Kings*, Adventures Unlimited Press, 1966

Hearn, Chester G, *The Illustrated History of the United States Navy*, Salamander Books Ltd, 2003

Hough, Richard, *Captain James Cook*, Hodder & Stoughton, 1994

Howse, Derek, and Sanderson, Michael, *The Sea Chart*, David & Charles (Publishers) Ltd, 1973

Huntingford, G W B, *The Periplus of the Erythrean Sea*, The Hakluyt Society, London, 1980

Hydrographic Department Admiralty, *Professional Paper 13*, London, 1950

Ireland, Bernard, *Naval Warfare in the Age of Sail*, HarperCollins, 2000

Jordan, David, and Wiest, Andrew, *Atlas of World War II*, Silverdale Books, 2004

Kaman, Henry, *Philip of Spain*, Yale University Press, 1997

Keegan, John, *A History of Warfare*, Hutchinson, 1993

Keegan, John, *The Price of Admiralty*, Century Hutchinson Ltd, 1998

Kemp, Peter, *The Oxford Companion to Ships and the Sea*, Oxford University Press, 1976

King, Dean, *A Sea of Words*, Henry Holt and Company, 1997

Knox-Johnston, Sir Robin: www.robinknox-johnston.co.uk

Lainema, Matti, and Nurminen, Juha, *Ultima Thule, Arctic Explorations*, John Nurminen Foundation and WSOY, 2001

Lavery, Brian, *Building the Wooden Walls*, Conway Maritime Press Ltd, 1991

Lavery, Brian, *Nelson's Navy*, Conway Maritime Press, 1989

Lavery, Brian, *The Island Nation: A History of Britain and the Sea*, Conway Maritime Press Ltd, 2005

Machiavelli, Niccolò, *The Prince*, first published as *Il Principe* 1531-2, translated by George Bull, Penguin Books, 2004

Mahon, Alfred Thayer (edited by Antony Preston), *The Influence of Sea Power upon History 1660–1805*, Gallery Books, 1980

Maritime History and Naval Heritage web-site: www.cronab.demon.co.uk

Moreland, Carl, and Bannister, David, *Antique Maps*, Phaidon Press Ltd, 1983

National Maritime Museum, Greenwich, *Royal Armada, 400 Years*, Manorial Research (Armada) Ltd

National Oceanic and Atmospheric Administration USA (NOAA): www.noaa.gov

Natkiel, Richard, and Preston, Antony, *Atlas of Maritime History*, Bison Books Ltd, 1986

Nordenskiöld, A E, *Periplus: an Essay on the Early History of Charts and Sailing Directions*, PA Norstedt, Stockholm, 1987

Padfield, Peter, *Armada*, Victor Gollancz Ltd, 1988

Padfield, Peter, *Maritime Supremacy and the Opening of the Western Mind*, John Murray (Publishers) Ltd, 1999

Perkins, Roger, and Douglas-Morris, Captain K J RN, *Gunfire in Barbary*, Kenneth Mason, 1982

Peron, F, and Freycinet, L, *Voyage de decouvertes aux terres australes*, Paris 1807-16

Phillips-Birt, Douglas, *A History of Seamanship*, George Allen & Unwin Ltd, 1971

Porch, Douglas, *Wars of Empire*, Cassell & Co., 2000

Pumfrey, Stephen, *Latitude and the Magnetic Earth*, Icon Books Ltd, 2002

Randier, Jean, *Marine Navigation Instruments*, translated from the French by John E Powell, John Murray Publishers Ltd, 1980

Reagan, Geoffrey, *The Guinness Book of Naval Blunders*, Guinness Publishing Ltd, 1993

Rémi Monaque, 'Trafalgar 1805: Strategy, Tactics and Results', *The Mariner's Mirror*, Vol. 91, No. 2, May 2005

Richardson, W A R, 'An Elizabethan Pilot's Charts (1594): Spanish Intelligence regarding the Coasts of England and Wales at the End of the XVIth Century', *Journal of Navigation*, Volume 53, No. 2, Cambridge University Press, May 2000

Ritchie, Rear-Admiral G S, *The Admiralty Chart*, Hollis & Carter Ltd, 1967, reprinted 1995

Ritchie, Rear-Admiral Steve, *As It Was*, GITC 2003

Robinson, A H W, 'The Evolution of the English Nautical Chart', *Journal of Navigation*, Volume 5, No. 4, Cambridge University Press, October 1952

Rodger, N A M, *The Command of the Ocean*, Allen Lane, 1994

Rodger, N A M, *The Safeguard of the Sea*, Allen Lane, 1994

Roskill Captain S W DSC RN, *The Navy at War 1939-1945*, Collins, 1960

Ruddock, Alwyn, 'The Earliest Original English Seaman's Rutter and Pilot's Chart', *Journal of Navigation*, Volume 14, No. 4, Cambridge University Press, October 1961

Sanderson, Michael, *Sea Battles*, David & Charles Ltd, 1975

Sider, Sandra, *Cartographic Treasures of the Hispanic Society of America*, Fundación Caixa Galica, 2005

Sider, Sandra, *Maps, Charts, Globes: Five Centuries of Exploration*, The Hispanic Society of America, 1992

Smyth W H, *The Sailors Word Book*, originally published in 1867, Conway Maritime Press, 1991

Spavens, William (edited by N A M Rodger), *Memoirs of a Seafaring Life*, originally published by R Sheardown & Son, 1796, re-printed by The Folio Society, 2001

Still, Professor William Jnr, *The Confederate Navy: The Ships, Men and Organization, 1861–65*, Conway Maritime Press, 1997

Sun Tzu (Denma Translation Group), *The Art of War*, Shambhala Classics, 2002

Taylor, E G R, *Mathematics and the Navigator in the 13th Century*, Institute of Navigation

Taylor, E G R, *The Haven-finding Art*, Cambridge University Press, first published in 1956, augmented edition, 1971

Thomas Donald, *Cochrane: Britain's Sea Wolf*, Cassell Military Paperbacks, 2001

Tibbetts, G R, *Arab Navigation*, The Royal Asiatic Society of Great Britain and Ireland, 1971

Turnbull, David, 'Cartography and Science in Early Modern Europe: Mapping the Construction of Knowledge Spaces', *Imago Mundi* (International Journal for the History of Cartography), No. 48, Imago Mundi Ltd

Vale, Brian, *The Audacious Admiral Cochrane*, Conway Maritime Press, 2004

Von Clausewitz, Carl, *In the Nature of War*, first published as *Vom Kriege* in 1832, translated and published by Routledge & Kegan Paul, 1908, published by Penguin, 2005

Wallis, Helen, *Sir Francis Drake*, The British Library, 1977

Warner, Oliver, *Great Sea Battles*, Weidenfeld & Nicholson, 1963

Waters, David, *The Art of Navigation in England in Elizabethan and Early Stuart Times*, National Maritime Museum, 2nd edition, 1978

Whitfield, Peter, The *Charting of the Oceans*, The British Library, 1996

Williams, Glyn, *The Prize of all the Oceans*, HarperCollins, 1999

Winton, John, *An Illustrated History of the Royal Navy*, Conway Maritime Press, 2005

Index